SPIRIT

TO

SPIRIT

SPIRIT

TO

SPIRIT

POETIC PRAYERS, PRAISES, AND MEDITATIONS

By
DEANNA HOFFMANN

Spirit To Spirit
Poetic Prayers Praises, And Meditations
by Deanna Hoffmann

Printed in the United States of America

ISBN 978-1-60791-222-4

www.xulonpress.com

Dear Kelly,

Come away My Beloved to where I AM
The God who is mighty, who has the plan,
To take you & make you His bride & His wife
To set you on high above trouble & strife!
So ascend dear daughter & let His love,
Always & ever take you up above!

God Bless You Always,
Conrad & Deanne

ACKNOWLEDGEMENTS

First and foremost I want to thank
Father God for loving me and making me His Child,
My Lord and Saviour Jesus Christ for saving me,
And The Holy Spirit for bringing me to faith in Christ Jesus.

Next, I want to thank God for His Holy Word, The Bible,
For in it, I have found the path to true life.
God's Holy Word is my source for leading me into all truth!

Then I want to thank God for giving me Christian parents who
taught God's Word to me, and took me to church whenever
The doors were opened

Next, I want to thank The Lord, for The Pastors and Teachers,
Apostles, Prophets and Evangelists,
Whom God has used and is using,
To equip me to do the work of the ministry

Finally, I want to thank my husband, my family and my friends in
The Body of Christ, for their love and support,
In good times and bad.
Your prayers, and examples of love and faith,
Have encouraged my heart,
To Press on to The Goal to be
More like Christ!

My life verses are found in
Philippians Chapter 3:7-16

MY DECISIVE DEDICATION - Inspired by Romans 12

To My Lord and Saviour, I now devote,
  These words, to give men life and hope,
May every word, bring forth His Light,
  To illumine all, to give fresh sight,
Into all what God, in His mercy gave,
  For those who heed, His will and crave,
His Holy Presence, His Abiding Love
  And His Joy for strength, to rise above.

I sincerely thank You, Holy Spirit,
  For Your power enlightens, so I can inherit,
The promises in, God's Word that show,
  Your Way to walk, so I can grow,
Into the knowledge of who I am,
  Your child, Your heir, by Your great plan.
For without what You, have given to me,
  I would not know, The Truth that frees.

To God Almighty, I give my thanks,
  For what You give, yields more than banks,
Your mercy and Your faithfulness,
  Have graced me with, Your righteousness!
You've given me words, to show Your love,
  To lead men to, Your Throne above.
I pray these words, will show to all,
  Your grace, Your love, Your Holy call!

I want to also, thank right now,
  Those who encouraged, taught me how,
To hear, then write, what I had heard,
  From God, The Spirit, through His Word.
I thank God for His Body, The Church,
  For His family encouraged me, always to search,
The Scriptures for in them, God gives life,
  The life that frees, from every strife!

RING THE BELLS

Ring the bells, let the earth rejoice,
    For the Lord has come to give a choice
A choice to live and love and be free,
    Free to live through eternity
So let us all stand up and sing,
    And glorify our coming King
For Christ alone is Lord of all,
    To Christ alone on our knees we fall
Let's worship Christ with grateful hearts
    And then from Him we'll never depart.

COME AND SEE.

Oh come my friend come see this sight,
    A Saviour is born this very night!
No ordinary babe in a manger is He,
    He is come to set His children free;
Free to live and free to love,
    Free to worship our God above;
Free to enter His courts with praise,
    Free to worship Him all of our days,
Free to look on His holy face,
    Free to bow in the Holy Place;
Free by His grace without our merit,
    Free to receive by faith His spirit.
Free to proclaim His message of life,
    Free to forgive all malice and strife.
This is the freedom He offers us now,
    Eternity beckons-bend your knees-make a vow!
For Christ is the King and Christ is the Lord,
    Our Saviour is He—our God to adore!

CHRISTMAS LIGHT.

On Christmas Eve a special sight,
    Came to our eyes to give us light.
This Light became The Light of men,
    To set us free from all our sin;
To give us hope and joy and peace
    And love from God to bring release.
Oh come with me, let's worship The King,
    For He is The One to whom we sing
Glad praises now Oh Lord we bring,
    For You Oh Lord, cause the bells to ring!

LOOK TO THE LORD

As Christmas comes again this year,
    Our hearts are filled with joy and cheer.
Joy because our Saviour came;
    Cheer because we're never the same.
What an awesome gift is ours,
    Look to the Lord who made the stars!
The God of all made heaven and earth,
    Then sent His Son to give new birth.
The birth of Christ gives us new life,
    Then frees us from all sin and strife.
So as this Christmas comes once more,
    May your hearts be filled, and your spirits soar,
To offer praise and thanks anew,
    For all that He has given you!

GOD'S PERFECT TIME: - Inspired by Romans 5:6-11

In the fullness of time, God sent His Son,
    In the fullness of time God's will was done.
A star arose from Jacob's line,
    A Sceptre pure in Israel's time.

The Lord himself declared The Sign,
    A virgin conceived in God's own time;
Conceived by the power of the Holy Ghost,
    His birth proclaimed by the heavenly host.

Proclaimed to shepherds that starry night,
    Proclaimed to bring men holy light.
A light to lighten the hearts of men,
    And free them from the trap of sin.

A child was born, A Son was given,
    A Saviour came from the courts of heaven!
Came to free us from our sin,
    Free to have His peace within,

Free to live and serve Him now,
    Free to make a solemn vow.
A vow to give our lives to Him,
    A vow to live our lives in Him.

YOUR WORD - Inspired by Psalm 119:11

Lord You gave Your Word to me,
    To set my soul and spirit free,
To make me Yours and Yours alone,
    To worship You upon Your throne.
Forgive me now oh Lord I pray,
    From all that cause my heart to stray.
Make me a temple pure and true,
    A holy place to worship You!

SING TO THE LORD - Inspired by Psalm 96.

Sing a new song to the Lord,
    For He is a God who keeps His word.
A Saviour He promised to free us from sin,
    To make us whole and alive again
He came to the earth as a human babe,
    Then gave His life so all can be saved.
Saved from sin and pain and strife,
    Saved to live a victorious life.
A life that offers to all mankind,
    The gift of salvation, and a transformed mind.

COME AND WORSHIP - Inspired by Psalm 95:1-5

Come worship The King, in the heavens above,
    Come sing of His mercies, His goodness and love.
For He is our God, to Him we give praise,
    And He is the God, who gives life to our days.

This life He gives free, to all who would choose,
    To give Him their lives, for they've nothing to lose!
The life that Christ gives, is abundant and free,
    The life that Christ gives, gives us liberty.

Liberty is ours, not license you see,
    Liberty to stand, and to make us free.
Free from sin, and free from strife,
    Free to give us a brand-new life.

Free to love, and free to hope,
    Free to believe, and not to grope.
For the freedom Christ gives, gives sight to all,
    A sight to see, and not to fall!

BOW TO THE KING - Inspired by Psalm 95:6

Bow down, and Christ will lift you up,
    Bow down, and Christ will fill your cup.
Bow down and worship, The King of Kings,
    Bow down, He'll give a song to sing!
A song of praise, a song of love,
    A song to our God, in the heavens above;
A song that lifts, your heart to sing,
    A song that makes, the rafters ring.
Jesus The Christ, has come today,
    For hearts to rejoice and spirit's praise!

THE ANGEL'S PROCLAMATION: Inspired by Luke 2:11

The angels proclaimed, a King is born!
    A Saviour, Redeemer, on this Holy morn!
Oh what can we bring, to this Saviour, this King?
    Let's bring Him our lives, and the songs we sing.

For He alone, is God of all God's,
    He alone, holds the Shepherds rod!
A rod to guide us, into perfect paths,
    A rod that leads, to His cleansing bath.

For the Blood of Jesus, is the bath that frees,
    The Blood of Jesus, cleans you and me.
The Blood of Jesus, alone can save,
    His precious life, for us He gave.

Life eternal, is the gift He gives,
    So choose The Christ, this day and live;
Live in the grace, His life bestows,
    Live in the life, of His Blood that flows,
From His precious side, His Blood poured out,
    So, trust in His love and never doubt

JOY - Inspired by John 15:11

Oh what joy, is ours who believe,
    Who live in The Christ, to Whom we cleave.
For Christ is our God, our King and our Lord,
    Our Saviour, Redeemer, The Living Word!
Do you know Him my friend, He is waiting now,
    So open your heart, make a solemn vow,
To love Him and serve Him, all of your days,
    To offer up worship, and prayer and praise.

This life He offers, is abundant and free,
    It's a life of God's grace, and liberty.
This liberty was purchased, by our Saviour's Blood,
    So we could experience, God's ultimate good.
This goodness that comes, from heaven above,
    Is a goodness that gives us, the choice to love.
To love our God, with a love that's true,
    And to love one another, as God loves you.

So in this special, season of time,
    Open your hearts, to this message of mine;
Choose life from our Lord,, give Him your all,
    And though you may stumble, you'll never fall.
For underneath you, are His eternal arms,
    He will keep you from trouble, from dread and alarm.
You'll be safe forever, in His strong right-hand,
    He will bring you safe, to His promised land

For heaven is waiting, and the joy that it holds,
    Are wonders unceasing, and our Lord to behold.
For our greatest joy, is to behold His face,
    Then worship our Lord, who gave us His grace.
Grace to receive, His life for free,
    Grace to praise Him, for eternity!
Grace to give Him, our highest goals,
    Grace to believe, He holds our souls!

A GIFT OF WORTH - Inspired by Revelation 19:7-8

There is a song that I must sing,
   A song of worship to my King,
He saved my life from sin and strife,
   Now I am His bride, His cherished wife.
What can I offer, what gift can I bring?
   What can I give, to my Lord and my King?
I will give Him the love, that He gave to me;
   I'll give Him my life, for He set me free!

LORD OF LOVE - Inspired by Psalm 119:111

I write a poem to You my Lord,
How I love Your precious word.
For in Your Word You gave to me,
A Word of life, a grace that is free!
Free to love you Lord of love,
Free to worship God above.

ONE ACCORD - Inspired by John 17 & Ephesians 4:1-6

Precious Jesus, Holy Lord, make us all of one accord.
One in faith and hope and love, one to serve our God above;
One to live in purity, one to set the captives free.
Free to love You Lord of Love, free to enter Your courts above!
Free to worship, free to praise, free to serve You all our days!
For You're a God, who lives to give,
A God who gives us, grace to forgive.
A God who redeems, a God who restores,
A God who gives life, forevermore.
This is the God, I want to show,
So others may see, and others may know,
How much You love, Your children below.

HEAR THE WORD - Inspired by Ecclesiastes 5:4 & 5

Hear the Word, I give you know,
 As you make, your solemn vow.
For the vow you make, is before the Lord,
 And He is the God, who keeps His Word.
So think it through, take time to pray,
 Before you make, your vow today.
For a vow before God, is a solemn pledge,
 A vow with God, protects like a hedge!
To keep within, a line of faith
 And keep without, what leads to death.

So as you make, your vow today,
 Heed the Words the Lord would say;
For in His Words, are life and peace,
 And all His Words, bring sweet release.
Release from all, that troubles man
 And gives to us, God's perfect plan.
A plan that gives us, life and hope,
 A plan that shows us, how to cope:
Not with human strength, to stand,
 But in the power, of our God's hand.

For once we enter, with this solemn vow,
 To be His child, forever now,
His arms protect, His love defends,
 His grace provides, our fears He ends.
So come to Christ, this day my friend,
 His love for you, will never end.
Eternal life begins, right now,
 His blessing, as you make your vow,
A vow to always, live for Him,
 A vow that frees, our lives of sin.

DO YOU HEAR? - Inspired by John 14:6

Hear and listen, learn and obey,
    The Word I give, to you this day.
The God you serve, is not a man,
    His truth, His way, His life, His plan!
This is the way, to life my friends,
    The way of life, without an end.
For the ways of God, are pure and true,
    And what He says, is what He will do.
So seek His truth, His way, His life,
    In Christ alone, is the path that's right.

Cease from striving, cease from sin,
    For in His life, comes peace within.
A peace that calms, our deepest woes,
    A peace that triumphs, over our foes,
A peace that passes, every thought,
    A peace, The Blood of Christ has bought!
This peace the world, can never give,
    But Christ has given, so you can live!
So live my friend, in His dear love,
    Then join the courts, in heaven above.

Seek His kingdom, and His alone,
    For Christ Himself, is The Cornerstone.
The Stone to hide in, The Rock of shelter,
    A place of safety, like no other.
For faith in Him, and His Precious Blood,
    Faith will save you, from the flood.
So turn to Him, call out today,
    And from His call, turn not astray.
Real life He offers, strong and true,
    Real life He gives, to me and you!

REMEMBER - Inspired by Ecclesiastes 12:6

Remember your Creator, in the days of your youth,
>   For He is The Way, The Life and The Truth.
He alone, is the God who reveals,
>   And what He reveals, is what He heals!
He gives to us, a life that is free, a life that brings us liberty.

Liberty is freedom, bought with Christ's blood,
>   Freedom to live, for our Holy God!
Freedom from all, that would hinder man,
>   Freedom to choose, our Master's plan.
So remember now, don't put it off;
>   Remember now, your life He bought!

Remember now and enter in, remember now, and cease from sin.
>   For He is God, and He alone,
He gave His life, our sins to atone.
>   Christ has made us, right with God,
He keeps us with, His Shepherds Rod,
>   Keeps us free and pure within, keeps us living all for Him!

PRECIOUS LORD - Inspired by John 13:34-35

You are precious, Lord to me,
>   Give me sight, that I might see;
See the wonders, of Your face,
>   Feel the warmth, of Your embrace.
A touch from You, is all I need,
>   So I can love, by word and deed.
Love you Lord, with all I am,
>   Then love Your children, while I can.
Let me love, with Your sweet love,
>   So all can know You, God above.

BELIEVE AND RECEIVE - Inspired by John 12:12-14

Believe in Me, and what I say,
    Believe in Me, trust and obey!
Believe in Me, and My power to do,
    The works that I, have given you.

My kingdom shall come, and My will be done,
    When the Father, is glorified in the Son!
The greater works, you then shall do,
    By the power of the Spirit, that lives in you.

Power to proclaim, the Living Word
    And power to use, the Spirits sword!
Power to set, My people free,
    Power to live, through eternity,.
In the grace and love, and power of God,
    With thanks in your heart, now give Him laud!

CHOSEN - Inspired by John 15:6

Lord I praise, Your holy name,
    From heaven to earth, for us You came
The Father's love, You came to show,
    To save the fallen, to lift the low!
To give us hope, and peace today,
    To be our God, and Lord always.

You chose us, we didn't choose You,
    You came to us, to make us new
By the life You led, and the Blood You shed,
    You paid the price, for our lives instead.
You set us free, You gave Your grace,
    Now let us Lord, behold Your face.

TRADERS - Inspired by Zechariah 14:21 b

No more traders, in the House of The Lord,
    But grace and prayer, to spread My word.
My Word and Blood, have the power to save,
    From all, that soul and body crave.
So cleanse your hearts, and minds right now,
    Hear My call, and make your vow-
A holy temple I will be,
    A place from where, I worship Thee.
For you alone are God The Lord,
    We give our lives, to spread Your Word.

WHAT TIME IS IT? - Inspired by John 4:34-38

The time is right, the time is now,
    The time has come, to reap and plow
Reap the harvest, already white,
    Plow for the seed, to be planted right.
Prepare the ground, with praise and prayer,
    For then My Word, can enter there.

The seed that enters, shows no life,
    It's power is hid, from sin and strife.
But when it dies, it changes form
    And God brings life, a child is born!
A child who hears, the Voice of God,
    A child who worships, The One True God.

This child whose heart, is free from sin,
    Is a child who has, God's Spirit within.
This child's true strength, is in the Lord,
    With a word from God, like a blazing torch.
To light the path, of those who stray
    And bring them back, to God today!

21

HEAR AND LIVE
Inspired by Matthew 13:9 and Hebrews 4:12

Hear Me now, thus says The Lord,
    Trust in Me, and trust My Word.
My Word is sharp, like a scalpel true,
    Will cut from your life, all that hinders you.

Fear not God's scalpel, for what it cuts,
    Will set you free, from deadly ruts.
Now free to soar, on God's Spirit wings,
    You're free to live, with a song to sing!

So sing your song, to your God alone,
    A song of hope, to those He atoned.
It is finished, Christ paid the price,
    Paid our debt, with His sacrifice.

Come unto Me, The Saviour calls,
    Then from My side, you'll never fall.
My arms protect, the ones I love,
    I bring them to, My courts above.

So heed God's voice, and heed His call,
    Come to Him now, surrender all.
For your life, has just begun,
    Serve your God, behold His Son!

CHECK MY HEART - Inspired by Matthew 10:39

What will you give, so man may live?
    Will you give your all, or will you stall?
Is your heart God's own, His royal throne?
    Do you live for Christ, and Christ alone?
These are the questions, to check my heart,
    So from my Saviour, I will never depart.

GOD'S VOICE - Inspired by Romans 12:1

Lord I give, my life to Thee,
    Hear my heart, set my spirit free.
Free to hear, Your lovely voice,
    For I love you Lord, I make my choice.

What You will say, that I will do,
    For I desire, to worship You.
To see the wonders, of Your grace,
    To feel the warmth, of Your embrace.

For it's Your love, Oh Lord I crave,
    Your love alone, has the power to save.
You saved me Lord, I am Yours alone,
    I bow before, Your Holy Throne.

MY CHILDREN - Inspired by 1st Thessalonians 1:5

Out of My children, My Word goes forth,
    From West to East, from South to North
It touches all, for all can hear,
    All can see, all draw near.
To hear the pure, and living truth,
    Of The Word from God, with signs and proof.

My Word will have, free course this day
    And then My flock, will never stray!
My Word is The Word, and My Word is true
    And what I have said, is what I will do.
Obey My Word, do not delay,
    Give Me your life, this very day.

CREATOR GOD - Inspired by Genesis Chapter 1

In six short days, God made the earth,
  With man and beast, He gave them worth.
A plan to live, in life and peace,
  With joy and love, to never cease.

Then man fell for, the tempters lies,
  It seemed God's plan, for man had died.
The earth was filled, with strife not peace,
  Until the Lord, brought sweet release.

His coming timed, by God's wondrous grace,
  To show to all, God's loving face.
For when we see, The Face of God,
  With love and faith, by The Spirit of God,
Our lives are changed, our hope is restored,
  God's love is revealed, by our precious Lord.
So hear His call, give Him your all,
  For on bended knee, you'll never fall.

MY PRAYER

Lord I love Thee, keep me near,
  Cause me to love, and cease from fear.
Let me see, Your lovely face,
  Hold me in, Your warm embrace.
Then from this place, of Your pure love,
  And with Your power, Oh God of love,
I will show, by word and deed,
  That You Lord God, are all I need.
So that your truth, alone be told,
  Please make Your Word, alive and bold.
To decree and declare, that God alone,
  Gives power and grace, our sins to atone!

YOUR VOICE

Let me hear, Your voice so sweet,
　　As I kneel, to wash Your feet.
Then wash the feet, of those You love,
　　Prepare them for, Your courts above.
Cause me to love, with Your acts of grace,
　　To help them, see Your loving face.
For it's only by, the deeds we do,
　　That Your love is shown, as pure and true.
Let my words, be Yours alone,
　　As I bow, before Your throne.
May I Lord, Your servant to be,
　　Now and through eternity.

TELL THE TRUTH.

Tell the truth, to each other in love,
　　For this is the will, of your Father above.
Let mercy and grace, temper your tone,
　　For God is God, He is Lord alone.
For as you speak, His truth in love,
　　The Word alone, from God above,
The chains that bind, are broken clean
　　And men are from, their sins redeemed.
Redeemed to live, a brand-new life,
　　A life that's free, from sin and strife.
My love I give, to set men free,
　　That I might then, their Saviour be.
For this is why, I came to earth,
　　To give to all, My free new birth.

GOD'S PROMISE

Lord I give myself to you,
Cleanse me Lord, and make me new.
Wash me in Your Precious Blood,
Heal me by Your Cleansing Flood.
A pure temple I would be, wholly given unto Thee.

I will cleanse and purify,
Lest you stumble, fall or die.
Take your fingers, from your ears,
Hear Me now, and hear Me clear.
Check your motives, search your mind,
Was it for Me, that you were kind?

Judge your heart, now honestly;
Were your thoughts, on self or Me?
Is your heart, My royal throne,
Are you Mine, and Mine alone?
Think it through, let your heart be true,
For a new temple, I would make of you!

At temple not, with brick or stone,
A temple made, with flesh and bone.
A living temple, a fresh new start,
A temple with, a brand-new heart,
A heart that follows, after Me,
A heart to set, the captives free.

Free from guilt, and every stain,
Free to live, for Christ to gain
His mercy, and salvation too,
For Jesus gave, His life for you.
So show God's mercy, and His love,
The kindness of, our God above.
Then My temple, you will be,
Mine for all eternity!

PURE RELIGION - Inspired by Proverbs 14:31

I have spoken repeatedly, in My Word,
    Not to oppress, but always to bless.
Reach out to orphans and widows, God says,
    The foreigners and poor, in their duress.

I AM The Father, to the fatherless,
    I AM the spouse, to the one in distress,
So reach in My Name, with My love to bless,
    For then they will know, My love, My caress

Give to the poor, so they'll know My love,
    The ones who don't know Me, to take up above.
Reach out in the natural, and spiritual too,
    Give them My word, for My Word is true.

I AM The Fountain, of Life that lives,
    I AM The God, who saves and forgives,
Peace and prosperity, I'll give unto all,
    Who give me their life, to save from the fall.

Then I will rescue, and will save from the grave,
    I will make you a symbol, of a life that's been saved,
For all men will know, that I rescued you,
    They will see that My grace, has brought you through.

TRUE CHRISTIANITY - Inspired by James 1:27

God has spoken, in His Word,
    Clothe the naked, feed the poor.
Cheer the lonely, heal their hurt,
    Then with His love, lift from the dirt.
Reach out to those, for whom He came,
    The weary, worn, the blind, the lame.
Then all may see, and all my know,
    That Jesus came, God's love to show!

GRACE TO FAST - Inspired By Matthew 6:16

Dear Lord I pray, make a way, grant me grace to fast and pray.
Fast to set the captives free, pray to walk in liberty.
This is the day and this is the way, to see My face, fast and pray.
One day a week is what I ask, to fast and pray, this is your task.
Fast to see My will made known, pray to come before My throne.
Fast from all the cares of life, pray to cease from sin and strife.
Here Me now, this is the way, the way to hear My voice today.
Fast from all that life demands, pray to follow My commands.
Eternal life is yours today, and from My side you'll never stray.

WHY DO WE FAST - Inspired by Joel Chapter 2

What does it mean, to fast and pray?
    Why do we wander, from God's way?
We fast to see, the face of God,
    We pray to walk, the path He trod.
For when we see, His holy face,
    And feel the warmth, of His embrace,
Our hearts rejoice, to hear His voice,
    And make His perfect will, our choice.
His will to see, men's souls set free,
    He gave His life, for all to see;
His love so wondrous, His grace so true,
    His Blood was shed, for me and you!
Shed to give, to all who call,
    The faith we need, to give our all.
For when we give, our all to Him,
    He sets us free, from every sin.
Free to live and free to love, free to enter His courts above.
    Free to give, of His mercy and grace,
Free to walk, in His loving pace.
    You will not grow weary, or worn this way,
When you walk with the Lord, your God this way!

THE ARROWS OF GOD - Inspired by Isaiah 49

Like an arrow, He shoots me forth,
   To west and east, to south and north.
To give His Word, to all who hear,
   To spread His love, to far and near.
Here Me now, says our God and Lord,
   Listen clearly, to My Word..
Is this the time, to feast and play?
   In times like these, Fast and Pray!
Fast to see, My saving grace,
   Pray to know, and see My face.
My glory shown, to all who care,,
   My love to cover, the naked and bare

What My love covers, My love cleans,
   My Blood purifies, My Blood redeems.
Buys back My own, that sin and stray,
   And sets them on, the narrow way:
The way that gives, eternal life,
   The way that frees, from sin and strife.
Choose now my friend, today is the day,
   Choose now my friend, to fast and pray.
Then you will see, My will is done,
   My grace extended, to all who come;
Who come to gain, the life I give,
   Who come to Me, so they may live.

My loving Grace, will set you free,
   To live and love, set captives free.
Free to know Me, free to love,
   Free to serve, their Father above.
For this is why, I came to earth,
   To give to all, a second birth.
Not of flesh, but by My Spirit given,
   To live for Me, on earth and heaven!

ZION - Inspired by Jeremiah Chapter 31

My love for Zion, is passionate, strong,
  My love that cleans, from sin and wrong.
My love abounds, my love sets free,
  From sin and strife, and immorality.
My love defends, My holy bride,
  My love redeems, from deadly pride.
Grace and prayer, come from My Spirit,
  Poured out on all, without their merit.
The gift to pray, is given to all,
  His grace He bestows, to those who call.
So call upon, the Lord today
  And from His side, you'll never stray.
For He who gave, His life for you,
  Is The One who stands, and pleads for you.
Stands in prayer, at The Father's right hand,
  Stands to defend, His holy band.

GOD'S WAYS - Inspired by Psalm 25:10

All the ways of the Lord, are mercy and truth,
  His love is abundant, much greater than Ruth's.
She left home and country, because of her love
  She left with Naomi, to serve God above.
So let us all, in the same spirit of love,
  Leave the things of this world, on the wings of a dove.
To soar above all, that would drag us down,
  To lift the Lord's name, His name of renown.
For His mercy and love, and grace He gives free
  To all who would trust, in Him and believe.
So love not the world, and the wealth it provides,
  Love the Lord your God, and stay by His side.
Receive His mercy, and grace today,
  Cling to Him now, and never stray.
He keeps His own, with His strong right arm,
  His love has no limits, He saves us from harm

HOPE AND LIFE. - Inspired by Psalm 42:5

There is hope, and life for you,
    If by My Word, you live what's true.
For it is not, by words alone,
    That you approach, My holy throne.
It's by your deeds, you show My love,
    And lead men to, My throne above.
Let words of faith, be spoken true,
    Then deeds of love, extend from you,
Then all will know, the God you love,
    Is God alone, The God above.
He offered all, His life He gave,
    So we can from, our sins be saved,
Saved to live, for God alone,
    Saved to stand,before His throne.

SPEAK TO THE ROCK - Inspired by Mark 11:22 & 23

Speak to the rock, that stands in your way,
    Speak to the rock, in the Lord's name today.
The rock was not put there, to hinder your walk,
    But to seek the Lord, for His message to talk.
So speak to the rocks, that the Lord has placed,
    With the words that He gives, by His love and His grace.
The rocks will move, when they hear what you say,
    If you'll speak in faith, God's will to obey..
If you'll speak and walk, in the Word of God's power,
    His Name and His fame, will be honoured this hour.
Oh forgive me Lord, for taking from You,
    The glory and praise, and worship that's due,
To You our Lord Jesus, and to God Most High,
    So all of men everywhere, may live and not die.
For when Your glory, to men is revealed,
    They turn from their sin, and their souls You heal
By the incoming power, of Your love and Your grace
    They can worship You now, and behold Your face!

WHEN YOU PRAY - Inspired by Matthew 6:5-8

When you pray, don't babble about,
    Pray in faith, and do not doubt.
For when we pray, in faith we know,
    God hears our prayers, and His answers go
    From heaven to earth, to meet the need,
    Of those who call, to Him for seed.
Sow the seed, He gives to you,
    Sow that men, may know the truth.
    Sow in faith, and sow in love,
    Sow to bless, the ones God loves.
For as you sow, with love and grace,
    All who receive, can see God's face.
    His face is love, in purest form,
    And by His Word, He stills the storm

GIVING - Inspired by Matthew 6:1-4

When you give a gift, to one in need,
    Don't brag about, this special seed,
For God is The One, who gave the seed,
    So you could give, to meet their need!

SPEAK TO ME - Inspired by Isaiah 50:4

Holy Spirit, speak to me,
    Give me eyes, to really see.
Help me hear, Your Word today,
    Help me walk, the narrow way.
Shed Your light, upon the path,
    That leads to life, and not to wrath.
For You are love, in purest form,
    Your love alone, redeems, transforms.
Immerse me fresh, in Your holy love,
    So I may enter, Your courts above!

DEDICATION - Inspired by Romans 12.

Dear Lord I give, my life to You,
    Let my heart be Yours, and my spirit true.
True to love You, all my days,
    Yours to follow, in every way.
For You are God, and God alone,
    I bow before, Your holy throne.
Thank you Lord, for loving me,
    You set my soul, and spirit free.
Holy Spirit fill me now, as I make this solemn vow.
    To love and serve, to give and forgive,
And always for, my Saviour live.
    To live for Christ in all I do, to show His love to others too.
Not by words alone I pray, but with deeds, along the way.
    So all may see, and all may know,
That Jesus came, God's love to show.
    A love that frees, from the grip of sin,
A love that gives, The Spirit within.
    To hear and know, God's loving voice,
To make His will, our only choice.
    For then we'll, know our God above,
And love Him, with a Holy love!

GOD'S HOLY WILL - Inspired by John 7:17 & 18

Do My will, and you will live,
    Do My will, and you will give,
Do My will, and you will love,
    On earth beneath, and heaven above.
For I AM God, and God alone,
    Worship then, before My throne.
As you worship, you are changed,
    To enter paths, that I arrange,
Paths of love, and hope and peace,
    Paths that bring, your soul release!.

THE WATER OF LIFE - Inspired by John Chapter 4

Are you thirsty? Come and drink,
 From The Water of Life, The Living Link!
For Jesus is The Link, to God,
 He leads us by, the path He trod!
If you would like a life refreshed,
 Come now to Jesus, and be blessed.
His coming is like, the morning dew,
 His life He gave, for me and you.

A perfect life, is what He gave,
 So we from death, can now be saved.
To live for Him, with joy and love,
 To freely enter His courts above.
To worship, sing and praise our Lord,
 To come together, in one accord.
To hear His voice, and do His will,
 To hear Him speaking, "Peace be still".

So allow His peace, to fill your heart,
 Then from His side, you'll never depart.
For His peace alone, can calm our fears,
 Can soothe our mind, and dry our tears.
This peace will guide you, in His will,
 And then His plans, you will fulfill.
Oh what joy, and what delight,
 For in His plan, there is no night.

His plan gives light, that comes with love,
 Only the light, from The Father above.
Light to lighten, every way,
 Light to choose, God's ways today.
So come to Christ, The Water of Life,
 He'll make you clean, from sin and strife.
He is waiting now, do not delay,
 His Spirit is calling - come today!

THE WORD OF THE LORD - Inspired by Hebrews 4:11-16

I need a word, from You my Lord,
    I need Your guidance, strength, and sword.
Your Word, a sword, that separates,
    So we can enter, Your holy gates.
Cut off from us, what would defile,
    So we can go, the extra mile.

Hear Me now, thus says The Lord,
    Hear My voice, proclaim My word.
Give ear to Me, come near and see,
    The plans I have, prepared for thee.
The plans I give, will help, not harm,
    My plans will shield you, from alarm.

Let My Word, your teacher be,
    Let My Spirit, strengthen thee;
To do the work, for which you're called,
    To lift the fallen, heal the stalled.
With the words, I have given you,
    Speak My life, to many or few.

Use the words, that I have given
    To save the lost, to lead to heaven.
Then give to men, while on this earth,
    The life to live, by My new birth.
My birth will bring, your soul's release,
    My birth will give, a life of peace.

This peace the world, can never give,
    This peace I give, so all can live.
In grace and love, of God alone,
    Faultless to stand, before God's throne,
Robed in white, by His precious blood,
    Saved by grace, through faith for good.

REVELATION TO SEE - **Inspired by Romans 16:25-27**

Your revelation, is what we need,
    To purify, Your holy seed,
To see You Lord, in Your holiness,
    To receive Your grace, and righteousness.

To You Oh Lord, we humbly come,
    To cleanse from all, our sins not some,
That we would see, Your holy face,
    And then equipped, to run the race,
We'd tell the world, to far and wide,
    Come to Jesus, precious side;

From His pure side, His Blood did flow,
    To cleanse us from, all sin and woe.
His Blood, the only sacrifice,
    That will atone, that will suffice.
Now by His Blood, we are set free,
    From all the devil's, tyranny!
Free to worship, free to praise,
    Free to love God, all our days,

We are cleansed to be, His holy bride,
    Free from all, our sin and pride,
Free to give, to Him our all,
    Free to answer, when He calls,
Free to say, Oh Lord send me,
    To set the bound, and captive free;
That all would hear, His voice so dear:
    "I'll wipe away, your every tear,
I'll give you life, forever true,
    Born again, born brand new!

THE LIGHT OF GOD'S LOVE - Inspired by John 8:12

The light of Your Love, is shining Oh Lord,
    Shining, to all the earth.
The Light of Your Love, is leading Oh Lord,
    Leading all men, to new birth.
The light of Your Love, is guiding Oh Lord,
    Guiding, to a life of truth.
The Light of Your love, is healing Oh Lord,
    Healing, that brings love to birth.

Jesus, You are the Light of the world,
    You, are the hope of mankind.
Jesus, You are the love that keeps giving,
    Jesus, You healed my mind.
Jesus, You are the source of my joy,
    Jesus, You give me peace,
Jesus, You give me life everlasting,
    Jesus, You bought my release.

Now at this very special time,
    The time we honour Your birth,
Cause us to speak to the nations,
    Jesus, The Christ came to earth!
Not just for one man or two,
    Jesus, You came for us all.
You came to bring victory and freedom,
    Freedom, to answer Your call.

We come to You now, Dear Saviour,
    We come to answer, Your call
We want the true life, that You offer,
    We come, to give You our all.
We want this peace, that You give,
    Your joy and Your love, divine;
We ask that You take and make us, Lord,
    Always and forever Thine.

REJOICE! REJOICE! - Inspired by Philippians 4:4-9

Rejoice, Rejoice, Oh people of God,
    Give God the glory, and give Him laud,
Let your praise, to Him arise,
    For Christ became, our sacrifice.

A pure and holy God is He,
    He came, and set our spirits free.
Free to walk, this world in light,
    For we've been made right, in His sight.

Then trust and believe, have faith today,
    And at His feet, your burdens lay.
Christ has set us, free from sin,
    Now by His Blood, we enter in.

We come into, God's courts above,
    Equipped to walk, this world in love.
His love will conquer, fear and doubt,
    His love will shut, the tempter out.

His love will bring, our soul's release,
    His love will give us, joy and peace.
So enter into faith, my friend,
    Christ died for you, on Him depend.

His life He gave, because He loved,
    Paid our price, with His precious blood.
He paid for us, to be set free,
    With Him, we'll live eternally!

THE WILL OF GOD - Inspired by Colossians 1:9-12

Do My will, and you will live,
    Do My will, and you will give,
Do My will, and you will love,
    Here on earth, and heaven above.

For I AM God, and God alone,
    Worship then, before My throne.
As you worship, you are changed,
    To enter paths, that I arrange,
Paths of hope, and paths of peace,
    Paths that bring, your soul release.

I came to set, your spirit free,
    To walk in love, and liberty;
So tarry not,, do not delay,
    Enter into, My truth today.

Receive My gift, of life right now,
    Give Me your life, and make your vow.
Joy and love, like you've never known,
    Will flood your soul, and spirit hone.
By My Word you'll know, what is right,
    My Spirit makes, My word a light.

FLEE - Inspired by 2nd Timothy 2:22

Flee from sin, from debt and pride,
    Flee to Me, My holy side.

I will make, a way for you,
    A way that's pure, that's right, that's true.

For you are still, My own dear child,
    My life I gave, to make you mild.
        (mild means kind and gracious.)

<u>HEAR ME</u> - Inspired by Isaiah 55:3

Hear Me now, thus says The Lord,
　　Trust in Me, obey My Word.
My Spirit will, reveal to you
　　The life I have, prepared for you.

I paid the price, I gave My life,
　　To set men free, from sin and strife.
For striving only, causes pain,
　　And traps you to, a life that's vain.

So give to God, The Lord, your all,
　　Leave off your pride, and hear His call.
He'll cleanse your heart, from every sin,
　　He'll make you pure, and whole within.

His life will bring, your soul's release,
　　A life that gives you, perfect peace.
His peace is like, you've never known,
　　This peace comes from, God's heart alone.

This peace will conquer, every fear,
　　This peace that says, come here, draw near.
This peace, the world can never give,
　　This peace God gives, so you can live.

So live a life, of joy and love,
　　Established by, The Father above.
And when you hear, God's Spirit's call,
　　To give to Christ, your life, your all.
He will come in, He'll set you free,
　　He'll give you life, and liberty.

WHO CAN SEPARATE - Inspired by Romans 8:35 - 39

Who can separate us, from God's love,
    The love God gives, from heaven above.
The love of Christ, has shown to all,
    A love that's pure, He gave His all;
That we His temple, now could be,
    Here on earth, and for eternity.
Oh listen to, The Spirit's call,
    Come to The Christ, come one, come all.
He has a life, for us to live,
    A life of love, a life to give.
A life that sets us, free from sin,
    A life of love, from The Spirit within.
Oh what joy, and peace He gives,
    When we invite, our Saviour in.
For when we bow, and make Him Lord,
    Our hearts come in, to one accord,
With Father's will, and plan for us,
    To set us free, from sin and lust.

Now free to live, and love His way,
    For nothing keeps, God's love away.
Fear or worry, or powers of hell,
    None can conquer, His love dispels.
Despite these things, the victory is ours,
    For Christ has broken, every bar.
So reach out My child, with grace and love,
    Reach out with the touch, from God above.
His mercies are, forever new,
    His peace will guide, and comfort you.
And in the grace, which you've been given,
    You'll lead men to, the courts of heaven,
Cleansed, redeemed, healed and restored,
    You'll lead them to, their Redeeming Lord.
Where with the saints, in full array,
    They'll praise and worship, God that day.

HOLY SPIRIT HEAR MY PRAYER

Holy Spirit, hear the words I pray,
    What should I speak, what should I say?
What should I write, what should I pray,
    How may I gladden, God's heart today?
I'll sing to Him, a brand new song,
    I'll make it sweet, and make it long,
For a heart of love, He's given to me,
    To make my heart, and spirit free.

Dear Lord I sing, this song to You,
    A song of love, to worship You,
For You are all, my soul's desire,
    You light my life, with holy fire.
Let my life, an offering be,
    To be Your own, for eternity.
You alone, are my soul's delight,
    You illumine, the darkest night.

You give me peace, and joy within,
    Your love redeems, my soul from sin.
Oh how great, Your sacrifice,
    You gave Your life, You paid the price.
Your Blood You poured, on the mercy seat,
    You gave us life, so we could meet,
With You Lord God, The King of all,
    To humbly kneel, to hear Your call.

You call to come, and enter in,
    You call to bring, Your peace within.
Oh Precious Lord, I love You so,
    You've set me free, from every woe.
I'm free to worship, all my days,
    Free to offer, up my praise,
Free to sing, and free to dance,
    Free from living, a life of chance.

Now my heart, can enter in,
    To hear Your voice, of love within.
Oh Father God, receive my song,
    For You I live, for You I long.
A holy temple, I would be,
    For You, for all eternity:
A place where You, can live and dwell,
    For You have set me, free from hell.

Let my words, and life proclaim,
    The glory of, Your Holy Name;
For Your Name is The Name, above all names,
    It is by Your Name, that we are saved.
Saved to worship, saved to praise,
    Saved to love, You all our days!
Saved to serve, and saved to give,
    Your Light to all, so all may live.

HEAR MY WORD - Inspired by Nehemiah 8:8 & 1st John 2:27

Hear My Word, take heed I say,
    To all My Word, this very day,
Don't pick and choose, just what you want,
    For then your soul, is lean and gaunt.
But if you want, a full clear life,
    A life that's free, from sin and strife,
Then let My Word, do it's perfect work,
    To clear your sight, from lies that murk.
For lies will cloud, your heart and mind,
    They'll keep you in, the sin that binds.
So listen clear, this very day,
    Listen with, your heart and say:
Come Holy Spirit, speak to me,
    Explain Your Word, and set me free.

CRY TO THE LORD - Inspired by Hebrews 4:16

Cry to the Lord, from the place you are bound,
    Cry to Him now, let your voices resound.
Give glory and praise, to His Holy Name
    Lift your hearts and your voice, His fame to proclaim.
When you lift your voice, to the Lord on high,
    With praise and worship, God hears your cry.
For the place of praise, is where Father God lives,
    In this place of praise, you receive what He gives.

Don't whine your prayers, you're a child of the King,
    Come boldly to enter, His courts and sing.
Sing a new song, to our God of love,
    Sing a new song, join the Angels above.
Fill the courts of heaven, with worship and praise
    For the God of all gods, is the Ancient of Days!
He sits enthroned, in The Holy Place,
    His glory shines forth, from His Holy Face.

This glory has power, to change you and me,
    His glory in Christ, has set us free.
Now free from the bonds, of sin and shame,
    We are free to respond, to His Holy Name.
We are free to give Him, our worship and praise,
    We are free to love Him, for all of our days.
We are free to share, His message of grace,
    We are free to live, with His joy on our face.

This joy comes from knowing, Christ Jesus our Lord,
    From hearing His voice, and reading His word.
His Word He has given, to lead as along,
    The path He has chosen, to make us strong.
Strong in His love, and strong in His power,
    Strong in His faith and His hope in this hour.
For He has come, to set us free,
    To enjoy His life, for eternity

OH PRECIOUS LORD - Inspired by Ephesians 1:7-14

Oh Precious Lord, You sets me free,
    Your precious Blood, You shed for me.
You died upon, that awful cross,
    To set me free, from sin and loss.

Redeemed my soul, from sin and death,
    Redeemed and gave me, life and breath.
Oh what joy, that now I know,
    I'm cleansed and changed, Your love to show.

To You Oh Lord, my God and King,
    I praise Your Holy Name, and sing;
I sing and speak, of Your great love,
    To lead men to, Your courts above.

For it's not by works, that we have done,
    But by the Blood of Christ, God's Son.
For when we put, our trust in You,
    You set us free, You make us new.

You give us faith, to give our all,
    And answer yes, to Your holy call.
Life in Christ, is ours to share,
    With words and deeds, with love and care.

So come my friend, let us tell to all,
    This word of hope, Christ died for all.
Then joining with all, the hosts of heaven,
    Let's praise His name, for what He has given!

SONG OF LOVE - Inspired by John 1:12-14

There is a song, that I must sing,
    A song of love, to You my King!
So I lift my heart, and I lift my voice,
    For you have given to me, freedom of choice.
Oh Lord my God, to you I raise,
    This song of love, this song of praise.
For Who is like, my Glorious Lord,
    Whose voice can cheer, by just one word.

My love I offer You, Oh Lord
    Keep and hold me, with Your cord.
Bind me to, Your holy heart,
    Let me never, ever part,
Now to You Lord, my God and King
    Let my voice resound, let my praises ring.
For there is none, like You, Dear Lord,
    You gave us love, Your Blood You poured.

You poured Your Blood, on heaven's mercy seat,
    So we could enter, we could meet
With God our Father, Lord of all,
    To hear His voice, to give our all,
To bow before, His holy throne,
    To worship God, and God alone!

So come my friends, come one and all
    Our Lord has come, come hear His call
He calls to all, with voice so dear,
    His love He offers, pure and clear.
His love can cleanse, make whole and new,
    His love completes, gives hope anew.
So tarry not, make this the day,
    To hear His voice, respond and say,
Forgive me Lord, by Your merciful love,
    I receive Your grace, from heaven above.

ROSE OF SHARON - Inspired by Romans 8:38 & 39

Oh Rose of Sharon, Precious Lord,
    Loving Saviour, Living Word.
I lift my heart, to You alone,
    I bow and worship, before Your throne.
Oh God of gods, and King of kings,
    I lift my voice, to You and sing.
Oh God my refuge, and my strength,
    Your love is eternal, it has no length
Nor breadth or width, or height to know,
    Your love transcends, your love bestows
To all who call, upon You Lord,
    To love and stand, in one accord.
To live in love, and unity,
    In holiness, and purity.
You give the grace, and power to all
    Who answer yes, to Your holy call.

So work a work, in us we pray,
    A work to cause, our hearts to say:
Jesus is Lord, and God alone,
    As we approach, Your holy throne.
May we with all, of heaven proclaim
    The glories, of Your Holy Name.
That all who live, now here on earth
    May know your love, receive new birth.
A birth not done, by the plans of men,
    A birth conceived, by The Spirit within,
A birth of life, and love for God,
    A birth that lifts, from this earthly sod;
A birth that gives us, life and hope,
    A birth that shows us, how to cope;
Not with strength, of human ways,
    But by His Spirit, for all our days!

WHICH WAY LORD? - Inspired by Proverbs 14:12

There is a way, that seems right to men,
    But these are not, God's plans for them.
For the plans of God, are higher still,
    The plans of God, will His power fulfill!
So cause me Lord, this very day,
    To hear Your voice, and then to say:
Not my will, but Thine be done,
    That The Father be glorified, in Christ The Son!
For the glory of God, must be revealed,
    So the hearts of men, can be opened, unsealed,
Open to hear, the voice of God,
    Open to feel, His Shepherds Rod.
For His Rod protects, and keeps His sheep,
    He watches us, He never sleeps!
He lives to ever, intercede,
    Before The Father's throne, He pleads.

He pleads for us, for whom He died,
    Pleads for all, whom He justified.
By Jesus Holy sacrifice,
    He shed His blood, He paid the price!
So all who call, upon His name,
    Can come to Him, without sin's shame.
For Christ has opened, up the door,
    The door to life, forevermore;
A pure and holy life, of love,
    A life of love, from God above.
So come my friend, say yes to Him,
    He will set you free, from every sin!
You'll know the love, that sets men free,
    Right here on earth, and to eternity.
This life He gives, brings hope and peace,
    It's a life of love, for our souls release.

LIVE HIS LIFE - Inspired by 1ˢᵗ Thessalonians 4:1-7

Live a life, that pleases Me,
    I'll make your heart, and spirit free;
To bring men freedom, is why I came,
    So all could trust, My Holy Name.
For all who call, upon My Name,
    To set them free, from sin and shame,
Can enter in, to a life that's new,
    A brand-new birth, that's given you.
It is not by works, by which you have done,
    But by your faith, in Christ, God's Son.
For He is The One, who set us free, to walk in love, and liberty.
So call to Christ, do not delay, He'll save your soul, this very day.
Then you will have, real joy and peace,
    His Holy Blood, bought your release.
Release from fear, and sin and doubt,
    Released to give, the Lord a shout.
So give a shout, of thanks, and praise,
    A shout of worship, to The Ancient of Days!

God alone, is the King of Kings,
    He alone gives, a song to sing:
So sing a song, when the path is bright,
    Or a song to sing, in the darkest night.
For His presence is with us, wherever we go,
    He loves, He comforts, He lifts every woe.
So bring Him your heart, your spirit and soul,
    He will hold you real close, your life to console.
He'll console and comfort, restore and redeem,
    By the love of The Father, to give His esteem.
He will raise you to where, He is seated above,
    Then you'll know what it is, to be truly loved.
For you will experience, such love and such grace,
    As you look with love, on His Holy Face,
That never, no never, will you ever depart,
    From the Fathers love, from the Father's heart.

CHOSEN - Inspired by John 15:16

You are chosen to know Me, thus says the Lord,
  Chosen to live, by My holy word.
Chosen to walk, with the Saints in light,
  Chosen to worship, My Name with delight.
Chosen to trust, and to understand,
  Chosen to come, chosen to stand.

You are chosen to leave, this world behind,
  Chosen to think, with a brand-new mind.
Chosen to choose, the Lord as God,
  Chosen to witness, the love of God.
Chosen to declare, God's mercy and grace,
  Chosen to behold, God's holy face.

Now you can walk, through deep waters and fire,
  For you're chosen to walk, and never to tire.
For the Lord is with us, wherever we go,
  He quells our fears, as His Presence we know.
He never leaves us, or turns aside,
  So now we can know Him, whatever betide.

God is God, and God alone,
  No one else, sits on His Throne.
He alone, is The God Who saves,
  He alone, stills the wind and waves.
He is the fourth man, in the fire,
  He redeems, from sin and mire.

He is the One, who gives us life,
  He is The One, who saves from strife.
He is the One, who gives us peace,
  He is The One, that brings release.
From all that causes, fear and doubt,
  Our lives are free, to never pout!

GOD OF ALL - Inspired by The Love of God

God of all god's, Lord of all lord's,
    It is You that I worship, You I adore
You alone, are the One that I love,
    You alone, in heaven above.
You give me the grace, to walk in this place
    To walk and to live, from the light of Your face
The glory that comes, from You alone
    Is the glory that gives, the grace that atones.
You lead us from glory to glory, to You
    We are changed by Your glory, our faith is renewed
For it is not by any, works we have done
    It's only by, Your Blood, Holy Son!
You come and cleanse, by Your Righteousness,
    When we come in faith, our sins to confess.

So Father we come, to You now on this day
    In Jesus' Name, wash our sin away.
Forgive us, for all of the wrong we have done
    Wash us and cleanse, with the blood of Your Son.
We want to be pure, Your holy child,
    Saved from sin, and undefiled.
A vessel of glory, of God and of grace
    So that we may enter, Your holy place.
Enter to worship to live, to abide,
    Enter to walk, by Your holy side
There to worship, before Your throne
    There to live, for You God alone!
And then You impart, to us anew
    Your grace and Your love, to walk with You.

Now led by Your Spirit, beholding Your face
    We come to You, in that holy place.
There to worship, to love and adore
    You, our Dear Lord, forevermore.

TRUST AND OBEY - **Inspired by Proverbs 3:5-10**

Trust and obey, The Lord your God,
    Trust and obey, His holy Word
Trust and obey, your life He'll fulfill,
    You'll joy and delight, in His Holy Will.

For His will is not, so grievous or hard,
    He gives us His will, and His blessings impart
Such joy and peace, like we've never known,
    Such love poured out, from His holy throne.

This love will nurture, and care and tend,
    This love will heal, and forgive and mend.
His love is the key, that opens the door,
    For a life that's fulfilling, of more and more.

His love brings blessing, and peace we can know,
    Blessings and peace, that bring overflow
Of love and joy, and grace to forgive,
    A love and joy, that give life to live.

Let us live and love, before all of mankind,
    For the love of The Saviour, gives sight to the blind.
So that all can see, the Saviour's face,
    And enter with joy, His Holy Place.

Let us worship and sing, of His holy name,
    To tell of His love, His grace to proclaim.
For He is our God, our Saviour and Lord
    He forgave us our sins, He gives us His Word.

He promised our parents, Adam and Eve
    That He would deliver, by His Holy Seed!
Jesus came, our souls to redeem,
    And by His blood and His love we are clean!

Now when we choose, to believe in Him,
    We're set free from death, and hell and sin.
Free to give, our highest praise,
    Free to worship, for all of our days.

We are free to tell, the world of His love,
    We're free to proclaim, the power of our God.
So come now dear children, and enter in,
    To a life of real peace, for salvation He's given.

To all who call, and trust and believe
    Who will open their hearts, their Lord to receive.
Then with eyes open wide, and hearts of love,
    We'll behold our Lord, our Saviour above.

We'll abide in Him, and look on His face,
    We'll behold His love, His mercy and grace.
His grace will change and make our hearts new
    This grace He so lovingly, gives me and you.

This grace is not given, for ourselves alone
    But a grace to extend, to call others home.
Home to the Lord and His holy will,
    Home to fulfill, by His Spirit still.

For it's not by our power, we walk in His way,
    But by Holy Spirit, we trust and obey.
To live in the love, His Spirit imparts,
    Then share this love, He has given our hearts:

This love will seek, the lost and forlorn,
    This love will heal, the broken and torn
His love will save, redeem and restore,
    His love will bring joy, forevermore.

<u>WHY DO YOU STRIVE?</u> - Inspired by Matthew 6:24-34

Why do you strive, for that which is gold?
  Strive for what's good, and true riches unfold!
For the wealth of this world, is passing away,
  The wealth from the Lord, comes day by day.
Day by day, He provides what we need,
  Day by day, He provides what we seed.
For His mercies are new, to us every day,
  So our minds will not wander, along the way.
For wisdom from God, is given each day,
  When we trust in His word, His will to obey.

Dig deep in His Word, have faith when you pray
  For our Father delights, when His children pray.
So pray for wisdom, for grace and for love,
  Pray for His will, to be established in love.
His love is the key, that opens the door,
  For a life that is blessed, by God evermore
So love the Lord God, with all of your heart,
  And give Him your life, right from the start.
He will take your life, when you give it to Him,
  He'll give you more pleasure, than the pleasure of sin.
For the pleasures of sin, go swiftly away,
  In the wake of their passing, is grief always.

But the pleasures of God, bestowed from His hand
  Bring joy without measure, and life without end.
Eternal life, is given to you
  When you look to Christ, for salvation true.
He is the Saviour, who paid the price,
  His Holy Blood, The Pure Sacrifice.
The only worthy, atonement for sin
  The only way, we can enter in.
To the saving grace, of God above,
  To receive His mercy, His grace and His love!

HOLY! HOLY! HOLY! - Inspired by Revelation 4:8

Holy, Holy, Holy, are You Lord,
    You're God alone, The One adored!
We will worship, You alone,
    You're The One, upon The Throne.

There is no one, quite like You!
    You're ever faithful, ever true,
You deserve, the highest praise,
    We cast our crowns, before You today.

For there is no one, else who saves,
    Our souls from sin, Your life You gave,
To ransom us, Your blood You shed,
    To redeem us, from the lives we led.

So on this day, at the very start,
    I give my life, I give my heart,
To be Your child, and yours alone,
    So I can stand, before Your throne.

Now I give, to You all praise,
    I will thank, You all my days.
For You redeemed, my life from hell,
    You healed my heart, You made me well.

You gave me purpose, joy and light,
    Your love, You brought me in the night!
For when my soul, was deeply sad,
    You turned my grief, you made me glad.

So now with joy, I tell men too,
    Jesus will do, the same for you.
He'll take your heart, and bring you life,
    He'll give you joy, and peace from strife!

CHRIST JESUS SAVES - Inspired by 1ˢᵗ Peter 1:18 & 19

Christ alone, has the power to save,
    He redeems, from death and grave.
He lifts the ones, who are cast down,
    He gives a smile, to erase a frown.

The joy Christ gives, will make you new,
    He heals life's hurts, our hope is renewed.
For the life He gives, brings love and peace,
    He gave His life, for our soul's release.

Christ Jesus is standing, at your hearts door,
    To give you His life, forevermore!
So turn to Him, do not delay,
    Just ask Him now, ask today.

Jesus, be my Saviour now,
    Save me from sin, I make my vow,
To live for You, from this very day,
    To hear Your voice, and then obey.

I want to do, Your Holy Will,
    I want Your Grace, to then fulfill,
The plans You have, prepared for me,
    To walk in faith, and liberty.

In love and faith, in truth, and might,
    Help me to lead, to Your perfect light,
All those for whom, You bled and died,
    To bring them to, Your precious side.

For You alone, are The Light of the world,
    Your Blood alone, is a banner unfurled,
With a message clear, fro all to see,
    Christ paid the price, for you and me.

HE IS LORD - Inspired by Romans 14:11

He is The One, who gives us faith,
    He is The One, who conquered death.
He is The One, who took the keys,
    He is The One, who always sees.

He is The One, who gives His Word,
    His Word is still, The Spirits sword.
His Word has power, to heal and save,
    His Word delivers, from death and grave.

His Word became flesh, and lived with us,
    Full of love, and faithful trust.
Full of Mercy, full of Grace,
    So we could come, to The Holy Place.

So come and worship, the Lord our God,
    Bow to Him, and give Him laud.
Come and believe, accept Him now,
    Trust His love, and make your vow.

Then you will become, a child of God,
    You'll walk in the power, and love of God,
You'll know His love, and joy and peace,
    You'll walk in life, your fears will cease!

So offer up, to Him this prayer:
    Lord I am sorry, I know you care,
Save my soul, oh save me now,
    Forgive and cleanse me, to You I bow.

I'll live for You, by Your great power,
    I will walk with You, from this very hour.
Thank you Lord, for saving me,
    Thank you Lord, for setting me free.

FAITHFUL GOD - Inspired by Deuteronomy 32:1-4

Who is a God, like unto You,
    Ever faithful, ever true.
Full of mercy, full of love,
    Full of kindness, from above;
Full of Grace, and full of Glory,
    Living Witness, of God's story!

Jesus came, to earth for man,
    To fulfill, God's holy plan,
For when we sinned, He gave His life,
    A Perfect, Holy Sacrifice
What love, can be compared to His?
    What sacrifice, to bring such bliss!

This bliss comes from, our being loved,
    By God Incarnate, in heaven above
No gift can ever, be compared,
    To this, The Gift, God has prepared
Prepared for all, to now partake,
    Of life abundant, of grace so great!

Holy God, to You I come,
Cleanse me by, the Blood of Your Son
I've sinned and I, have missed the mark,
    I've wandered far, in the world's dark.
Now I come, into Your light,
    Free me from, the darkest night

You gave me life, and have given me hope,
    You freed me, I no longer grope.
You are the Light, of the world to all,
    So we can walk, and never fall.
But grow in grace, and mercy too,
    Then show to all, Your love that's true!

BE STRONG - Inspired by Ephesians 6:10

Be strong in the strength, of your mighty God
    Be strong in the Lord, in His holy Word.
Be strong in faith, in love and power,
    Be strong in the Lord, this very hour!
Press into Me, thus says the Lord,
    Press in, to claim My holy Word.
Press in; receive, what I have for you,
    Press in to experience, a life that's true.
No man on earth, can offer you,
    The blessings I have, prepared for you.
Miracles come, from My mighty hand
    My grace and glory, make you stand.
My love unhindered, full and free,
    Is the love that sets, your spirit free.
Now free to live, and free to love,
    You're free to praise, your God above;
You are free from your guilt, and sin today,
    Free to hear, My voice and pray!

So come my child, do not delay,
    Hear The Spirit's call, today.
A life of blessing, is prepared for all,
    Who hear and answer, The Spirit's call.
A call to leave, this world of sin,
    A call to come, and enter in.
Salvation is yours, by the blood of Christ
    Salvation is yours, by Christ's sacrifice
Say here am I, I. answer Your call,
    Wash me, clean me, heal me now.
I want to be, your loving child,
    Free from sin, and undefiled
I've sinned and wandered, far from You,
    But I'm coming drawn, by love that's true
Thank you Lord, for saving me,
    Thank you Lord, for setting me free!

BY GOD'S SPIRIT - Inspired by Zechariah 4:6

By the Spirit, You've given me
   My eyes are opened, and I can see
      The wonders of, Your love divine
         Your love outpoured, to make You mine.
Holy God, what love is this:
   That straightens all, that was amiss,
      That heals the hurt, forgives the sin,
         That brings, the broken sinner in?
I am brought to the courts, of heaven above,
   Redeemed, made clean, by the Saviour's love.
      You heal our hurts, erase our pain,
         You give us life, Your love we gain.
This love so rich, so undeserved,
   You pour on us, so we can serve,
      This gift of grace, and mercy true,
         To all, so they can know You too.
For knowing You, is the greatest gift,
   And loving You, makes our spirits lift
      Your precious love, none can compare
         This love You've given, for us to share.
So help us see, the world You love,
   See anew, with Your eyes of love.
      See each one, for whom You died,
         Bring them to, Your precious side;
Where your Blood, by love was shed,
   Saved from sin,, to raise the dead.
      For without Your saving, precious Blood,
         We are dead in sin, no earthly good.
You saw us in our wretched state,
   You died for us, became The Gate,
      To life eternal, life with You,
         A life of love, that is pure and true!

So I thank you Lord, for loving me,
   And I thank you Lord, for saving me!

<u>THE WAYS OF MEN</u> - Inspired by Ephesians 2:1-10

The ways of men, seem right to all,
    Who have never heard, The Spirit's call.
They wander in, the darkest night,
    Thinking, living, without The light;
        The Light that comes, from heaven above,
          The Light that shows The Saviour's love.
This Light is hidden, from their eyes,
    By the world's wiles, and the devil's lies.
But darkness cannot, snuff The Light,
    That comes, with Holy Spirit sight;
        The sight to see, the sin we're in,
          The sight to see, the results of sin.
But hope is given, when we realize,
    That in Christ's love, and sacrifice,
        We can repent, from all our sin,
          And be redeemed, to enter in;
To a life in God, by trusting Him,
    To eternal life, our souls we win.
        To once again, by love to choose
          A life of good, no more to lose,
The freedom purchased, by Christ's blood,
The freedom given, for our greatest good.
God has given, to all who ask,
    The will to live, and love the task,
        Of showing love, to all alike,
          So men can see, The Saviour's light,
So forsake the dark, and what it holds,
    Come into The Light, and there behold,
        The One who came, in the darkest night,
          The One who came, to bring us light.
For Jesus Christ, is The Light for all,
    To all who answer, The Spirit's call.
        So come to Him, and the life He gives,
          You'll not regret, new life you'll live!

WHY DO YOU TARRY? - **Inspired by Revelation 3:20**

Why do you tarry, Why do you wait?
    The Saviour is standing, right at the gate!
Standing and waiting, to enter in,
    Waiting to hear, you call from within,

Come in Lord Jesus, come in right now
    Come in and cleanse me, cause me to vow,
To live for You, and love You always,
    To hear Your voice, to hear You say,
I love you child, I have made you Mine,
    My grace and glory, will make you shine
With light that comes, from God above,
    The light that glows, with Jesus love.

His light brings life, to all who call,
    Upon The Lord, both great and small.
There is no one, He will not hear,
    His voice He speaks, Come here, draw near.
I have a life, prepared for you,
    A life of love, that is pure and true.

His life will show, you how to live,
    In love with God, who always gives
A life of purpose, full of praise
    A life of joy, for all your days
For peace and love, and joy abound,
    When in the Saviour's, arms you're found

He cleans and washes, those He has freed,
    He plants in us, His holy seed,
Then waters it, by His holy Word,
    His Spirit quickens, our hearts are stirred.
To reciprocate, His precious love,
    And worship God, forever above.

PRECIOUS LORD - Inspired by God's Love

Precious Lord, God and friend,
    Let me love You, to the end.
Let me be, Your child always,
    To love and serve, You all my days.
Help me to love, what' ere the cost,
    To love the poor, the sad, the lost,
With all the love, You've given me,
    So they can know, Your love so free;
Free to all, who call on you,
    For life abundant, grace that's true.

You alone, can give us life,
    You free us from, all sin and strife
Free us to call, upon Your name,
    To call and come, be cleansed from shame.
Your blood alone, has made us clean
    Your sacrifice, our lives redeemed,
From sin and fear, from pain and doubt,
    From hurt and harm, within, without.

Oh Holy Lord, and God of all,
    I bow my knees, I humbly call
Be Lord and God, and King always,
    Cause me to love You all my days;
For in Your love, new life I've found,
    And in Your peace, my joy abounds.
A life of joy, like I've never known,
    A life of peace, coming from Your throne.

Oh God You are love, in the purest form,
    You give Your love, our spirit's transformed.
Like a worm to a butterfly, we're made brand new,
    With a heart that's free, and a spirit true,
To live in love, and grace and truth,
    To show the world, Your love anew!

<u>COME NEAR</u> - Inspired by Jeremiah 31:3

Come near my child, come near and hear
    The words I speak, words pure and clear
I'll make the darkness, light for you
    For the words I speak, bring light that's true
A truer light, you will never find
    My light gives sight, unto the blind

Some are blind, and some are bound
    Some are lost, can't hear the sound,
For the love of the world, has blinded them
    Has shut the ears, and eyes of men
But the Light of the World, has not gone out
    It shines through the lives, of those who don't doubt
Who trust in Me, and My love for them
    Who hear My voice, above the din.

They come apart, to find in Me
    True life and peace, and joy that's free,
Free to all, who call My name
    Freed by love, from sin and shame
Free to give, their hearts to Me
    Free to live, in love with Me.

Oh My child, I died for you
    I gave My life, so you could choose,
A life that's free, to live with hope
    A life of light, no more to grope
For in the life, I give you child,
    Is light and love, that's undefiled.
This purity, gives light to see
    Brings joy and grace, and liberty!

LIVE BY GRACE - Inspired by Ephesians 2:5-10

Live according, to the Spirit's power, live by grace, this very hour
Live in power, to conquer sin, live the life, Christ paid to win.
For the old has gone, the new has come,
Life and liberty by Christ God's Son!

So leave the past, it's memories too,
Cleave to Christ, He died for you
Died, that you might never die, lives, to plead your case on high;
Intercedes, before God's throne, for those He calls, His very own

What an awesome love is ours,
For Christ has come, to give us power
By His Spirit, to live His life, freed from evil, sin and strife.
Nail old passions, to His cross, leave behind, your fear and loss.

His Spirit is come, to lead our lives,
To produce His fruit, that satisfies
Not for us and us alone, but to give, so all may know,
The God of Love, who came for all,
Who hear and heed, The Spirit's call.

The Spirit says: Believe the Lord, Forsake your sin, and all it's cords
For Christ has set you, free from sin, call to Him, invite Him in
There with you Saviour, to abide, there to dwell, by His Holy Side,
There to enjoy, His Warm Embrace, there to behold, His Holy Face
There to worship, there to praise, there to receive, His loving gaze

For in His face, we see His Love, the love that left, His throne above
To come, to save, to pay the price,
Christ set us free, from the devil's device!
So let us all, with one accord, give praise to God, our Holy Lord
For He has ransomed, us from sin, He took the keys, we enter in,
To God's eternal, courts above, there to worship, there to love!

I THANK MY GOD - Inspired by Philippians 1:3-11

I thank my God, when I remember you,
For your love for God, shines pure and true.
It shines through deeds, and works of love,
It shines with the light, of heaven above.
It shines by grace, through The Spirit's power,
To show to all, God's love each hour!

What God has given, to you, you share,
To all He brings, your love is there;
There to give, so full and free,
There to share, so all can see,
That Christ is Lord, in all you do,
That He has given, His life for you.

May your life abound now, by His grace,
May you always give Him, thanks and praise.
In everything, may His love abound,
So all can hear, the great glad sound:
Christ has come, to ransom thee.
Christ has come, to set you free!

So spread this word, to all you meet,
Arise, approach, God's mercy seat,
With boldness that is, imparted by faith
Approach God's throne, receive God's grace.
His mercy is, forever yours,
If you will open, your heart's door.

For Christ has risen. and waits to impart,
To all for whom, He gave His heart
All who come, to Him to save,
All He has ransomed, from the grave,
There to live, in His courts above,
There to bask, in His awesome love.

PURE HUMILITY - Inspired by Philippians: Chapter 2

Pure humility, Christ has shown,
    For He left His home, His heavenly throne
He came to live, to love, to forgive,
    He came, so we could truly live!.
What awesome love, and grace is ours,
    When we accept, His grace this hour
A saving grace, a pure sacrifice,
    His Holy Blood, to atone, to suffice;
To cover, to cleanse, and redeem all men,
    To bring us back, to The Father again.

What can we say, to this precious gift?
    He gave His life, to seal the rift,
That sin had made, between us and God,
    So give God praise, and give Him laud.
Then as He's shown, His love for you,
    Share this love, with others too.
Prefer one another, as better than yourself
    Humble yourselves, for the greater wealth
Of knowing that Christ, is formed in you
    When you love the Lord, and your neighbour too.

For the Word of God, is never bound,
    When grace and love, and truth are found,
In the hearts of those, who live in love
    Who worship God, in heaven above.
For by our deeds, we let men know,
    That Christ is Lord, His glory to show.
Then when His glory, lights the earth,
    All men can see, and receive new birth;
Not by flesh, or the will of man,
    But by His Spirit, new life is given
A life that honours, and gives God's praise,
    A life of worth, for all our days.

PRICELESS GIFT - Inspired by Philippians 3:12-14

Oh what a priceless gift is ours,
    To know and trust, this God of ours;
To hear His voice, of love so dear
    To see His face, so pure and clear;
To know He loves, and answers prayer
    To know our Lord, is always there.

He is there to comfort, and console,
    There to lift, our deepest woe,
There to give, us joy and peace
    There to bring, our souls release.
So let us all, in one accord,
    Give praise and worship, to our Lord,

For He has given, to us such love
    He's made us right, with God above.
Love so pure, so good, so whole,
    Has set us free, redeemed our souls.
So let's forget, all that is past,
    Press into love, and joy that lasts,

Press in to hear, our Dear Lord's voice
    Press in to make, His will first choice
For He who gave, His best for us,
    When we were dead, in sin and lust
Has opened heaven's gate, right now,
    To all who hear, and make their vow,
To give to Him, their life their all
    To answer yes, when The Spirit calls!

WHERE ARE YOU?

What has captured, your heart and mind?
    What has caused you, to lag behind?
What has led, your life astray?
    What has kept you, from His way?
What has caused you, fear and strife?
    What has taken, up your life?

Think on this, and ponder still,
    What Christ did, by His perfect will!
He left His throne, in heaven above,
    Then came to earth, to show His love,
He died for all, so all may live,
    Free from sin, and free to give.

Now free from fear, and free from doubt,
    We're free to shut, the devil out!
Free from sins, that wound and kill,
    Free to approach, God's holy hill..
Free by the Blood, of Jesus, The Christ,
    The only price, that would suffice.

The only gift, that could atone,
    The only way, to approach God's Throne.
Is to come to Christ, receive His gift,
    Salvation, is this Holy gift!
His Spirit lifts us, to behold,
    The treasure that, will never mold!

God lifts us to, His holy place,
    Enfolds us in, the Lord's embrace.
To know the love, and grace He gives,
    To know the joy, and peace to live,
Ever loved, by God above,
    Ever to live, a life of love!

THE IMAGE - Inspired by Colossians 1:15

Christ is The Image, of The Invisible God
He came so we, could know our God.
He rules supreme, over all God made,
His glory shines, it never fades.
He is The Image, of The Unseen God,
So give Him glory, praise and laud.

He is the Head, of His Holy Church
He is over all, He is The First!
He took our sins, He was reviled,
Now by His death, we are reconciled.
He made us right, He cleansed our sin,
He made us clean, and pure within.

No one could match, this sacrifice,
No one has paid the price, but Christ!
So come to Him, do not delay,
His Blood He shed, the price is paid!
He ransomed us, from sins allure,
To make our hope, and calling sure.

Now we are holy, in His sight,
Free to live, and do what is right.
We are free to stand, for truth alone,
Free to come, before God's throne.
So stand in the love, and truth received,
Stand by faith, don't ever leave.

Receive Christ's love, and grace outpoured,
Behold His face, and be transformed.
For in His face, His love He shows,
So all may see, and all may know.
That by His name, and His alone,
We now can enter, to God's throne!

RAISED IN CHRIST - Inspired by Ephesians 2:1-6

Since you have, been raised with Christ,
    To receive His love, His sacrifice,
Worship Him, in all you do,
    Let your mind be pure, and your spirit true.
Be true to the Lord, who rescued you,
    Who saved your soul, delivered too:
From all that sin, and strife had caused,
    From all that put, your life on pause!

Now your real life, is hidden with Christ
    So don't be greedy, for the things of life.
Greed allows, the devil in,
    To lure your heart, away to sin.
So put away, what does defile,
    Set your heart, on what is worthwhile.
Set your affection, on heaven above,
    To behold God's face, and receive His love.

Then your life, will have true worth,
    You will lead men, to their own new birth
In Christ, for there, we all are justified
    By His free gift, we are made His bride.
Now we are clothed, in righteousness,
    Clothed with grace, and gentleness.
We are clothed with mercy, and kindness too,
    Clothed by God, in all we do.

So let Christ's Word, be rich in you,
    To teach and lead, and counsel too,
To forgive, as He has forgiven you,
    To extend His love, in all you do.
Let His peace, surround your days
    Give Him honour, love and praise
Give Him thanks, for all He has done
    Worship Christ, The Lord, God's son!

WHO IS LIKE YOU LORD? - Inspired by John 1:1-14

Who is like unto You, Oh Lord?
　　You alone, are The Living Word.
You came down, to earth from heaven,
　　You gave Your life, Your side was riven.
Your side was riven, for all to see,
　　The love of God, on that cruel tree.
You became sin, because You loved,
　　You paid the price, You shed Your blood.
You washed us clean, You made us new
　　You forgave our sins, our hearts renewed.

Our lives were cracked, and dead in sin,
　　Too dry to let, your life flow in.
You saw us there, in our wretched state,
　　Redeemed us from, all sin and hate,
So we could know, Your precious love,
　　Transformed, made ready for courts above.
What an awesome love, is this,
　　To be made new, no more to miss,
Your saving grace, that makes us new,
　　Your perfect love, our souls renewed.

Oh Lord, my God, what can I give?
　　Oh Lord my God, my life I give,
To be made new, by Your grace and power,
　　To live for You, from this very hour.
Forgive me Lord, forgive I pray,
　　Take and make me, change me this day.
I want to be, Your child alone,
　　I want to worship, at Your throne,
With all the saints, who have gone before,
　　There to worship, and adore
For only You, deserve the praise,
　　You, I will worship, all my days

THE GOD, WHO SINGS! - Inspired by Zephaniah 3:17

If there's a crown, of life for me,
    I will cast it down, before your feet!
For You Oh God, are God alone,
    You paid the price, my sins to atone.
So now I come, before you Lord,
    Cause me to walk, in one accord,
With You my Holy God, and King,
    To hear Your voice, to hear You sing,
The words of love, You sing to me,
    The words of life, that set me free.

Oh cause my ears, to always hear,
    And by Your Word, to me draw near;
Nearer to my God, to Thee,
    Nearer to Your Face, to see,
The love and grace, and glory shown,
    So I can then, to men make known,
Your perfect love, Your grace bestowed,
    Your holy gift, salvation showed.
This is what, I want to give,
    The Word of God, so man can live,
Free from sin, and all it holds,
    Free to let, Your Spirit mold.

God, mold us with, Your love divine,
    Make our faces, truly shine:
Shine with glory, and with grace,
    As we behold, Your holy face.
Oh let us see You, Lord today,
    Oh let us hear, Your voice always,
So that with all, Your body true,
    We'll live in love, and worship You.
For You are God, and God alone,
    We bow and worship, before Your throne!

IF THERE'S A SONG - Inspired by Psalm 98

If there is a song, that I must sing,
    If there is a way, for bells to ring;
        If there is a love, that calms my fears,
            If there is a peace, that dries my tears;
Then this is what, I want today,
    This is what, I humbly pray.
        To know the Lord, who gives a song,
            Who frees my soul, from sin and wrong;

Christ gave His life, to ransom me,
    To set my soul, and spirit free;
        Free to worship, Christ as Lord,
            Free to live, in one accord,
With God as Father, what' ere betide,
    With Christ as Saviour, by my side.
        With Holy Spirit, guiding me,
            To speak His Word, set captives free.

For when Christ's freedom, is proclaimed,
    When God's Name, is not defamed,
        The bells of heaven, will all ring out,
            As saints in light, rejoice and shout.
Give praise that's due, to Christ The King,
    And heaven with earth, rejoice and sing!
        For God Himself, has given His peace,
            A peace that comes, from lives released.

Now we're released, from sins that bound,
    Released to worship, with holy sound.
        Released to worship, Christ our Lord,
            Released to come, with one accord.
So let us present, our lives to Him,
    For we've been freed, to enter in,
        To heaven's portals, open wide,
            There to live, by His precious side;

PEACE BE WITH YOU - Inspired by John 20 & 21

Peace be with you, says the Lord,
   My peace I give, to seal the Word,
      That I have spoken, to your heart,
         So from My side, you'll never depart!
This peace I give, is not like the worlds,
   For this is a peace, by grace unfurled;
      A grace that comes, to conquer sin
      A grace that heals, the wounds within.

This grace and peace, to all are gained,
When all with faith, and hope unfeigned,
      Receive My love, and life outpoured,
        Receive Me, as their God and Lord.
For this is why, I came to earth:
   I came so all, could have new birth.
      This birth by Spirit, and By My Word,
        This Birth designed, to give them worth.

Christ's birth came not, by human hands,
   For Christ alone, paid the laws demands.
      By Holy Spirit, Christ was conceived,
        By Holy Spirit, we can believe.
Now by His Spirit, we are called,
   To faith in Christ, to break the walls,
      That held us captive, in our sins,
        That kept us bound, without, within.

But Jesus broke, the walls that day,
   When "It is finished," He did say
      He paid the price, with His own blood,
        He saved us for, our greater good.
He saved us by, His Holy grace
   To then behold, His wondrous face,
      Now changed from glory to glory now
        We are free to worship, free to bow!

COME LET US KNEEL - Inspired by Psalm 95

Come let us kneel, before God's throne
    Come let us make, His glories known.
For when we worship, and adore,
    Our lives are changed, for evermore.
Now we can come, before all men,
    To offer life, and grace to them.
For life in Christ, by faith is given,
    When we bow down, with all in heaven.

Trust and believe, in Christ as Lord.
    As Saviour, Jesus Blood was poured
To ransom all, who come to Him,
    To save us from, a life of sin.
So let us all, with gladsome voice,
    Proclaim to all, you have a choice,
To believe and trust, in Christ as Lord,
    Forsake all sin, believe His Word.

God's Spirit then, will take Christ's Blood,
    And cleanse us for, our greater good:
A good that puts, His will before,
    That opens up, a heavenly door.
A door to serve, our Christ, The King,
    In all we do, His praise to bring.
For then a life, like we've never known,
    Becomes a life, by grace atoned.

This life of freedom, and His peace,
    This life that brings, our soul's release,
Frees us to live, and to forgive,
    Frees us to give, so all may live;
Live for Christ, and Him alone,
    Live for Christ, before His throne.
Live to offer, up our praise,
    Live to love, Him all our days.

DO YOU LOVE ME? - Inspired by John 21:15-17

Do you love Me, asks the Lord? Do you love Me, love My word?
   Do you cherish, what I say, do you want, My will today?

Then feed the lambs, I bring to you,
   Feed them with, The Word that's true,
      Feed and care, for them with love,
         The love that comes, from heaven above.

Then once again, the Saviour asks, Do you love me, love the task?
   Love me with, your heart and soul?
      Then feed my sheep, to make them whole!
         Make them whole, and free from sin,
            By My Word, and Spirit within!

By Holy Spirit, we are called, to faith in Christ, to be enthralled,
   By love and grace, that Christ poured out,
      When by His death, He broke the clout,
         Of sin and death, of hell and grave,
            He gave His life, so we'd be saved!

He saved us for, His love to show,
   Saved us as well, so others may know,
      That Christ the Lord, has come to save,
         To save and ransom, from the grave!

Now we are given, life and peace,
   We're saved, redeemed, our souls released!
      Now in the freedom Christ has given,
         We now can tell, all men of heaven,

Of life and love, of peace and grace,
   That come when we, behold His face.
      So let us answer, when He calls,
         Say yes, my Lord, I give my all!

TAKE HEED - Inspired by 2 Samuel 9- 12 and Ruth

Take heed and listen, take heed and pray,
   Take heed to the word, I say this day.
For even the beloved,, can stray and fall,
   When they do not listen, when I call.
Temptations come, to lure and stray,
   To lead men, from My perfect way.
But I have given, grace to you,
   To hear My voice, and choose to do,
The will of God, to walk the walk
   To walk His way, and talk His talk.

You have a dream, you have a goal,
   I've placed within, your very soul,
A dream to tell, the world of Me,
   To lead them, heal them, set them free.
Lead not by words alone, of love,
   But by your deeds, show them My love.
Then when My will, becomes your own,
   You'll worship Me, before My throne.
Now when you worship, when you praise,
   You'll get My answer, of The Way.

I have a way, prepared for you,
   To hear My voice, and do what's true.
Dear child of Mine, I open doors,
   That were not open, to you before,
Doors to enter, and then possess,
   What I've prepared, by righteousness
Not by righteous works you've done,
   But by The Righteousness of My Son.
For when your sins, He did atone,
   By giving up, His life alone,
He made the way, for you to come
   Into My plan, all sin to shun!

So leave all doubt, and fear aside,
    Come walk with Me, here by My side
Walk in faith and love and truth,
    Walk in hope, like faithful Ruth.
She forsook, her father's home,
    And left the way, that she had known.
She left it all, to choose what's right,
    She left the darkness, and the night.

She left to walk, in faithfulness,
    Led by God's, own righteousness.
For God had planned, a path for her,
    A path to make, her goings sure.
She became, a wife again,
    The chosen one, by God's good plan.
As she was faithful, to work and toil,
    She reaped and gathered, from the soil.

God saw her heart, and spirit true,
    Prepared a place, for her to do,
What He had planned, long time ago,
    To show His grace, and love bestow.
He took her shame, and widowhood,
    And turned them, for her greater good.
She married Boaz, and in time gave birth,
    To a son who restored, Naomi to mirth.

Her son, Obed, became the grandfather,
    To David the King, a man like no other.
Then in David's line, our Saviour was born,
    Jesus, The Christ, that holy morn.
In human form, God became man,
    To save all who, would trust His plan!
So follow Christ, and trust Him now,
    Hear His voice, fulfill your vow,
To always do, God's perfect will,
    To hear His voice, and then be still.

JEWELS IN A CROWN - Inspired by Zechariah 9:16

Like jewels in a crown, like jewels in a crown,
> I will make of My children, those of renown.
They will look to Me, as their only source,
> I will set their lives, on a plain straight course.
For those who look to Me, will live,
> For I am The God, who restores and forgives.
They'll not wander again, for My love holds them close,
> My Spirit reveals, that I love them the most!

Those I love I protect, with My sword and My shield,
> My sword is The Word, that My Spirit wields.
It will cut away all, that deforms and destroys,
> And make them as strong, as the strongest alloy.
Then they will stand, in the day of My power,
> They will stand and not falter, for this is the hour;
The hour to show, to My world My love,
> So that all can attain, to My courts above.

We cannot attain, by the deeds we have done,
> But by faith in God, in Christ Jesus, His Son.
For it's faith in Christ Jesus, and Him alone,
> That our sins are forgiven, and our lives are atoned.
This faith is a shield, that protects us from harm,
> This faith in Christ Jesus, destroys Satan's charms.
For his charms are deceitful, and lead men to hell,
> But faith in Christ Jesus, destroys Satan's spell.

So come to the Lord, and trust in His Word,
> He'll lead you and guide you, for He is The Lord.
His staff will protect you, His arms hold you near,
> His voice reassures, He calms all our fears.
So quiet your heart, be still in His arms,
> His presence brings peace, His love keeps you warm!
His power enables, to walk then by faith,
> Forever abounding, in His love and grace!

REJOICE IN YOUR KING - Inspired by Zechariah 9:9

Shout and rejoice, in your God and your King,
  He is righteous, victorious, to Him let us sing.
This King came humbly, on a colt to say,
  To Jerusalem City, with the message that day;
A message of peace, and joy and love
  His message proclaimed, that God is love!
Because of the covenant, God had made,
  To redeem His people, the price was paid.
Not by anything, that we could do,
  Our Lord Jesus gave, for me and for you.
His life was the ransom, He died on that cross,
  So we then could be, restored from our loss.
He restored what we lost, in the garden that day,
  God restored by the blood, of Christ Jesus to pay;
The debt we could never, pay on our own,
  Christ Jesus gave freely, His Blood to atone.

So now, we can come, in the name of The Christ,
  In faith believing, for He paid the price
He ransomed our lives, and our souls from hell,
  His Blood paid the price, to reverse death's knell.
Come back to the place, of safety God calls,
  Come up, there is hope, in His heavenly halls.
Come up and see, what our Lord has prepared,
  Come up, enter in, to the joys He shares.
For to all who come, to answer His call,
  To all who respond, to give Him their all,
He takes them away, from the state they are in,
  He cleanses, restores, redeems from all sin.
He grants life eternal, with joy and with love,
  Unlimited access, to His courts above.
Now all it takes, is a humble cry,
  Jesus I'm sorry, redeem my life!

THE PRICE - Inspired by Zechariah 11:12 & Matthew 26:14-16

What was the price, of a slave that day?
  Thirty pieces of silver, was the going rate!
For that princely sum, our Lord was betrayed,
  Into hands of men, full of anger and hate.
For Jesus came, not obeying their laws,
  He came to live, as God's Spirit calls,
To live by the voice, and will of His Father,
  To show to all men, a love like no other!
For men in their pride, had tried to replace,
  The Fathers love, and His saving grace.

They added their rules, to God's alone,
  Rules they used, to make their deeds known.
They used these rules, to make them look good,
  So they need not submit, and live as they should.
They were called to live, by God's love up above,
  To show to all men, His mercy and love.
In their pride they listened, to the devil's lies,
  They left their first love, and compromised.
They traded the image, of God up above,
  For an image of self, they rejected God's love.

We cannot point only, to them as the cause,
  Our sins and theirs, put our Lord on the cross.
Jesus came to redeem, by His precious blood,
  He came and He gave, for our greater good.
He came to restore, all who call upon Him
  Who repent and renounce, all their previous sin;
Who call out to Him, for His mercy and grace,
  For He gave His life, our sins to erase.
Then on the third day, He rose from the grave,
  Broke open hells gates, He redeemed the saved.
So now we can live, by heaven's rules
  And receive His power, no longer fools!

LIFE-GIVING FOUNTAIN - Inspired by Zechariah 13:1

A fountain of cleansing, was opened that day,
  A fountain that washes, our sins all away.
A fountain of Blood, from our Saviour's dear side,
  A fountain that cleanses, from sin and from pride.
Pride is the first listed, of deadliest sins,
  Pride keeps us back, from entering in,
From coming for cleansing, to Jesus alone,
  From coming to Christ, for our sins to atone!
When we think we can live, on our own without Christ,
  When we hinder the message, of His sacrifice,
When we suffer in silence, because of our pride,
  This deadly deception, casts us aside.

Pride casts aside, from God's holy embrace
  Outside and away, not receiving His grace.
Pride was the sin, that cast Lucifer down,
  Pride caused him to covet, God's Holy Crown.
Then some of the angels, believed Lucifer's lies,
  So they joined his departure, joined his demise!
Their destructive weapons, are all based on lies,
  For they cause men to boast, yet tremble inside.
They portray to men, a false picture of God,
  As a vengeful, unmerciful, and hateful God.
They appeal to the sinful nature, of man
  To deceive and destroy, to thwart God's plan.

But God is a God, whose plan will succeed,
  For all who will call out to Him, and believe:
That Christ is The Answer, for redemption from sin,
  Whose Atoning Blood, cleared the path to come in;
To enter the Presence, of our God up above,
  To experience His grace, His mercy and love.
So call to The Lord, for forgiveness today,
  He'll respond to your call, our price He has paid!

THE BREAD OF LIFE - Inspired by John 6:32-40

Oh Holy Saviour, Son of God,
    To whom can we go, while on earth we trod?
You alone, have the gift of life,
    You alone, redeem from strife!
You alone, are all we need;
    You alone, are The Bread that feeds!
You are the Living, Bread from heaven,
    The Bread of Life, without sin's leaven!.
Give us Your Bread, so we can live,
    By what Your Word, declares and gives.

We cannot live, by bread alone,
    Your life we need, our lives to atone.
Only Your love, redeems our souls,
    Redeems and cleanses, makes us whole.
Without You Lord, we are incomplete,
    Without Your love, there is only defeat.
You alone, have the power to give,
    You alone, give a life to live.
You give a life, of love and power,
    To live, to give, Your love this hour;

Cause me to love, with all my heart,
    So from Your side, I'll never depart.
Help me to love, as You have loved me
    To share the love, You have given me.
A love that came, with word and deed,
    A love that shows, to us our need.
We need to be, complete and whole,
    To live and love, with heart and soul.
So now I come, to Your Holy Word,
    Use it Oh Lord, as Your Holy Sword.
Cut from me, the cords that bind,
    Free my, spirit, soul and mind.

LIVING BREAD - Inspired by John 6:48-51

Lord, Your Word, is Living Bread,
 In Your Word, is life instead,
A life that sets, our spirit free,
 A life to live, through eternity
So Holy Spirit, open to me,
 Your Word, to set my spirit free,
To see You Lord, with eyes of love,
 To see anew, my God above.
To see the glory, of Your throne,
 To worship You, and You alone

For when I see, Your holy face,
 And when I feel, Your warm embrace,
My soul takes wings, and leaves behind,
 All fear and doubt, and sins that blind.
Take me above, to where you are,
 Cause me to cross, the heavenly bar,
There to join, the saints in light,
 To worship You, with all my might!
For You alone, are worthy of praise,
 I bow before You, Oh Ancient of Days.
I cast my crown, at Your holy feet,
 Your love alone, makes my life complete!

Baptize me fresh, now Lord I pray,
 So I can give, Your love away,
To all You bring, across my path,
 To receive Your love, Your cleansing bath.
For when we are bathed, by Your cleansing blood,
 Then we are saved, from sin's dark flood.
Now to enter, Your courts above,
 Now to experience, Your precious love.
What can I give, in response to this,
 I seal Your love, with a holy kiss!

<u>WHO IS A GOD LIKE YOU?</u> - Inspired by Micah 7:18-20

Who to is a God, like unto You,
  Who loves and shows, His mercy too?
    To all who call, upon Your name,
      You save from sin, and remove the shame.

You remove the shame, that comes from sin,
  That steals our life, and hope within!
    To You alone, our praise we bring,
      To You alone, our spirits sing.

You trample our sins, under Your feet,
  Then throw them in, to the ocean so deep,
    Never to be, remembered again,
      Now fully redeemed, from all of our sin!

Oh, what wondrous, love You show,
  Your grace and mercy, on us bestow!
    What can we say, to this great love,
      This love come down, from heaven above?

Your love You portrayed, on a cruel cross,
  Your love that paid, for our sin and loss!
    Your love redeems, and sets us free,
      To live right now, and for eternity,

By faith in Christ, and Christ alone,
  We live by grace, and mercy shown,
    To do what is right, love mercy too,
      Walk humbly with our God anew.

By this we come, to justly act,
  To show His love, to state as fact:
    That God is God, upon the throne,
      The One we worship, Him alone!

DEAR LORD, I COME - Inspired by Romans 3:18-20

Dear Lord I come, to the foot of Your cross,
   To worship You, to receive what's lost;
      To once again, behold the price,
         You paid by love, and sacrifice.

I have sinned my Lord, I've turned away,
   My mind has led, my heart to stray,
      To look for things, instead of You,
         To seek what others, have that's new.

Dear Lord, I realize my loss,
   I come for cleansing, to Your cross.
      Wash me Saviour, lest I die,
         Wash me, cleanse me, Lord I cry.

I come to You, for Your pure gold,
   For Your fire to cleanse, so I can behold,
      Your face, Your truth, Your loveliness,
         Your beauty pure, Your holiness!

Clothe me in, Your righteousness,
   So I may enter, your gates so blessed.
      Anoint my eyes, so I can see,
         All that You, have done for me.

Correct me now, Oh Lord I pray,
   So from Your side, I'll never stray.
      I hear Your knock, on my heart's door
         Come in Dear Lord, I want You more.

I want Your love, I want Your grace,
   I want to see, Your holy face.
      For when I see, Your face I'll know,
         The grace and love, that You bestow.

BE STILL MY SOUL - Inspired by Isaiah 26:3 & 4

Be still my soul, wait patiently,
    For God's clear voice, to speak to thee;
        His voice so dear, so pure, so right,
            He brings us hope, and joy and light.
His light will lighten, every path,
    His joy will give, our soul a bath!
        His hope will cheer, and strengthen faith,
            His Word in faith, cuts like a lathe.
It cuts and trims, all fear and doubt,
    Removes the sins, that keep us out;
        Out from His grace, and from His love,
            Out from God's Presence, up above.

Christ the Lord, prepared the way,
    When He gave us, His life that day.
        He made the way, to enter in,
            Then shed His Blood, to cleanse our sin.
He rose to conquer, hell and grave,
    He gave his life, for us to save.
        His light came in, dispelled the sin,
        He made the way, to enter in.
So come my child, sit at His feet,
    Submit your life, to Christ so sweet,
        So pure, so loving, and oh, so kind,
            He'll give you life, a brand-new mind!

This mind will act, and think like His,
    A mind that knows, and loves the bliss,
        That comes from God, in heaven above,
        His love He gave, His purest love.
For when God gave, His Only Son,
    He showed to us, The Perfect One.
        The Christ came down, from heaven to earth,
        He gives to us, a brand-new birth.

Oh come into, His light this day, forsake all sin and let us pray,
    This sample prayer, with all our hearts:
    I'm sorry Lord, please cleanse my heart,
    Forgive me now, Oh Lord I pray,
    Make me your child this very day.
    Keep me close, and keep me near,
    So I can hear, your voice so dear.
    Your voice that calls: Come unto me,
    All who are weary, I'll set you free,
    Free to enter, into My best, Free to give eternal rest!

Please read Matthew 11:28-30

<u>A CROWN FROM GOD</u> - Inspired by 2nd Timothy 4:8

Grace was given, when God came down,
    Grace was given, to give a crown;
A crown of righteousness, to all who believe,
    Who trust the grace, of Christ to redeem.

Christ alone, has the power to save,
    To redeem from hell, and death and grave.
So let His grace, purge out the leaven,
    Of sin and pride, that bars from heaven.

Trust instead, in the mercy given,
    Leave all sin, and yearn for heaven.
Live today, in the light of God's word,
    To receive the joys, of His grace assured

For then you will have, such joy and peace,
    You'll know the love, of a soul released
You'll enter the courts, of heaven above,
    To receive of His grace, His mercy and love.

IS CHRIST YOUR LORD? - Inspired by Matthew 10:32 & 33

Will you acknowledge, Christ as Lord,
    Before all men, right here on earth?
Will you accept, His saving grace,
    Receive His love, behold His face?
Will you forsake, all sin and wrong,
    So you can to, your Lord belong?
If you will now, confess this faith,
    This faith that conquers, is no wraith!
It is strong and mighty, like a shield
    Has power to cause, our wills to yield.

Now when we yield, to the will of God,
    To believe in Christ, as Son of God,
Then we are promised, in God's Word,
    That our salvation, is assured.
Now if we declare, before men on earth,
    That Christ has given, to us new birth,
Then He will declare, before God above,
    He'll say we are His, to our God of love!
But there is another, side as well,
    If we don't believe, we are doomed to hell.
For Christ alone, is the only way,
    To enter heaven, on Judgment Day.

For it's by our faith, in Christ alone,
    That we approach, God's holy throne.
So leave the sins, of this world behind,
    Come to The One, who is loving and kind.
Come to this Saviour, for His new birth,
    Come to the Lord, He will give you worth.
For you are created, in The Image of God,
    And without His Spirit, you are only sod.
The breath of God's Spirit, quickens, gives life,
    Raises us up, from death and strife.

He raises us up, to God above,
    Raises us up, to experience God's love.
His love and grace, no words can express,
    Such peace and joy, such perfect rest.
Now when we yield, ourselves to Him,
    And give our life, acknowledge our sin,
Repent from all, that leads to hell,
    He makes our souls, and spirits well
He washes us clean, makes us His own,
    Presents us to God, as His alone!

PREACH THE WORD - Inspired by 2nd Timothy 4:2-5

Preach The Word, and preach it true,
    Christ gave up, His life for you!
Whether the time, seems right or not,
    Preach in love, your life He bought!
He bought it with, His precious blood,
    Bought it to give, us lives of love.

Be patient, yet persistent too,
    Encourage and strengthen, to renew,
The lives of those, Christ came to save,
    From all that lead, to hell and grave!
For a time is coming, when some will leave,
    Will refuse the truth, and lies believe.

They will listen to what, they want to hear,
    Reject the truth, their conscience seared!
So keep a strong, and pure clean mind,
    Speak the truth, to heal the blind,
To give them eyes, to really see,
    The Lord who comes, to set them free!

WHAT DOES IT MEAN TO WALK WITH GOD?

What does it mean, to walk with God?
How can we walk, the path He trod?
Christ Jesus came down, from heaven above,
He came to show, The Fathers love!
He showed compassion, for all the lost,
Compassion and love, to pay the cost!
Now the price, is fully paid,
Our Saviour came, His life He gave.
He'll ransom all, who come to Him,
To redeem their souls, and cancel sin.
To you He has given, the message of hope,
To live in this life, not just to cope.
If you'll live this life, and give His love,
You'll lead men, to their God above!
Open your eyes, and you will see,
The fields are ripe, for eternity.

I have placed eternity, in men's souls,
Without this hope, they've dug a hole.
They've crawled inside, in their despair,
Not knowing Christ, would find them there.
But child of Mine, I've given to you,
And to all who love, this message too,
The power and will, to seek the lost,
To save them from, their sin and loss.
So bring them to, My precious side,
There to be healed, restored, abide.
I cleaned you up, I made you whole,
So you could go, restore, console.
It is not by words, or prayers alone,
But by your deeds, My love is shown.
So hear Me now, do what I say,
And walk the paths, I have today.
Paths that lead, to those I show,
To redeem their souls, and make them whole

WHICH WAY WILL YOU GO? - Inspired by John14:6

There is a way, that seems right to men,
    That seems real good, a definite plan.
But only the plans, of God will bless,
    Only His plans, yield righteousness.
For it's by the plans, of God we see,
    The way that leads, to eternity!
So look at your plan, take a careful look,
    Does this plan follow, the path Christ took?

Is it the way, that leads men to Christ,
    That leads them to, His sacrifice?
For it's only by leading, all to the cross,
    That sins are forgiven, with no more loss.
Redeemed, set free, to live in the light,
    Restored and ransomed, to give all sight.
So check your lives, in the light of God's Word,
    Do your lives lead men, to The Living Word?

For it's not alone, by the words we say,
    It's by our deeds, and the words we pray,
That all can see, God's Precious Face,
    Behold His love, receive His grace,
Enter His courts, with faith to abide,
    Forever and always, by His dear side.

Oh come Holy Spirit, come fill me now,
    Refresh my sight, I make this vow,
To see the way, my Saviour sees,
    To hear His heart, I bow my knees.
Now from this place, I'll do my part,
    To show Your love, reveal Your heart.
So all can know, from great to small,
    The Lord redeems, gives grace to all
To all who give, their lives to Him,
    He heals their souls, gives life within

THE FRIENDS OF GOD - Inspired by John 15:14-17

You are My friends, if you obey Me,
   These are the words, God speaks to thee.
No more His servants, for now He confides,
   To those who by, His Word abide.
To abide forever, in His love,
   To lead men to, His courts above.
This is why, the Saviour came,
   To redeem our souls, free us from shame.
He has chosen us, who seek His face,
   To receive His mercy, and His grace,
He has chosen us, go and tell,
   Chosen us, to redeem from hell,
      The souls He came on earth to save,
        To ransom, pardon, from the grave.
Now to all who receive, His saving grace,
   Who enter in, to see His face.
      He lifts the sting, of sin and death,
        He gives eternal, life and breath.
This breath of God, imparts to our souls,
   So we with all, can now behold,
      The wonders of, His holiness,
        Partakers of, His righteousness.
For it is by the Blood of Christ alone,
   Our sins are cleansed, our lives atoned.

What's your response, to this great love,
   What's your response, to God above?
      Say yes my friend, to His holy call,
        Give Him your life, your love, your all.
For in His life, you will have life,
   No more to live, in sin and strife.
      Now free to walk, by His holy side,
        You are free to live, and in love abide.
You are free to grow, in love each day,
   Free to hear, His voice today!

TO WHOM DO YOU CALL? - Inspired by 2nd Corinthians 6:2

Was it to Me, that you did call,
    When the trials of life, on you did fall?
    Or did you rely, on your strength alone,
    Instead of coming, before My throne?
What kept you away, from My saving grace,
    Why, oh why, did you hide your face?,

I will tell you why, Oh child of mine,
    Sin and deception, had made you blind;
Blind to My glory, and My grace,
    Blind to behold, My loving face
Guilt and fear, kept you away,
    They kept you from, My grace that day.

But My light shines brighter, in the darkest hour,
    When My children call, for My holy power
My power was shown, to all that day,
    When I gave My life, on that cross to say:
I love you child, I came for you,
    I came to make, your life brand-new.

I long to hear, you call to Me,
    Oh set my heart, and spirit free!
For if you call, for help My friend,
    Your fears and doubts, and strife will end.
They'll end, when you call out to Me,
    They'll end because, I will set you free.

For all who call, upon My name,
    Receive My grace, that erases shame.
For by My love, and sacrifice,
    I made a way, I paid the price,
To cleanse, redeem, and restore all men,
    To bring them near, to My presence again.

COME TO THE SAVIOUR - Inspired by 2nd Corinthians 4:6-7

Do you feel crushed, on every side,
　　Perplexed and broken, suffering inside?
Then come to the Saviour, of our souls,
　　He will save you now, He will make you whole.
For in His Presence, you will get the power,
　　To stand with grace, and love this hour.
For He who called you, stands with you,
　　His strength gives power, your soul is renewed.
For trials come, to all mankind,
　　They test our body, spirit and mind.

So when trials come, and cause you distress,
　　When worries and fears, bring you unrest,
Call out to The One, who has power to save,
　　Call out to the Christ, who rose from the grave.
For death has no sting, to the one who trusts Christ,
　　He took the keys, He paid the price.
He ransomed our souls, He poured out His blood,
　　The only atonement, for sin's awful flood!
Sin and death, were our destiny,
　　The result of rebellion, and tyranny.

If you call to Him now, and do not delay,
　　He will save you from sin, this very day.
He will light up your life, by just what He says,
　　This light brings the glory, of Christ to the dead.
For when we were dead, in our trespass and sins,
　　By the god of this world, who had trapped us within,
The desires and will, of our sinful minds,
　　Had deafened our ears, had made us blind.
But God in His love, sent Jesus to save,
　　To pay sins price, from hell and the grave.
So receive His life, and His love this hour,
　　His glory to shine, with His grace and His power!

AWAKE, OH SLEEPER! - Inspired by Ephesians 5:14

Awake Oh sleeper, and rise from the dead,
    Climb out of your coffins, partake of The Bread!
The Bread of Life, has come for you,
    To give you strength, your life renew!
For He who gave, His life to pay,
    Removed the nails, on your coffin that day.
The nails were sins, that trapped you in,
    To graves of death, and hell and sin.
But the Power that raised, Christ from the dead,
    Is yours today, so you can be led,
By the Spirit of God, into faith this hour,
    To walk in love, and grace with power.
We cannot walk, this life on our own,
    We would trip and fall, over boulders and stones.
So call to The Spirit of God, this day,
    He will smooth the path, and make a way.

Holy Spirit will clear, all that hinders and blocks,
    So we can walk, like our Saviour walked.
For love is the key, that opens the door,
    Love is the path, to joy evermore.
His joy gives strength, to our hearts and our souls,
    It brings us His peace, and His life to bestow.
Do not let sin's fleeting pleasures, this hour,
    Keep you from seeking, for more of Christ's power.
He has so much more, to give unto you,
    Blessings untold, to give others too.
This is the way, He wants us to share,
    Out of His fullness, His love to care.
So show His care, to all of mankind,
    The love of our God, gives light to the blind.
The Light of our God, will give us new sight,
    Will brighten and light up, the darkest of nights!

WAIT FOR THE LORD - Inspired by Isaiah 40:31

Wait for The Lord, wait patient today,
 His coming is sure, He will not delay!
At just the right time, He comes on the scene,
 To restore your hope, and fulfill your dream!
The dreams He puts, in your heart and mind,
 Are dreams and visions, to restore in kind.
When our sight was dimmed, by all our sin,
 Our vision was darkened, no hope within.
But The Spirit of God, gives visions and dreams,
 In day or night, with a light that beams,
To waken, to brighten, in every dark place,
 To behold the beauty, of His glorious grace.
By the mercy and grace, of our Saviour and Lord,
 Our hope is restored, to receive our reward;
The reward for giving, our lives to Him,
 By trusting His grace, to remove all sin.

Now by The Power of God, we see,
 The plans He has destined, for us to be,
His living light, while on this earth,
 A light that brings, men's souls to birth.
We are born again, into the kingdom of God,
 By Word and Spirit, to give Him laud!
Praise and worship, knit our hearts to His,
 To enter in, partake of His bliss.
The bliss of God, Oh, what love,
 The love of God, from heaven above!
Oh draw near, wait upon your Lord,
 Ask for His Spirit, to quicken His Word,
For in His quickening, we are given His light,
 To walk His walk, in the darkest night.
So in the night seasons, prepare to hear,
 The voice of your Saviour, so sweet and clear.

GOD'S HIGHWAY - Inspired by: Isaiah Chapter 40

Make a highway, for The Lord,
    Make it straight and plain, restored.
Fill up the valleys, and level the hills,
    For the Word God speaks, to be fulfilled.
He is coming in glory, to reveal His name,
    He is coming to wash, and cleanse all shame.
He is coming in power, to receive His bride,
    To clothe Her in glory, by His side to abide.

Shout to the world, and tell the good news,
    Your God is coming, to cleanse and renew.
His coming gives hope, to all on the earth,
    Gives life to all, by The Spirit's rebirth.
He will feed us all, as a shepherd does,
    Protect and keep us, without a pause.
He will carry us in, His loving arms,
    Holding us close, away from harm.

He will gently lead us, to pastures green,
    Restore our vision, and make us clean.
By the Precious Blood, of our Saviour true,
    He grants salvation, to me and you.
He prepares our hearts, and spirits to live,
    In grace and faith, and joy to give;
To give to all, the message of love,
    To tell to all, Jesus came from above.

He came to be, The Saviour for all,
    So we could stand firm, and never fall,
Never fall or stray, away from His love,
    But stand by the grace, He gives from above,
This grace is mighty, sure, holy and true,
    It was purchased by The Blood, Christ shed for you.
For you and me, and all who trust,
    In The Son of God, The Pure and The Just!

THE UNSEARCHABLE RICHES OF CHRIST
Inspired by Ephesians 3:8

What are the riches, in Christ our Lord?
    How are His mercies, and grace outpoured?
By The Blood of Christ, we've been redeemed,
    By the Love of God, we are esteemed!
Esteemed by God, what a precious thought,
    Made worthy by, the fight Christ fought!
He redeemed our souls, from death and hell,
    Then restored our souls, and made us well!

This wellness comes, from trusting Christ,
    By receiving His grace, and His sacrifice.
He descended into, the realms of hell,
    Took back the keys, so we could tell,
Of His wondrous love, His saving grace,
    Then behold the beauty, of His face.

Oh believe on Him now, and trust His Word,
    Then allow that word, to be a sword,
A sword that severs, every sin,
    To make us clean, and pure within.
For we're made pure, by Christ's own blood,
    Made pure to see, the face of God!
Oh, realize, your need for Him,
    Come quickly now, He'll forgive your sin.

An honest prayer, is all it takes,
    Admit your sin, and then partake,
Of a love that gave, His life on a cross,
    So you could count, all things as loss;
For the knowledge of God, in Christ as Lord,
    For the blessing of God, and peace restored,
For the love of God, ever transcends,
    Is forever, always, without an end!

BUILD AN ALTAR
Inspired by Ezra 3:2 & 3 and Romans 12:1

Build an altar, to The Lord your God,
Build together, in one accord.
Build with hope, and build in love, build to worship, God above.
Then bring to God, your offering,
With songs of worship, let praises ring,
To God alone, who reigns on high,
Present yourselves, your very lives.
For Christ who offered, up His life,
Became the Perfect Sacrifice.
He gave Himself, because of love,
Came down to earth, from heaven above.
He came to serve, to live, to die, for such a one as you and I.

Then on the morning, of that third day,
He rose and tore, death's cords away,
So we could live eternally, with Christ our Lord, forever free.

So in the words of Paul, I say,
Present yourselves, to Christ this day,
A holy, living, sacrifice,
A body pure, and cleansed from vice.
Now we're made pure, by Christ, God's Son,
Made pure by what, His death has done.
For He alone, is The One who saves,
He alone, raises up from the grave.
Sin had trapped us, by its power,
But Christ redeemed us, in that hour.
So come today, come enter in,
Receive His grace, be free from sin,
Present yourselves, before His throne,
For Christ, to be His very own.
You'll not regret, this choice you've made
The choice to be, The Lord's today!

BE GLAD - Inspired by Romans 12:6-12

Be glad for all, God is planning for you,
Be glad, for He has a work for you,
A work to lift, the fallen and sad,
A work to make, His children glad.
So use the gifts, that God has given,
To free men's souls, for life and heaven.
For in this life, God has given you,
The life of Christ, to live through you,
You'll have a love, to give to all,
The truth of God, to hear His call.

So if your gift, is serving others,
Serve with love, to sisters and brothers.
If your gift, is teaching men,
Teach them how, to love again,
To love The Lord, with heart and soul,
To love all men, to make them whole;
Whole by Christ's, redeeming power,
To live and stand, for Him this hour.
If prophecy, is the gift God's given,
To lead men to, His courts in heaven,
Then speak in faith, a word that's true,
A word that tells, men what to do.

If your gift from God, is encouragement,
Encourage and strengthen, make a dent.
With love and hope and faith, speak out,
The words of Christ, to bring about,
New hope and faith, new love and cheer,
To all who love, our Saviour Dear.
Be patient in trouble, and always in prayer,
Knowing that God, is always there.
He hears each prayer, whether thanks or need,
To love in faith, and hope and deed!

LOVE LIKE JESUS - Inspired by Romans 12:21

Does evil get the best of you?
  Then conquer it by living true!
    Be true to God by doing good,
      Be true by living as you should.
By the love that God has given,
  When He came to earth from heaven,
    Give the love He's given you,
      When His Spirit made you new!

For if you love like Jesus did,
  And if you love as The Spirit bids,
    Your lives will be an offering,
      That frees your heart to shout and sing.
So sing a song of love to The Lord,
  A song of joy to strengthen the cords.
    These cords will bind your heart to His,
      They'll free your soul to live in bliss!

For if you share with men God's love,
  Always responding in love from above,
    Then the words of God will prosper and grow,
      And men will see and men will know,
That God alone is The God who saves,
  Who saves from death and hell and grave!
    In His love He cleansed our sin,
      He paid the price to ransom men.

His blood, His death on Calvary,
  He gave so all could be set free!
    So if His Word men don't receive,
      Pray for their souls to be released,
From all the lies the devil told,
  That keeps them from our Saviour's fold.
    For when you pray in faith to tell,
      You will save a sinner's soul from hell!

CREATE A CLEAN HEART - Inspired by Psalm 51

Saviour, Healer, Friend, Divine,
    Cleanse, redeem, this soul of mine.
Create in me a heart that is clean,
    Make my spirit. renewed and redeemed.
For only by Your Precious Blood,
    Does Your mercy cleanse me for my good.
I need Your Spirit more each day,
    So from Your side, I'll never stray.

Reveal to me, how much You've cleansed,
    Cleansed so I could enter in,
To courts of heaven with joy and love,
    To worship God in heaven above.
Oh, Saviour Dear, I bow my knees,
    I cast my crown, at Your holy feet.
Who am I Lord, that You loved me?
    Who am I Lord, to be set free?

Yet Lord, You loved me, from the start,
    You loved me with, Your perfect heart.
You saw me in, my wretched state,
    You knew I'd die, in sin and hate.
But You did come, to make me clean,
    And from my sins, my soul's redeemed
Take not Your Spirit, Lord from me,
    Your Presence is, the place I seek!

What can I bring, to thank you Lord,
    What can I give, for a life restored?
A broken spirit, You'll not despise,
    A repentant heart, without, compromise.
Restore again, Your joy to me,
    So I can teach, all men of Thee.
I want to love, and lead men to,
    Your holy throne, to worship You!

RIVERS OF PRAISE - Inspired by Psalm 46:4-7

Let rivers of praise flow from my heart,
  To refresh my soul, to make a start,
    A start to this day, of life You've given,
      A day to prepare, my soul for heaven.
I praise You God, my Lord and King,
  You bring me life, and a song to sing;
    A song of joy, a song of praise,
      A song to worship, through the day.

Oh Lord my God, You have given to me,
  Your life, Your love, to set me free;
    Free to be, Your holy child,
      Free from sin, and undefiled.
Now free to live, for You alone,
  Free to come, before Your throne.
    I am free to cast, my every care,
      Free to know, You answer prayer.

Your Precious Blood, has set me free,
  Cleansed me from, sins tyranny.
    Though sin had damned, my soul to hell
      You gave Your life, to make me well.
Now well and whole, cleansed and free,
  I am free to live for eternity.
    You have freed me from the cares that bind,
      Free to think with a purified mind.

You have offered to me Your loving hand,
  You've received me now, so I can stand,
    Before You God of heaven and earth,
      To give You thanks for my new birth.
I cast my crown before Your throne,
  To worship You and You alone.
    God, You alone are God Most High,
      And by Your grace, I'll never die!

THE PRINCE OF PEACE
Inspired by Zechariah 9:9 and John 12:12-16

You came Oh Lord, on a foal that day,
    You came to proclaim, to all to say,
        The Prince of Peace, has come to men,
           To redeem our souls, to free from sin.
We receive Your Word, Oh God, and say,
    Come in, Oh Lord, come in and stay.
        Come in, abide, forever Lord,
           For then salvation is assured.

Your Word is living, pure and true,
    And by Your Word, You make me new.
        I am free to live, before You Lord,
           I am free by Holy Spirit's sword.
You birth by Spirit, and by Word,
    A child who does, what he has heard,
        The Word that comes, from Father's heart,
           To love all men, right from the start.
My eyes were blind, my ears were deaf,
    Before Your Spirit, gave me breath.
        I did not know, what You had planned,
           To help me show, Your love, Your hand.

But in Your grace, and mercy Lord,
    You cleansed my sin, Your Blood You poured,
        Upon the Mercy Seat in heaven,
           You made a way, for sins forgiven.
Your blood has cleansed, restored my soul,
    I walk before You, pure and whole,
        Not by anything, I have done,
           But just by trusting Christ, God's Son.
Christ is the only way to Life,
    So come to Him, to end the strife,
        That comes by trusting, in your ways,
           He'll lead and guide you, all your days!

WHAT DOES IT MEAN?

What does it mean, to believe in Christ,
  To trust His Blood, His sacrifice?
It means that you, forsake your ways,
  Then turn to Him, for faith always.
Forgiveness comes, when we call to Christ,
  Call upon Him, for His Blood will suffice.
Only His Blood, can cleanse our souls,
  Can save from sin, and make us whole.

When we were dead, in all our sin,
  Doomed forever, so blind within,
Christ Jesus, came from heaven to earth,
  Lived and died, to give new birth.
Christ was no ordinary man,
  He was God in the flesh, by God's own plan.
In order for us, to be forgiven,
  A sinless offering, had to be given.

No sin was found, in This Son of God,
  For He walked and talked, on this earthly sod,
By what The Father, had said to do,
  Christ showed to all, The Way of Truth.
Then on the cross, that fateful day,
  He took all sickness, and sin away,
He became for us, the pure sacrifice,
  To pay for all, our sin and vice.

Oh believe on The Lord Jesus Christ today,
  Confess your sins, to Him and pray,
Forgive me Lord, restore my soul,
  I want Your grace, to make me whole.
He'll take you in, to heaven's door,
  He'll save your soul, and give His more.
His hand provides, for all you need,
  His Blood, the price, the total deed!

REBUILD MY HOUSE
Inspired by Haggai 1:8, 1st Corinthians 3:9-17 & John 17:21

Rebuild My house, The Lord would say,
    Rebuild it now, do not delay.
Rebuild the temple, where I can dwell,
    Rebuild it now, and build it well.
Come up to where I AM, this day,
    Receive My plans, so I can stay,
Into the temple, I've prepared,
    A temple where, My Word is shared.
This temple is not, of wood and stone,
    This temple where God, now sits enthroned,
For He alone is, The Head of His Church,
    And we His Body, for Him must search.

Let's search for His Presence, and will to bless,
    Let's search for His blessing, of Righteousness.
Consider now, The Lord would say,
    Consider where you, have gone astray.
You've built on what, men's words have said,
    Instead of all, My Word has said.
You have taken parts, of what is true,
    And built the walls, that separate you.
You have stayed alone, before My throne,
    To offer up your prayers alone.

Oh come My Church, come to Me know,
    Come one and all to make a vow,
A vow to live in unity,
    So that My blessing can flow free;
Freely from My head outpoured,
    Free to all who have been restored,
Restored to God, by The sacrifice,
    I gave to pay, sin's awful price.
For when you are one, before My Throne,
    The world will know, I AM God alone!

GRACE IS NOT GRAY - Inspired by Ephesians 2:8-10

Grace is not gray, my husband did say,
    For it comes by The Blood of Jesus to say:
Though your sins are like scarlet, I purify,
    By My precious Blood, I justify!
To all who come, to My Throne for grace,
    For My blood to cleanse, to run My race,
I redeem, I replace, I make whole, restore,
    The lives of those, who want Me more.
Those who want the life, I alone can give,
    I grant real life, and the grace to forgive.
So as you start, your life each day,
    Remember dear child, the price Christ paid.
When you are tempted, by the lure of sin,
    Remember the price, Christ paid for our sin!
He lovingly came, from His throne up above,
    Suffered and died, out of pure sweet love.
He redeemed and ransomed us, from the grave,
    Rose to proclaim, from death we are saved!

Consider carefully, the plans you make,
    Listen to His Spirit, all sin forsake.
Walk in the Light He has given you,
    And to Him your Lord, be faithful true.
Don't tolerate sin, in any form,
    For it muddies the lives, Christ came to transform.
Ask instead, for His strength to abide,
    And love, first love, to stand by His side.
Then behold with eyes, made pure and clean,
    Your Lord, His Love, for you've been redeemed.
Then you will know, and realize,
    That sin is not worth, the compromise!
Sin only leads, to hell and death,
    Holy Spirit comes, gives life and breath.
So ask for His Spirit, to empower you,
    Then you will live, in love that's true!

<u>MY PEOPLE</u> - Inspired by Zechariah 10:12

My people have wandered, here and there,
    Tossed and scattered, by worry and care.
But, now no more, for I AM calling them,
    Calling them to, forsake their sin.

I AM calling them, to come to Me,
    I AM calling them, to be set free,
For I have come, to save My flock,
    The flock that by, Christ's blood was bought!

Christ bought, redeemed, from sin and loss,
    He cleansed and saved there, on that cross,
Now in the Name, of Christ alone,
    Our sin is erased, our lives atoned!

I AM The Lord, their holy God,
    I hear their cries, their cries out loud.
They have cried to Me, in their suffering,
    They have cried, Oh Lord, remember me.

So now, My Spirit has come to speak,
    Into the hearts, of all who seek,
My face, My love, My comfort true,
    So I can make, all things brand new!

I have come to take, their stony hearts,
    That kept men, from My side apart,
To give a brand new heart to all,
    For in My love, I have come for all.

I'll redeem their souls, from death and sin,
    I will give them grace, to enter in.
Then in My Presence, and in My power,
    I will give them strength, to stand this hour.

They will stand in power, and authority,
Wherever they go, by land or sea,
To witness and, proclaim My Name,
With the power that comes, My Name to proclaim.

All who call upon My name,
Are saved from death and hell and shame.
So hear My voice and what I say,
Receive My call and then obey.

The Words that I have given to you,
Will make your heart and spirit true.
For in My truth, My love abides,
And in My love, true life you'll find.

My love and joy, peace and power,
Will give My people, strength this hour.
My strength will, re-establish them,
Will give them strength to conquer sin;

Strength to love, what' ere the cost,
Strength to lift, and save the lost,
Strength to bring, new life and hope,
To all who struggle, just to cope.

The plan I have, for all mankind,
To heal the deaf, the mute, the blind,
Is life abundant, full and free,
A life to live, for eternity.

So go to the highways, and there proclaim,
The wonders of, My Holy Name.
For in My Name, all can be saved,
From sin and sickness, death and grave.

STAND FOR THE LORD - Inspired by 2nd Timothy 4:17 & 18

When you stand for The Lord, He stands with you,
    He gives you strength, to do what's true,
To say and do, with all your lives,
    The message given, without compromise.

For when we speak, the Lord's Good News,
    We set men free, from what confused.
The truth of God, when spoken in power,
    Will redeem the souls, who hear this hour.

Those who receive, the message given,
    That Christ has come, to purge sin's leaven.
Will then receive, a brand new mind,
    And a brand new heart, so they can find,

The way to God, on the road of life,
    The road that's cleared, of sin and strife.
Christ Jesus cleared, the way for all,
    Who hear His Word, and heed His call.

So now to you, who have heard His call,
    Who have answered yes, to give your all,
To Christ who has, redeemed your lives,
    Speak His Word, to remove the lies.

For when His truth, is spoken in love,
    It frees and redeems, to courts above,
There to worship, with all the saints,
    Almighty God, without restraint!

HOLY SPIRIT, LIVE IN ME - Inspired by 1ˢᵗ John 3:18

Holy Spirit, live in me,
  Teach me how, my life should be.
Conform me to, The Saviour's will,
  So all God's plans, can be fulfilled.
Increase my love, for God and men,
  So that my life, will show God's plan,
A life that's more, than speaking words,
  A life that shows, God's love by works.
For by God's love, we are justified,
  And by His love, our lives are tied,
To Jesus Christ, our Saviour Dear,
  To show His love, to bring His cheer.

By words and actions, let's live this Faith,
  For faith in Christ, redeems, makes way,
To show to all, by word and deed,
  That Christ has met, our every need.
He meets the need, for love and peace,
  He paid to give, our soul's release.
Now we're released, from sin and loss,
  Christ paid our price, upon that cross.
He alone, redeems makes whole,
  He gave His life, ransomed our soul.

Oh Father God, I come right now,
  I pledge my life, I make this vow,
To live for You, and You alone,
  To trust in Christ, before Your throne.
I stand by faith, in His righteousness,
  That cleansed me of, unworthiness.
Make me Your temple, undefiled,
  Your loving and obedient child.
So all can see by word and deed,
  That faith in Christ is all we need!

CONTINUE TO LOVE - Inspired by Hebrews 13:1

Continue to love, like The Father above,
    Continue to love, with true Christian love.
Show this love, to all you meet,
    To those you bring home, to those on the street.
God wants His love, to be shown to all,
    His children, who heed His Spirit's call.
We are called to love, as The Saviour loved,
    When He left the courts, of heaven above.
He didn't stay, in His privileged place,
    Ever beholding, His Father's face,
But came to us, to extend God's grace,
    So we could see His Father's face.
He came to live, and die for all,
    He came to cleanse us, from our fall.
As the second Adam, He came to redeem,
    To cleanse our hearts, and remove the beam!

This beam was pride, that blocked our sight,
    That kept our eyes, from seeing His light.
When Jesus gave, His life for all,
    He removed the beam, that caused our fall.
For the devil had blinded, our eyes with pride,
    To make us think, we were clean inside.
We thought that we, were doing well,
    But we were on, the path to hell.
We trusted in, the way we lived,
    Instead of trusting Christ, to forgive.
So let us come, to Christ right now,
    And make our pledge, a solemn vow,
Oh Lord, I ask, forgive my sin,
    Make me Your child, without, within,
So I can worship Christ as Lord,
    Behold You God, by all adored!

FORGIVE ME LORD - Inspired by Ezra 9:6- 10-17

Oh Lord, my God, I am utterly ashamed,
    For we Oh Lord, have profaned Your Name.
We have sinned by refusing, to do what is right,
    By tolerating sin, not walking in The Light.

For the Light of Life, came down to earth,
    Jesus The Christ, by His holy birth,
He came to cleanse us, from our sin,
    He came to give us, peace within.

But we have wandered, to and fro,
    Not serving Him, with heart and soul.
We've tried to walk, the narrow way,
    But let our minds, cause us to stray.

So Lord I come, to You this day,
    Forgive me Lord, and cleanse I pray,
From all that causes, sin and loss,
    From all that put You, on that cross.

Make me a child of Yours, today,
    A child who walks, Your narrow way,
For in that way, is life and peace,
    Is joy and love, which never cease.

Create in me, a pure clean heart,
    And a new right spirit, to never depart.
For in Your presence, is abundant life,
    A life made free, of sin and strife!

FOR GOD AND GOD ALONE - Inspired by Genesis 1& 2

Who is a God like You, Oh Lord,
  Who made the earth, by just one Word?
You made the sea, and all the dry land,
  By the power of Your Word, and Your mighty hand!
You made plants and animals, and all living things,
  Then man in Your image, to rejoice and sing!
From the dust of the earth, You formed a man,
  In Your holy image, to fulfill Your plan.
You breathed in him, the breath of life,
  Then created for him, a companion, a wife!
You gave them dominion, over land and sea,
  You blessed them with power, and authority,
To subdue the earth, and multiply,
  To live with You, and never die.
You gave for food, all the fruit bearing trees,
  And all seed bearing plants, to fulfill their needs.

You walked in the cool of the evening, with them,
  You imparted Your love, to their souls again.
Only the fruit of one tree, was forbidden,
  By the Word of God, the order was given:
From the tree of the knowledge, of evil and good,
  Don't partake of the fruit, of this tree for food.
If you eat of this tree, you will surely die,
  This was the Word, of God Most High!
But the devil came, to the woman one day,
  With deception and lies, to lead her astray,
To lead her to death, and hell like him,
  To tempt and condemn, her by this first sin.
He told her she would be, like God Most High,
  Knowing good and evil, she would not die!
But the devil is a liar and she swallowed his bait,
  She took of the fruit, and gave Adam a taste.
They ate of the fruit, then suddenly felt shame,
  They saw they were naked, with no one to blame.

God came to them later, in the cool of the day,
    But they hid themselves, for they'd gone astray.
Now when God spoke, they cowered in shame,
    Instead of repenting, they played the blame game.
Adam blamed God, for giving him Eve,
    And Eve blamed the serpent, for how he deceived.
They were banished by God, from the garden that day,
    And God placed His angels, to keep them away.
He sent them to work, by the sweat of their brow,
    To struggle and toil, for a living now.
The serpent God cursed, to crawl in the dust,
    An enemy of women, who they never would trust.
From now on a woman, would not have the power,
    To convince and control, a man in his hour.
Her desire would always, now be for him,
    And he'd be her master, without and within.

However, God's promise also was given,
    By God who is love, a word came from heaven.
The Seed of the woman, would crush Satan's head,
    To release men from sin, from hell and from dread.
Jesus, conceived, by The Spirit of God,
    Was born to a woman, with a love for God.
When she gave birth, God's Son was given,
    To deliver all men, to fit us for heaven.
He gave His life, on that awful cross,
    Redeemed us from death, and all that was lost.
Now we can live forever, with Him,
    Now we can live, in freedom from sin.
For Christ paid the price, with the cross that day,
    The price of our sins, He took away.

The curse that came, in Eden that day,
    When our parents sinned, and made a way,
For evil to enter into the earth,
    Prevented us all, from knowing our worth,
But God in His mercy, sent Jesus, His Son,

To redeem all of us, for what we had done.
Christ is The Way, The Truth, and The Life,
Come to Him now, put away sin and strife.
Confess you are sinners, to Christ who can save,
From death and from hell, from sin and the grave.
When you confess, your sins unto Him,
He opens the door, to enter in,
To a life of love, and joy and peace,
To a life eternal, where joys never cease!
This life can begin, for you right now,
If you come in faith, and make a vow,
A vow to give, your life to Him,
To let His blood, and His sacrifice given,
Be to you, your righteousness,
The way to God, His Blessedness!

<u>ONLY YOU</u> - Inspired by Ephesians 2:4-5

Help me Lord, to hear Your voice,
To heed Your will, to make a choice,
To live for You with all I am, to enter in salvation's plan.
For only You can satisfy, only You can justify;
Only You, have saved my soul,
Only You, have made me whole.
So Lord I come, this day to You,
To make my heart, and spirit true.
Help me to live, in grace and love,
So men can know, their God above;
To fully see, that God is there,
To hear their hearts, and take their care.
You give to all, who come to You,
The power to put, their faith in You!

<u>YOU MUST BE BORN AGAIN</u> - Inspired by John 3:3-17

What does it mean, to be born again?
   How can a person, be cleansed from sin?
      How can we see, the Kingdom of God?
        How can we walk, like The Son of God?
Jesus came and lived a life, a life that freed all men from strife!

Be born of the water, and The Spirit, Christ said,
   To a man one night, whom The Spirit led.
The Spirit of God, had touched his mind,
   And he came to Jesus, the truth to find.
He studied God's Word, and saw the signs,
   Miraculous signs, like healing the blind.
He knew the words, but not The Word,
   For it is only by The Spirit, The Word is heard.
We are born through the water, by our earthly birth,
   But it is only by God's Spirit, that we're given new birth.
The Holy Spirit gives us, life from heaven,
   For the life He gives, purges out the leaven.
Sin is the leaven, that destroys and kills,
   The lives of men, and all their ills.
Our God came down, in human form,
   He gave us His life, to be reborn.

Oh, come to Him, and come right now,
   Don't put it off, your solemn vow,
Say: Jesus Christ, forgive my sin,
   Make me Your child, to enter in.
I receive Your love, and sacrifice,
   I look to You, You paid the price.
Your precious blood, it's cleansing flow,
   Has paid the price, to make me whole.
Now according to Your Word, I read,
   Your love has cleansed, my every deed.

LIVE TO LOVE

Live to love, beholding God's face,
  Live to love, receiving His grace,
Live to love, to testify,
  Of Christ The Lord, for you He died.
Then when we all, behold His face,
  Receive His love, and trust His grace,
We are restored, for God alone,
  Restored to stand, before His Throne;
To stand with boldness by His grace,
  With all the saints, who've run His race,
Who've kept the faith, who've stayed the course,
  Who've fought the fight, by The Spirit's force.
For it's not by might, or power of ours,
  By The Holy Spirit, we stand this hour.
So stand, my friend, stand firm in Him,
  Don't let the fire of faith grow dim.
Keep stoking it, with love and prayer,
  Then you with all the saints, will share,
The joys God, has prepared in love,
  The courts of heaven, His mansions above!

TO LIVE - Inspired by Philippians 1:20 -21

Help me Lord, to live for You,
  To always hear, and say and do,
The words of life, You have given to me,
  The words, that place eternity,
Into the hearts, of those You love,
  So they can come, to Your courts above;
Cleansed made whole,, by Your righteousness,
  Free to receive, Your holiness.
Lord set us apart, by Your mercy and grace,
  Set us apart, to behold Your face.
For in You Lord, we now have life,
  The life that frees, from sin and strife!

<u>WHY DO YOU WORK?</u> - Inspired by Isaiah 55

Why do you work, for what is not bread?
Why do you toil, for money instead?
Why spend your money, on what gives no strength?
Why pay for things, that have no length?
Do you want a life, that satisfies?
Do you want a life, that never dies?

Then come to The Giver of Life, my friend,
For His life is abundant, it never ends.
Come to The Lord, with arms open wide,
Listen real close, for He has come to abide.
He has come to abide, in the hearts of all men,
Who have heard by His Spirit, be born again!

He will make an eternal covenant, with you,
If you give Him your heart, to make it true.
He will give you His mercy, and unfailing love,
Reveal to all men, their God up above.
He will show you His glory, and redeem your soul,
He will manifest His Presence, and make you whole!

So seek The Lord, while He may be found,
Turn to Him now, for His mercy abounds.
His mercy He gives, to all who come clean,
Who confess that they're sinners, their lives to redeem.
Christ will pardon, and cleanse within,
He will take away guilt, and remove every sin.

The Christ of God, our Saviour is here,
His mercy is present, His love is near.
Receive His love, and His mercy today,
So you can enter, His presence and say,
Jesus is Lord, and He is my Lord,
I will live by His Spirit, I will trust in His Word.

GOD'S ORDER - Inspired by 1st Corinthians 12-14

What is the proper order of things?
　　What makes the courts of heaven sing?
Lord I ask, examine my heart,
　　Is my love complete, do I do my part?
You have made of me, a part of a whole,
　　A part of Your Body, in spirit and soul.
Just as You've placed, all the parts in us,
　　In Your perfect way, by Your loving touch,
Help us now, to really know,
　　That You have placed us, where we will grow;
To grow in to, Your perfect plan,
　　Serving God, by serving man.

Help us to serve, in such a way,
　　To lead all men, to Christ today.
There is so much, we need to do,
　　To be, to lead, to love like You.
Oh teach us Lord, to understand,
　　To live from the guidance, of Your hand.
Lead us to where, we need to be,
　　So all may know, and all may see,
That Christ is Lord, and Saviour too,
　　For that is what, we're called to do.
We are called to love, and not complain,
　　To make the way, to Christ real plain.

Remove from us, all sin and pride,
　　So we can lead men, to Your side;
There with grace, and mercy given,
　　To lead them to, Your courts of heaven.
Cause them to see, with brand new eyes,
　　Your will, Your plan, without the lies,
That the devil had used, to hinder them,
　　From trusting You and Your love for them!

Your love is pure, and undefiled,
  To make of all, Your own dear child.
For by Your Blood and sacrifice,
  You proved Your love, You paid the price,
To ransom all, who come to You,
  Who ask in faith, for life that's new.
So now Oh Lord, I speak to You,
  Make of me Lord, a child that's true:
True to all, You have given me,
  To set My heart, and spirit free.

I come Oh Lord, for Your cleansing power,
  Forgive me Lord, place me this hour,
Into the place, where I belong,
  The place where You, can make me strong;
Strong in faith, and hope and love,
  Strong to serve You, God above;
Strong to serve, my fellowman,
  So they can see, Your love for them!

A CLEANSING - Inspired by The Book of Nehemiah

A cleansing is coming, to The House of The Lord,
  A cleansing must come, for glory restored.
My glory is coming, to purge and refine,
  Revelations of glory, to purify mine!
My glory gives light, to illuminate men,
  To cause them to choose, My ways once again.
So prepare your hearts, for My glory to come,
  Prepare, make ready, all people, not some!
The Glory of God, is a sight to behold,
  The glory makes new, what was tattered and old.
The glory reveals, the hearts of all men,
  The glory causes worship, to rise once again!
This worship is pure, a worship that's right,
  A worship of God, that restores our sight!

<u>DO YOU LOVE?</u> - Inspired by: Matthew 5 - 7, Matthew 11:28-30 and 1st Peter 5:7

Love one another, as I have loved you,
Do unto others, what you want for you.
These are the words, of Christ The Lord,
To keep us living, in one accord.

For when we live, our lives this way,
We show to all, God's love this day.
His love, He proved by what He did,
His life, He gave so we could live.

Oh child of Mine, I hear Him call,
Give me your life, your love, your all,
For when you give your life to Me,
I'll make your heart and spirit free.

I will take your life, and make it whole,
I'll redeem each part, renew your soul.
Blessings abound, for all who believe,
Who trust in Me, to meet their needs.

Now when you trust, with all your heart,
God gives your life, a brand new start.
Now you are free, from all your cares,
Now God's strength, is there to share.

The weight and burdens, upon you now,
He'll take from you, for He has vowed:
If you will cast, all care on Me,
I'll make your soul, and spirit free.

<u>GRACE TO SHOW</u> - Inspired by John 13

Do you have the grace to show?
    Do you love so others know,
That Christ The Lord has come to earth,
    To pay the price for their new birth?

Then come to Christ, and come today,
    Come to Him, and hear Him say:
The fields are ripe, for harvest now,
    I showed the way, I showed you how.

So lead men to, My saving grace,
    Help them to see, My Father's face.
The way is love, the way I showed,
    Therefore, do share, what I've bestowed.

Give of My love, and mercy too,
    Give what I, have given to you.
While you were a sinner, I died on the cross,
    I forgave your sin, and redeemed your loss.

So forgive and live, and to others do,
    What you would, have them do for you.
By acts of love and kindness give,
    The hope so men, can know and live.

Oh, live for Christ, and for God's plan,
    Live with love, for every man.
Speak the truth, to show the way,
    Then hear His voice call, to come and pray.

Pray for peace, and patience too,
    To wait on God, to do through you,
His will that shows, His love for all,
    Who answer yes, when His Spirit calls!

JUDGE NOT - Inspired by Matthew 7:1-5

Do you judge, do you condemn?
    For others will trust, if you trust them!
        The measure you use, in your dealings with men,
            Is the measure that's given, to you again.
Look in God's mirror, and look real close,
    Ask for His Spirit, The Holy Ghost,
        To clean out the beam, that blocks your sight,
            That keeps you in, the dark of night.
He'll take that beam, right out of your eye,
    When in the name, of Christ you cry,
        For help to see, the needs of men,
            For help to love, like Christ again.

Our sins of pride, and foolishness,
    Will block our sight, to see the best,
        They'll keep us thinking, we're doing great.
            When all we're doing, is blocking the gate.
For Christ is The Gate, The Life, The Way,
    For men to receive, God's life today.
        Now if we judge, and we condemn,
            We're falling for, the devil's plan.

So if you see, your brother sin,
    Show the love, that brought you in!
        For you were dead once, in your sin,
            Until you came to Christ, for Him!
He cleansed, redeemed, restored, consoled,
    He did it all, to make you whole.
        So take the love, Christ's given to you,
            Take His love, and give it too.
For when we show, His love to all,
    They'll know He loves, they'll hear His call.
        They'll pray to God, to give to them,
            Hearts to hear, and eyes for Him!

ASK AND YOU WILL RECEIVE - Inspired by Matthew 7:7-11

Do you want to really pray? Do you want God's will today?
    Then hear these words, of Christ that say,
The way to touch, God's heart always.

Keep on asking, and you will receive,
    Keep on knocking, and doors will release.
Persistence with faith, is what God seeks,
    From the pure in heart, the humble, the meek.

God delights, to hear the call,
    From people who, surrender all.
He loves to give, His plans to men,
    Who hear His will, to work His plan.
His plans for us, are better still,
    For when we live, to do His will,
His blessings, overtake our lives,
    They meet our needs, and all besides.

Now when God gives, there is overflow,
    So we can share, so we can go,
To those He has called, to give of His love,
    Called to bring, to heaven above.
So let's call those, for whom Christ died,
    Let's call them to, His precious side,
There to receive, His love and grace,
    There to behold, His loving face.

So tarry not, do not delay,
    Act in faith, in Jesus' Name!
Ask for Him, to do through you,
    His plans and purpose, that give to you,
The way and will, of blessing to abound,
    To all who hear, His voice resound.
His voice resounds, with love to all,
    To bless, to hear, His voice, His call!

<u>YOUR PLAN</u> - Inspired by James 1:5

What is Your plan, for me today?
  Oh guide and lead me, on Your way;
The way that leads, to blessedness,
  To peace and joy, and righteousness.
It is by Your sacrifice, Oh Christ,
  That I'm redeemed, from sin and vice.
Give me Your wisdom, from above,
  That's pure and gentle, with peace and love.

Help me to yield, with willingness,
  So I may walk, in righteousness,
The righteousness, of Christ my Lord,
  Full of mercy, in one accord.
Cause the deeds, that I will do,
  Show God's love, is pure and true.
Help me to walk, in perfect peace,
  God's will to bring, to men release.

For it's by the seeds, of peace we sow.
  That goodness, is the harvest grown.
This harvest Lord, You'll truly bless,
  Will lead all men, to then confess,
That Christ is Lord, and Saviour too,
  The One who makes, our lives brand new.

So if your lives, are full of stress,
  Come to The Lord, your sins confess.
He'll cleanse your sins, He'll make you whole,
  Renew your life, redeem your soul.
You'll enter then, His blessedness,
  His joy and love, His righteousness.
This is the life, He offers you,
  Draw close to God, He'll draw close to you.

When you bow down, before The Lord,
    Admit you've sinned, transgressed His Word,
He'll lift you up, with arms of love,
    Give you the honour, from God above.
The honour that comes, from being His child,
    A child redeemed, from all that is vile.
Redeemed by the Precious, Blood of The Lamb
    His child forever, in His courts to stand!

REDEEMED - Inspired by Psalm 107:1-2 and Luke 1:67-79

What does it mean, to be redeemed?
    To be bought back, by love esteemed?
God counted our lives, such precious worth,
    That He sent His Son, to be born on earth.
He lived a perfect holy life,
    To set us free, from sin and strife.
Strife destroys, and sin condemns,
    The souls of men, to cause their end.
For the pleasures of sin, are fleeting at best,
    They give no hope, no peace, no rest.

God's life through Christ, restores our souls,
    He sets us free, He makes us whole.
What Christ redeems, He then restores,
    He brings to life, at the very core!
Our hearts were meant, to live for Him,
    To commune in joy, and love within,
His sheltered rest, His loving arms,
    To experience peace, be safe from harm.
So come dear child, receive His love,
    His mercy, His goodness, His grace from above!

<u>TO GROW IN GRACE</u> - Inspired by 1st and 2nd Peter

Grow in the grace, and the favour of God,
  Grow in the knowledge, of The Lord your God!
For as you grow, in your knowledge of Him,
  Your heart will be cleansed, from desire for sin.
Sin and its ways, lead to death and hell,
  But the ways of God, are salvation's well.
Salvation is God's, holy well of life,
  A redeeming spring, from sin and strife.
His spring of life, refreshes our souls,
  It makes us new, it makes us whole.
Only in The Lord, is redemption pure,
  Only He makes, our footsteps sure.
He will set your feet, on a straight clear road,
  A road that is free, from sin's dark load.
God never meant, for the burden of sin,
  To be cast upon men, to destroy within.

God's plan for man, was to be his friend,
  To give man life, without an end.
But when sin came in, death came too,
  To destroy all God, had planned for you.
But God in all His mercy and love,
  Sent Jesus, His Son from heaven above,
He sent His Son, as a Saviour for man,
  To redeem our souls, and destroy sin's plan.
For when we admit, that we have sinned,
  When we invite, our Saviour in,
He cleans our hearts, restores our souls,
  He frees our lives, from sin's control.
Now those in Christ, can freely choose,
  To walk by faith, and never lose,
The gift of life, Christ gives to men,
  The gift that gives, new life again.

Oh, tarry not, do not delay,
    Confess you've sinned to God today,
Receive His mercy, and His love,
    Receive His grace, from heaven above.
For Christ is there, at The Father's right hand,
    Ready to hear, to deliver, defend,
All of those who put, there trust in Him,
    To free their lives, from every sin.
He will give His Spirit, to those who ask,
    Equip you for, your special task.
Child, Christ has only good for you,
    His plans bring hope, and life that's true.
You'll walk in freedom, and in love,
    You'll walk in love, with God above.

Now when you walk, with God that way,
    You'll show by love, God's love today.
You'll show His love, to all you meet,
    With grace and kindness, you will greet,
The ones that come, along the way,
    The way that God, has planned today.
So show by words and deeds to all,
    The Christ of God, has come to call;
He has come to say, come one and all,
    Come unto Me, you'll never fall.
For Christ has come, to save the lost,
    He gave His life, upon that cross,
So you could choose, to live for Him,
    Choose to leave, a life of sin.
Choose to walk, with Christ as Lord,
    Choose to live, in one accord,
With God as Father, by His love,
    With Christ as Brother, up above!

PREPARE US LORD - Inspired by Exodus 14

Prepare us Lord, as You part the waves,
    Like You did before, so Israel was saved.
You led them forth, out of Egypt's land,
    You led them out, by Your strong right hand.
The miracles You did, were to show them how,
    You display Your strength, when the time is now!
Then they came to the sea, and were sore afraid,
    For it seemed they were blocked, from their escape.
The sea was before them, and Pharaoh behind,
    It seemed they were trapped, in their doubting minds.
But when they cried out, to You Lord God,
    You spoke to Moses: Lift up your rod:
Stretch out your hand, toward the sea,
    Divide the waves, dry land there will be.
A path that's clear, to walk straight through,
    A path I've made, for Israel and you.

So Moses did, as The Lord had said,
    Israel walked through, with all they had.
They left behind, what Egypt gave,
    And chose the path, by which God saved!
Pharaoh pursued, with chariots and men,
    But God closed the sea, right on top of them.
The Children of Israel, then praised The Lord,
    For then their freedom, was doubly assured.
No more would Egypt, hold fears for them,
    For God had delivered, He had done it again!
So when the sea, is before you rejoice,
    Call unto your Lord, with faith and voice.
He'll deliver you from, what seems like a trap,
    He'll make a way, so you'll have no lack.
He'll lead you on by His presence, and power,
    When you look with faith, in your present hour.

What enslaved you before, will lose it's power,
    For when The Lord delivers, you will not cower.
He gives new faith, to the trusting and meek,
    Gives hope and life, when His hand we seek.
For He is our God, and our Father by faith,
    In the work of Christ, by Whom we are saved.
What an awesome God, is this God of ours,
    Who delivers His children, by His mighty power.

He holds us in, the palm of His hand,
    He leads by His Spirit, to traverse the land.
So trust in The Lord, wherever you go,
    Then you'll see His deliverance, from every foe.
The Lord made the seas, He can dry them at will,
    The oceans and forests, and everything still,
Stands by The Word, of His Awesomeness,
    So we can stand, by His Righteousness!

Put your trust and faith, in this Holy God,
    Then you'll never fear, while this earth you trod.
He'll give you the faith, that you need to stand,
    By His Holy Spirit, and The Blood of The Lamb!
For only by grace, are our sins forgiven,
    Only by faith, in The Lamb God has given.
The Lamb of God, is Jesus The Christ,
    Who gave His life, as The Pure Sacrifice.
The Blood that Christ shed, on Calvary,
    Is the Blood that cleanses, and makes us free.

So trust in The One, who gave us His Son,
    To forgive our sins, to make us one;
One in hope, in faith, in love,
    He sealed us for, His courts above.
All we do, is confess our sins,
    Repent and turn, our lives to Him.
This is His key, this is His door,
    That gives us life, forevermore!

DRAW NEAR AND HEAR
Inspired by Ephesians 1:4-7,Colossians 1:13,14 & 20,
1st Peter 1:7, 1st John 1:7, & Revelation 1:5

Help me Lord to hear You clear,
    To hear Your voice, and then draw near;
Near enough to see Your face,
    Near to feel Your saving grace.
For when Your grace and love are seen,
    We can repent from all we have been.
We come now Lord with open hearts,
    We come to stay and ne'er depart.
Oh, Precious Lord to You we come,
    For You alone are The Only One,
Who cleans, redeems, restores, makes whole,
    Who satisfies the weary soul.
Oh take us Lord, into Your arms,
    Set us free from all alarms,
That trouble and confound our minds,
    That work to steal, destroy and bind.

Your Blood alone, is what makes us free,
    Your Blood has purchased, me for Thee!
So let me live my life for You,
    Always trusting, always true.
For You've destroyed, the sin that bound,
    My soul, Your saving grace has found.
You found me in my sin and loss,
    Redeemed me by Your death, Your cross.
You alone, are The Perfect Lamb,
    Only You, can redeem the damned.
We were damned, by our trespass and sins,
    Until Your Blood, redeemed all men.
Oh what can we say to this sacrifice?
    We give you our lives, You paid our price!

GOD'S STRENGTH - Inspired by Isaiah 40:29-31

Lord I need Your strength today,
    To walk the paths prepared this day,
Paths of love and perfect peace,
    Paths that give my soul release.
Give me the peace the world can't give,
    Give me Your peace so I can live:
The way of truth and hope and love,
    The way to bless my God above!
For that's the way I want to live,
    To live Your way Oh God to give!
Oh Lord, You gave Your life to me,
    You gave Your life to set me free.
You've set me free from sin and vice,
    You bought me with Your sacrifice!
Now Lord I'm Yours, so take control,
    You gave me life, restored my soul.

Let me Oh Lord, show forth Your love,
    The love You give, from heaven above!
Your mercies are new, to me each day,
    They give me life, they show the way,
To give your mercy, love and peace,
    To all to bring their souls release.
For only when we cast our cares,
    And lay our hearts and spirits bare,
Before You Lord for mercy true,
    Can we be born again, brand new;
Born of Your Spirit,, born from above,
    Born to live Your life of love.
Born to know Your saving grace,
    Born to look upon Your face,
There to behold Your wondrous love,
    Transformed by grace for heaven above!

IT IS TIME - **Inspired by 2nd Corinthians 6:2**

Why do you tarry, why do you wait,
    The hour is now, the hour is late.
The time has come, for the saints to arise,
    To rise to God's call, to look to the skies!

Look to The Lord for mercy and grace,
    Look to The Lord, behold His face!
See in His eyes, His love for you,
    See in His eyes, His hope for you!

For in His love, there is hope as well,
    That brings to faith, so we can tell,
To all alike, whether great or small,
    That Christ redeems to all who call!

WHY I WRITE

The Spirit came, like a dove with a scroll,
    He spoke to my heart, my spirit, my soul.
I wrote as one, by The Spirit led,
    He gave me words, to awaken the dead.
For we were all dead, in our trespass and sin,
    Until Holy Spirit, called us to Him,
For when we receive, the life Christ gives,
    Our souls are redeemed, and we truly live.
Oh hear the Spirit, call today,
    Come to The Lord, do not delay,
Come unto Christ, and He will bless,
    Your lives, your souls, with righteousness.

GOD'S MERCY - Inspired by Ephesians 2:5-10

When we were dead, in our trespass and sin,
    God sent us His Son, to redeem and to cleanse.
But if we choose to walk, in our foolish ways,
    Thinking our works, will gain us the way,
To enter God's courts, by our deeds alone,
    We have failed to realize, only Christ's blood atones!
His Blood is the only, pure sacrifice,
    Only The Blood, of Christ paid the price.
It is only by faith, in the redemption of Christ,
    That we enter God's courts, for our works won't suffice!

No work of ours, would be good enough,
    Our works amount only, to stubble and stuff!
Stubble will burn, when God's fire arrives,
    To judge all the earth, to purify.
No work of ours, could ever make a way,
    No work that we do, could ever pay,
The price that God, required of men,
    The price Christ paid, to redeem us from sin.
Only The Lord, can purify,
    Only The Lord, can justify!

Don't think you will come, when you've cleaned yourself up,
    You haven't the power, or the will to give up,
The things that cause, your hearts to sin,
    The things that bind, without and within.
Ask for His Spirit, to make you brand new
    He'll give you His power, to will and to do.
Oh, come now to Christ, The Redeemer of all,
    He paid sin's price, so give Him your all.
You will never regret, this choice you make,
    The Saviour is waiting, for you at His gate!

TO SERVE GOD
Inspired by Psalm 15, Micah 6:8 & Matthew 16:24-28

What does it take, for a man to serve God?
    What does it mean, to live for God?
Who may worship, on Your holy hill?
    Who may live, and abide with You still?
This is the one, who follows The Lord,
    Who places their mind, in one accord,
With The Lord of all, who gives this call,
    Abandon ambition for self, give your all!
Walk and live, in a blameless way,
    Speak the truth, from your heart each day.
Do not slander, or defame with your tongue,
    Extend God's grace, to all not some.
Do not lend, for worthless gain,
    Give from your heart, your Lord to proclaim.
Do not ever, take a bribe,
    Stand for God, what' ere betide.

Follow Me, and take up your cross,
    Forsake the world, it's sin and it's loss,
For if you keep, your life you will die,
    But if you give Me your life, you'll fly!
I'll take you places, you've never known,
    I will take you right up, to My Father's throne.
I am coming again, with My saints to reign
    I am coming to claim, those who call on My Name!
The choice is yours, before you now,
    Do you want God's will, then make your vow.
Seek The Lord, while He may be found,
    Seek His will, and His grace to abound.
For all that God, has planned for you,
    To make His call, assured in you
Is to take the step, He is calling you,
    Walk on the water, He will carry you!

PRESENT YOURSELF
Inspired by Romans 12:1 & 2 and Hebrews 13:8

Why do you fear, the call of God?
    Why do you hide, from The Shepherd's Rod?
        His voice He used, to calm the seas,
           His rod protects, and comforts thee.
Climb out of the boat, while there is still time,
    Climb out to experience, His call divine.
        Choose to do, the impossible task,
           Choose His will, He calls, He asks.
The ways of God, are not grievous or hard,
    So give Him your life, as your offering of nard;
        The pure spikenard, of a life lived for Him,
           A fragrance of worship, set free from sin.
For His Spirit will free you, to worship and praise,
    Will free you to live, for Christ all of your days.
        You will live by the light, of His Holy Word,
           In the faith of The Lord, His Word assured.

For when we walk in the path, He has ordained,
    Our hearts are released, from what sin restrained.
        Sin causes worry, and doubt and fear,
           Sin keeps us from loving, our Saviour so dear.
Oh, come now dear one, come to The Dear Lord,
    Confess and believe, He's a God of His Word.
        He'll hold you, and help you, and cause you to stand
           Forever and ever, with His mighty hand.
He will cleanse your heart, by His precious blood,
    He will give you His life, and all that is good.
        The life He has planned, is perfect for you,
           A life that is holy, and pure and true.
When you walk in His life, His love to show,
    His blessings come down, on you here below.
        His blessings make rich, and they add no sorrow,
           For He is the same, today and tomorrow.

THE CHRIST OF GOD - Inspired by John 1; 1-14

Who is this One, The One they call Christ?
    Who is The One, who paid with His life?
Why did He pay for one such as I?
    Why did He come to the earth to die?

The One they call Christ, is The Son of God,
    Who gave His life, as a ransom to God!
He paid the price, for your sins and mine,
    He paid with His Blood, for reasons sublime.

When our parents sinned, in the garden that day,
    A separation came, from God's holy way.
From that time on, our ways were profaned,
    We were doomed to live life, in sin and in pain.
But our God is so loving, and merciful too,
    He made a way, to redeem me and you;
A way that would cost, a terrible price,
    The death of The Sinless Lamb, The Christ!
For Christ became man, God's only Son,
    By His death on the cross, paid for everyone,
To receive God's pardon, and release from sin,
    To receive God's life, and communion with Him.

What a gift, what a ransom was paid for us all,
    When Christ, The Anointed of God, gave His all.
When He shed His Holy Precious Blood,
    Our lives were redeemed, bought back for God.
The choice is now ours, to live or to die,
    Eternity beckons, what is your reply?
There are only two places, at the end of our life,
    Hell and its horrors, or heaven and true life.
All it takes is surrender, my friend,
    Give your life to Christ, His life has no end.

He will take your life, and transform it to be,
    A life of pure joy and pure love that sees,
The way of God, and all that it holds,
    Is the way of Christ who redeemed our souls.
The choice is yours, free will He gave,
    The choice of heaven, or hell and grave.
The devil came in the garden that day,
    To steal from our parents, God's presence to say,
That we could choose, to disobey God's word,
    The Word by which, our lives are assured.
Now the devil's plan is to destroy and kill,
    But Christ paid our price on that awful hill!

He calls by His Spirit, to all right now,
    Oh give Him your life, with your solemn vow.
He will pick you up, in His loving arms,
    He will free you from all, of the devil's charms.
The charms of evil, are deadly still,
    They will try to rob you, of your free will.
They will try to blind, from the plans of God,
    They will try to deafen, from the voice of God!
But they cannot steal, from you your will,
    For God has given to all, free will.
You have free will, to make a choice,
    The will to speak, with your own voice.

When you declare, Jesus Christ is Lord,
    Your salvation is paid, your place is assured,
In heaven with Christ, by the Blood He shed,
    When He died for you, and rose from the dead.
This life is yours, if you turn to Him now,
    This life of yours, can begin right now!
Receive His love, His sacrifice,
    Receive your forgiveness, He paid the price.
Confess to Him, all of your sins,
    Receive by faith, new life from Him.

OPEN YOUR EYES - Inspired by Ephesians 1:18

Open your eyes, and refuse the lies,
　　The lies the devil, has used to disguise.
Ask The Father, of Lights to show,
　　By His Spirit, The Saviour to know.
You are called to know, and understand,
　　The hope to which God, has called for all man.
God has a glorious, inheritance too,
　　For all who will choose, His will to do.
Immeasurable, unlimited, surpassing greatness,
　　Is the power of The Spirit, that subdues our weakness.
By The Spirit's power, Christ was raised from the dead,
　　Was seated in heaven, by His Father instead.

When Jesus was crucified that day,
　　All of the hordes of hell were arrayed,
As part of the mob, that yelled for Christ's death,
　　Thought they had won, when Jesus gave His last breath.
But now He is over, all heaven and earth,
　　Seated with power, to give men new birth.
The Blood Christ gave, He gave to atone,
　　He poured out His Blood to God alone!
He paid the price to set us free,
　　From all of Satan's tyranny.

Our God is a God, of justice and love,
　　So the price to be paid, came from heaven above.
God in His mercy, sent Jesus, His Son,
　　To be our atonement, The Sinless One!
Only the Blood of Christ was pure,
　　A sacrifice for our lives to procure.
Oh do not delay, make this day the day,
　　When you open your heart to Christ and say:
Oh Lord, I confess my sins to you,
　　Redeem me and save me, make me brand new.

PRAYER OF SALVATION

Dear Lord I receive Your sacrifice,
    The price you paid to redeem my life.
Forgive me for all of the wrong I have done,
    I want to be one, with You, God's Son.
Make me one in Your Spirit and one in Your love,
    One to enter Your courts above;
One to live for You here on earth,
    One to experience Your brand new birth.
Lord Jesus, I give myself to You,
    Purify my life, make me brand new,
So I can live in the love You give,
    So I can give the love You give!
I want to give no matter what age,
    The love You gave so all can be saved.
This is the message I want to share,
    That God is love and God still cares!
So I come Lord God to Your throne of grace,
    I hear Your call to seek Your face,
You are The One who cares for me,
    Thank you Lord Jesus for setting me free!

PRESS ON - Inspired by Philippians 3:14

Press on to reach God's heavenly goal, the prize God has prepared,
Forget the past and all its gains, they can't redeem your soul.
Press in to know Me says The Lord, press in for power restored
Press in to know The Father's heart, press in, to know your Lord.

What seems to be an obstacle now, is removed by faith and prayer
My awesome power will part the waves, if you give Me your care.
Oh, don't be faithless, just believe, My power will be displayed.
One Word from Me is all you need, My Blood your life has paid!

So when the waves of doubt assail, to trouble and confuse,
Walk in The light I give to you, then you will never lose!

THE RANSOM - Inspired by John 3:3-21

What can a man give, to ransom his soul?
    What can he give, to be perfect and whole?
The right things we do, could never come near,
    To redeem our lives, from sin and from fear.
Only the Precious Blood of The Lord,
    Only His Blood can redeem, can afford,
The price He paid by His Holy Love,
    The Love of God from heaven above

The Lord looked down, on the earth He had made,
    And saw all men, in His likeness dismayed.
We had no life, without our Dear Lord,
    Our sin had broken, and severed the cord,
Of life that came, from communion with Him,
    The life He had planned, was cut off by sin.
So God in His mercy, sent Jesus, His Son,
    The Christ, The Anointed, The Holy One.

Christ set aside all, of what heaven contained,
    To become sin for us, who were dirty and stained.
By His death on the cross, and the stripes that were laid,
    Upon His dear body, our price was paid.
Now He alone has the power to save,
    He died and was buried, but rose from the grave.
He ascended to heaven, as the disciples looked on,
    To prepare a place, for the ones He had won.

By His love He now stands at The Father's right hand,
    There to intercede for the souls of all men.
So now when we call on Jesus The Christ,
    To confess our sins, our weakness, our vice,
The Lord our God, forgives our sin,
    And by the Blood of Christ, we enter in.
So do not listen, to the lies of men,
    Receive The Christ, and be born again!

TO THE END OF THE AGE - Inspired by Matthew 28:18-20

To the end of the age, Lord Jesus did say,
  I'll be with you My child, whatever the day,
All authority in heaven, and earth is mine,
  So go make disciples, for now is the time.
Make disciples for me, of women and men,
  Teach them to observe, the words I have given.
Baptize everyone, who believes on Me,
  Who receives by faith, My forgiveness so free.

When all obey, the words I have given,
  They will find release, from all of their sin.
My stripes paid the price, to redeem all men,
  My death accomplished, new life for them.
This life flows from My Spirit within,
  This life will give and give again.
This life of The Spirit like an artesian well,
  Springs up with refreshing to release from hell.

Now to the souls, I came to save,
  From sin and hell, from death and grave.
To all who receive, My saving grace,
  To all I will show, My loving face;
A face of compassion, and tenderness,
  A face of forgiveness, and righteousness.
So preach My Word and make it plain,
  My Blood will cleanse, men's every stain.

If you'll speak My Word, in faith to show,
  My Glory, My Presence to all below,
My Spirit will then, confirm My Word,
  Will heal and save, as hearts are stirred.
The power to turn from their sins, will be given,
  And faith to believe, will come from heaven.
Their lives will be changed, in that moment, that hour,
  When My Spirit confirms, with Holy Power!

HE CAME FOR YOU! - Inspired by John 1:12

Christ came to earth, from heaven above,
 Left all He had, to give us His love.
He took our sins, on Himself that day,
 On the cross of anguish, His blood did pay.

He paid for the sins, of all mankind,
 To release us from, the sins that bind.
So come to The Christ, do not delay,
 Come to The One, whose death has paid.

Christ paid the price, to redeem our loss,
 Paid the price, by His death on the cross!
But death could not hold Him, and on the third day,
 He arose triumphant, the price was paid.

He paid in full, and now He stands,
 To defend all men, at The Father's right hand.
So confess your sins, and rebellion to Him,
 He'll forgive and cleanse, from every sin.

To all who come, with repentant hearts,
 He will give to all, a brand new start.
You'll be born again, never to die,
 Born to live, for Your Father on high.

Death could not hold, our Saviour down.
 And it cannot hold, His children's crown.
For a crown of salvation, is waiting for all,
 Who hear and say yes, when His Spirit calls!

DO WHAT IS GOOD
Inspired by 1st Peter 2:15 and 2nd Timothy 4:2

Do what Christ said, in the words He has given,
   Do what Christ said, to lead men to heaven.
For this earth will perish, and cease to exist,
   So stand for what's right, and always persist,
In doing the good, and living for Him,
   So all can know, and all be forgiven.
The Love of God, in Jesus The Lord,
   Is the love He gave, our lives to restore.
So worship The Lord, in all that you do,
   Live always for Him, in a love that is true.
His love will touch, and heal and restore,
   His love is a love, that gives evermore!
Love is nothing, unless it is given,
   This is the love, of our God up in heaven,
Who gave us His Son, to save men on earth,
   To give us new life, new freedom, new birth.

Do not hold this message, to yourself alone,
   Tell the whole world, Christ came to atone.
Christ came to redeem, to cleanse and restore,
   He came to give grace, to all men evermore.
The life He gives, goes beyond the grave,
   It is life eternal, by which we are saved.
If this is the life, the life you desire,
   Come to The Lord, for His holy fire.
He'll purge and He'll cleanse, burn off all the dross,
   He took all our sins, by His death on the cross.
All He asks now, is that we come to Him,
   To ask for forgiveness, from every sin.
No sin is too great, or ever too small,
   He came to redeem, to cleanse us from all.
The Blood of Jesus, has paid the price,
   He gave His life, as our sacrifice!

<u>YOUR SINS ARE FORGIVEN</u> - Inspired by Mark 2:1-12

Your sins are forgiven, Jesus said that day,
    To a paralyzed man, to answer the faith,
Of the four who brought, their friend to Him,
    To heal and cleanse, and forgive their sin.
The people came, to hear The Lord,
    They came and heard, The Living Word.
His words brought life, and healed the hurts,
    Of all the ones, by sin besmirched.

The law could only, show their sin,
    It couldn't remove, the stain from them.
They might be able, to keep one or two,
    But never complete, what only God could do.
For God alone, can cleanse our sin,
    To make us whole, and alive again.
God sent to us, His Only Son,
    The Redeemer from heaven, The Chosen One!

Christ Jesus showed, how we could live,
    A life of love, to give and forgive.
So let's confess we've sinned, to Him,
    Receive forgiveness, from every sin;
Then be born again, by His Spirit's power,
    Be born again, this very hour.
By the Power of The Spirit, we are transformed,
    From glory to glory, our souls are reborn.

Each day He gives, His mercy anew,
    Each day we find, His grace renewed.
So choose the life, that Christ has given,
    Choose it now, choose His heaven.
Then if you are crippled, in body or soul,
    Like the paralyzed man, He'll make you whole.
He will cleanse your heart, and by His Spirit release,
    Your life, your spirit, to perfect peace!

PATCHES - Inspired by Mark 2:21 & 22

You come to The Lord, to patch the holes,
    Where sin has wrecked your lives, your souls,
But Jesus wants, to heal our whole man,
    Not just here and there, but to begin again!
Now when a garment begins to wear out,
    Holes appear within and without.
Our lives are like a garment, it's true,
    They show wear and tear, in the light of His truth.

When we see our lives, in His perfect light,
    We see the holes, and wear all right.
We think a patch, would do just fine,
    But The Saviour came to replace, not refine.
First we need to see our sin,
    See that we need, His cleansing within.
He wants us to give Him, all of our lives,
    So He can replace them, with His new life.

No more do we look, like a beggar now,
    For He clothes with His Rightness, when we make a vow,
A vow to give our all to Him,
    A vow to always live for Him.
So give Him your garment, of sin and of shame,
    He'll give a new garment, give a brand new name.
No more a sinner, but saved you are,
    A son or a daughter, without sins mar.

Now clothed in the righteousness, of Jesus The Christ,
    We are made brand new, by His sacrifice.
The Blood Christ shed, made the way for all
    To hear His voice, and respond to His call.
Say yes to The Saviour, He's waiting now,
    He will enter in, and hear your vow,
He will make of you, a child that's true,
    From all that hurt, and troubled you!

THE POWER OF GOD
Inspired by Mark 4:35-41 and Mark 5:1-20

As the day ended, Jesus spoke to His men:
"Let's cross to the other side,"
He went to sleep in the back of the boat,
For He was weary and tired.
As He was sleeping a storm arose,
High waves broke into the boat,
The disciples shouted and woke Him up,
For they didn't know how to cope.
Then Jesus awoke and spoke to the wind,
He said to the waves: "Quiet Down!"
The Master arose, The Master spoke,
And none of them did drown!
The wind then stopped, there was great calm,
For He rules the wind and the waves.
He asked His disciples: "Why were you afraid,
Do you still not trust Me to save?"

Immediately they arrived, at The Gerasenes,
When a man rushed up to Christ then,
He was possessed by devils so fierce,
That chains were no match for them.
The man ran and fell at Jesus' feet,
"Son of The Most High God," was the shout,
The demons in the man knew their power was gone,
For The Lord told them to get out!
Jesus cast them out of the man that day,
Into a large herd of pigs,
The pigs then rushed into the lake,
Then died, that herd so big.
The crowd who heard from the herdsmen came,
And were terrified to see,
The man with demons was clothed and whole,
For Jesus had set him free!

The people begged Jesus to leave them alone,
 They wanted no part of Him
But the man who was freed, begged The Lord that day,
 To take him along with them.
Lord Jesus then spoke unto the man,
 "Go tell your family and friends,
Tell of the wonderful things God has done,
 His mercy and love for all men."
So the man started off and told everyone,
 He told them what Jesus had done,
He told them of what he was before,
 Then they saw what he had become;
A man set free by the mercy of God,
 Set free to tell of God's love,
A man commissioned by Jesus, God's Son,
 To lead them to God up above!

So if you are weary or bound today,
 Jesus can set you free,
The Christ has come, He has opened the door
 To life and liberty!
Nothing can bind, the one who Christ saves,
 Nothing can hold you back,
If you will give your life to Him,
 He will put your life on track!
For all He has, He gives to all,
 To all who heed His call,
He gave His life, upon the cross,
 He gave His life for all!

Now just as He arose that day, to heaven above to stand,
He calls us now, come here My child, come let me take your hand.
I'll lead you into pastures green, to waters cool and clear,
I'll feed you with the food that feeds, your life, if you will hear.
Oh hear His voice of love dear one, and give to Him Your all,
He saves and heals, delivers too, He ransoms from the fall!

CHRIST THE HEALER - Inspired by Mark 5:28-34

A woman came up, to Jesus one day,
    For she had suffered long,
She pressed through the crowds, and made her way,
    To The Lord to make her strong.
She had spent all she had, to try and be healed,
    But her condition, only got worse,
So she pressed in by faith, to The Master that day,
    And was released, from her terrible curse!

She said to herself, if only I touch, the hem of His garment I know,
His power will come, His power will heal, and then I will be whole!
Immediately her bleeding stopped, for power went out from Him,

The Lord knowing this, stopped and looked at the crowd,
    And asked: "Who touched my hem?"
The woman though frightened, and trembling inside,
    Came close and fell at His feet,
She told The Lord what she had done,
    And how His power had healed!
The Lord then spoke, My daughter He said,
    Your faith has made you well,
Now go in peace you have been healed,
    His power had made her well!

His love and power are still the same, when we call out to Him,
    He'll save and redeem, He'll heal and make whole,
        From all of the curse of sin.
Sin brought a curse, on the whole human race
    And with it came sickness, as well,
        But God in His mercy, sent Jesus His Son,
            To redeem us from suffering and hell.
So come to The Saviour, and do not delay,
    He waits to hear our call,
        He'll come and He'll cleanse,
He'll heal all our wounds, He'll deliver, when we give Him our all!

RESTORED - Inspired by 2nd Corinthians 5:19

Restored to walk, in the light Christ gives,
    We're restored to live, and forgive.
For when we love, as God loves us,
    We're forgiven as we forgive.
When we forgive, wrongs done to us,
    We exhibit to all, God's grace,
And when we choose to love all, not some,
    They'll see the love, on God's Face.
So sing to The Lord, a brand new song,
    Sing His praises loud and long.
Let His voice be heard, always through you,
    For His love is gracious and strong.
Oh give to The Lord, your highest praise,
    Worship The King of all kings,
Our God alone, is The Ancient of Days,
    Let's join all heaven and sing!

His voice is saying: Come unto Me,
    All who are weary and sad,
I will fill your life, with joy and peace,
    I will wash away, all what is bad.
I will give you a joy, to make your life,
    Complete and safe and whole,
Then you will never fear again,
    For I have cleansed your soul.
Oh Holy Lord, what can we say,
    To give our thanks and praise,.
We give our lives, our thoughts, our plans,
    For You to use always.
Transform us so we'll never strive,
    To gain by our own power,
The great salvation You have won,
    But live in You each hour!

<u>ONE TOUCH</u> - Inspired by Luke 7:22

One touch from The Lord, was all it took,
    For the lame to walk, and the blind to look,
        For the sick to be healed, and the lepers cleansed,
            One touch from our God, who became a man!
A man of sorrows, and grief was He,
    But He looked on us, and saw our need.
        He saw us in, our lost estate,
            He came and saved us, from our fate!
Death and hell, are the fate of all,
    Who love the world, and heed it's call.
        But heaven, and life eternal wait,
            For all who call, on Christ to save.
One call in faith is all it takes, one call to Christ, all sin forsake;
Then life abundant, full and free, is what He gives to you and me.

When we obey, The Spirit's call,
    To come to Christ, to give our all,
        He takes us, as we come to Him,
            He cleans us up, from every sin.
Christ alone, has the power to save,
    He triumphed over, hell and grave!
        He took the keys, that had us bound,
            He smashed hell's gates, into a mound!
No more does Satan, have the rule,
    Christ made of him, a total fool!
        The power of Christ, is there for you,
            He gave His power, to all to choose;
So, choose the life He offers free, choose His life, His liberty.
Don't delay, make this the day, to enter into life today.

Say, Jesus Christ, forgive my sin,
    Remove the lies, and fears within.
        Make me Your temple, pure and clean,
            Make me Your child, reborn, redeemed

THE CANAANITE WOMAN OF FAITH
Inspired by Matthew 15:21-28

A woman came to The Lord one day, a woman in deep distress,
She asked The Lord for her daughter,
For her daughter was demon-possessed.
However, she was a Gentile, a Canaanite by birth,
Jesus replied to her begging, by saying His family comes first.
Bread for the children must not go to the dogs,
The children must be fed first.
This mother was not put off by His word,
Though her heart was ready to burst!

She knew in her spirit, one word from Christ,
Would set her daughter free,
Now with this faith she replied to Christ,
Even dogs get crumbs that fall free.
Then Jesus answered and said to her,
Oh woman, great is your faith,
Your prayer has been answered, your daughter is healed,
No more will a demon cause waste!

Sometimes our faith seems oh, so small, our problems look so big,
But still one word from God will save, from lies the devil rigs.
Lies will try to truss us up, and bind us with their chains,
But Christ has paid for our release, He washed us clean from stains.

The stains of sin had made us blind, they kept from us pure sight,
But Jesus came in mighty power, He brought us into light!
So when your path seems oh, so dark, come to your Saviour dear,
He is your Lord, Redeemer too, He will fill your heart with cheer.

He'll speak a word, a word of life, He'll bring His Presence near.
Then in that place you'll find release, from all that gave you fear.
No more will the devil trip you up, for now God's Spirit seals,
The ones who put their trust in God, the ones The Lord has healed!

155

WHO AM I? - Inspired by 2nd Samuel 7:28-29

Who am I that You should love me?
Who am I that You should care?
Who am I that You would save me,
From death and hell Your love to share?

I have saved you for a purpose,
I have saved you by My grace,
I have saved you in this season,
To show My love, to see My face.

Here I am then Oh, my Lord,
Touch and cleanse me by Your Word.
Let Your Spirit enter in,
Make me whole, alive again.

That is what I want to hear,
To hear you say come in, draw near,
For I Am waiting at the door,
To give you life forevermore.

Then enter in Oh, Saviour Friend,
Enter in My life to mend.
You alone are God and Lord,
Hold me close with Your love cord.

I'll hold you close right to My heart,
I'll make for you a brand new start,
My mercies new to you each day,
To show to you the perfect way;

A way of joy and hope restored,
A way of love and peace outpoured.
Your cup can never hold it all,
It's meant to overflow to all!

THE WAYS THAT SEEM RIGHT
Inspired by Proverbs 14:12

There are ways that seems right to men,
    But these are not My ways, My friend,
The way to life, forevermore,
    Is to hear Me knock, and open the door.
Your heart is the key, do you want it pure?
    Do you want My call, and election sure?
Then come to Me, submit your call,
    Hear and answer, when I call.

Why do you linger, and why do you wait?
    The Saviour is waiting, right at the gate.
He is ready to come, ready to reside,
    Ready to make, His home inside;
He'll come into your heart, to direct at will,
    So you can rest at peace, and be still.
So, be still my soul, The Lord is here,
    Be still, my soul, The Lord will cheer.

He will give to you, new hope and faith,
    To triumph over, the doubts that rage.
The doubts and fears, that assault your mind,
    He'll take and replace, with love that's kind.
For He is The Lord, of all He has made,
    He will give you a faith, that never fades.
For when Holy Spirit, comes within,
    He sets you free from fear and sin.

He will bring the light to show the way,
    The way to walk His path today.
So let tomorrow, take care of itself,
    Live today, in The Spirit's wealth.
You'll never suffer want or lack,
    For on His path, you'll stay on track!

HOW WIDE, HOW HIGH, HOW DEEP, HOW LONG?
Inspired by Ephesians: Chapter 3

How wide, how high, how deep, how long,
    Is Your love Oh God to us?
What wisdom and might, and power displayed,
    Is Your glory revealed to us!

When I think of You, and all You have done,
    Who are we, that You think of us?
We did not deserve, the mercy You have shown,
    The compassion, you've showered on us!

In Your Love and grace, You gave us Your Son,
    To redeem our souls, from sin,
Then You sent Your Spirit, to give us faith,
    To come and abide, within.

Oh, Wonderful Lord, Oh Awesome God,
    What can we say to this?
What can we offer, what can we give?
    In response, to this wondrous bliss?

So, we bow our knees, and our hearts in praise,
    We bow to You Lord of all,
We worship You Lord, and You alone,
    You saved us to stand straight and tall!

So rule in us, Oh wonderful Lord,
    Rule in us we pray,
Cause us to see and hear and know,
    Your will to do and to obey.

Help us to love, as You have loved us,
    So that all nations, can know,
Your love and Your grace, Oh Father above,
    In Christ, has been fully shown!

THE RIGHT TIME - Inspired by 2nd Corinthians 6:2

At just the right time, You saved us Oh Lord,
    On the day of salvation, You came,
Your timing was perfect, for You knew the way,
    To redeem, by Your holy Name

So make us pliable, in Your hands Oh Lord,
    Remove our hard hearts, we pray,
Make us tender, to hear Your voice,
    Remould our hearts like clay.

Oh place Your Spirit, within our hearts,
    To make Your will our choice.
Give Your direction, place us apart,
    Apart from all that destroys.

For what You give, has life and worth,
    What You give, brings peace,
What you give, brings the Spirit's rebirth!
    A life of sweet release.

You gave to us Your Only Son, to make us one with You,
He bought us back to live a life, of love and faith that's true.

We never could remove the sin, that damned our souls to hell,
The Precious Blood of Jesus Christ, has made our spirits well.

Only The Blood creates and cleans, from what our sin has caused,
Only The Blood of Jesus Christ, restores what once was lost.

Lead us along, with all you have cleansed, in Your victory parade,
Until with all the saints we'll raise, Your Name in Highest Praise!

This earth is not our permanent home, we look to heaven for then,
We'll join with all that You've atoned, To sing the Great Amen!

THE THOUGHTS OF GOD: Inspired by Isaiah 55:8 & 9

Your thoughts Oh God, are higher far,
    Higher than the farthest star.
So who are we, that You should care,
    To keep account of every hair?
You who know our deepest thoughts,
    Yet gave Your life. our souls You bought!

I cannot comprehend such love,
    How You could send from up above,
Your Son, Your Precious Holy Son,
    To save our souls, to make us one:
One with You, to fill our days,
    Filled with joy, to sing Your praise!

So Lord, I come again this day,
    To offer up my life and say,
Make of me a child that's true,
    To follow You in what I do.
For only You can purify,
    Only You can justify.
Only You can save my soul,
    Only You can make me whole.

Use me then Oh Lord I pray,
    To show to all, Your living way.
For in Your way, is life and peace,
    In Your way, our soul's release!
Clear our minds by what You say,
    Cleanse us from all doubt today,
Cause us to trust implicitly,
    So from You Lord, we'll never flee.
You alone, are The One who saves,
    You ransomed us, from hell and grave.
Lord make of us, Your temple true,
    Wholly devoted unto You.

GOD'S TEMPLE - Inspired by 2nd Corinthians 6:16

I will make of you a temple true,
    I'll make your heart and spirit new
For those who give their lives to Me,
    Will live with Me eternally.

So do not fret, and do not fear,
    The Saviour of the world, is here.
He came to save, all those who call,
    For Him to save, and ransom all.
From death and hell, from sin and grave,
    The Saviour came, His life He gave.
He took upon Himself, our sin,
    He died to give us, peace within.

So say good-bye, to sin and fear,
    Disgrace and shame, can't enter here.
For if you've made, The Saviour, Lord,
    To live for Him, in one accord,
He'll cleanse and clothe you, by His grace,
    He'll show to you, His loving face.
There you'll behold, a love so pure,
    His love that makes, your calling sure!

So run to Him, call out in faith,
    Jesus save me, keep me safe.
Wash me, cleanse me, make me whole,
    Redeem my life, my very soul.
For I indeed, am sick of sin,
    Forgive and cleanse me, deep within.
Give to me, Your brand new start,
    Holy Spirit, fill my heart,
With all that God desires for me,
    So I can live for God, and be free;
Free to stand by faith alone,
    Free to worship, Christ alone!

WHAT IS IN YOUR HAND?
Inspired by The Song of Deborah in Judges Chapter 5

What do you have in your hand My child?
    What do you have in your hand?
Use what you have in your hand My child,
    Use what you have in your hand.

What you have is the sword of the Lord, My child,
    What you have is the sword of The Lord,
The sword is the Living Word of God,
    The sword is The Word you have!

So fill yourself with The Word, My child,
    Fill yourself with My Word,
My word will sharpen your sword, My child,
    My Word will sharpen your sword.

Then use My Word, like a sword to strike, use My Word as a sword,
To cut the works of the devil away, to cut off his works each day!

Then strip off the things, that hold you back, strip them clear away,
So that My Word, will have free course, to keep all lies away.

Lies will hinder and confuse, distract and lead astray,
But when you use My word to cut, the lies are stripped away!

Then only truth will stand out clear, for Truth is Christ The Way,
So let My Word be the light for you, the light that leads your way.

My Word alone by The Spirit given, will save your life today,
My Word alone will lead to heaven, all those who watch and pray!

<u>GO OUT</u> - Inspired by Luke Chapter 5

Go out into the deep My child, go out and do not sleep,
The needs you have, the needs you see, by faith I then will meet.
Let down your nets at My command, let down into the deep,
For then I'll cause your faith to stand, on all the Words I speak!

Provide a place where I can preach, provide a place for Me,
A place where men can see My face, a place to live for Me.
Open your hearts and home to all, open to those I bring,
Open to speak My holy call, to make the rafters ring!

Right now this is the place for you, the place to bloom and shine,
Your home a place of love and peace, a home that I call Mine.
Wherever you go and whatever you do, know that you are Mine,
Mine to have and Mine to hold,. to let My glory shine.

Always look to Me for grace, always look to Me,
Your fears by faith will be erased, for I supply your needs.
You shall know My plan My child, you shall know My plan,
When all you give is unto Me, I'll strengthen you to stand.

So stand in faith and hope and love, stand for what is true,
Be quick to offer hope to all, to all I bring to you.
So fear not what your future holds, My hand is holding you,
Fear not, Fear not, I will protect, My grace will see you through!

Oh Lord, confirm Your Word to me, confirm Your Holy Word,
Confirm Your Word until I see, Your truth revealed to me.
For when Your revelation comes, Your path is clear to see,
So open up my heart to know, the way prepared for me.

Oh, write upon our hearts we pray, Your covenant, Your holy way.
Put Your laws into our minds, write them upon our hearts to bind,
Our will and spirit unto You, so we can always live what's true.
Then men can see and ever know, the love and mercy You bestow.

GIVE HONOUR
Inspired by 1st Samuel 30- 2nd Samuel 5

Give honour to whom, the honour is due,
    For this, is The Word of The Lord for you;
Then as you honour, the one in charge,
    To submit in matters, great or large,
I'll give to you, the authority,
    That comes by your, submission free!
For what you do, to the children of men,
    By humbly submitting, and obeying them,
I use as a tool, to show to all,
    The grace I give, to all who call.

The key to greatness, is servant hood,
    To lead men to, The One that is good!
Christ Himself, declared this truth!
    For that is what, He showed to you!
So ask of The Lord, what He wants done,
    Then do by the power, He gives each one,
Who ask for help, in their time of need,
    And He will provide, with special seed.
This seed is faith, that looks to Him,
To redeem and cleanse, from every sin.

Sin destroys, and leads to hell,
    But Jesus came, our faith to swell.
Now by His Spirit, we overcome,
    And use our voice, to bid men come,
To come to The One, who gave His all,
    To ransom, save, whether great or small.
For God imparts, to the hearts of men,
    To reveal to them, His sacred plan,
Now all who call, upon His name,
    Receive as Saviour, The Lord who came!

So receive this life, Christ offers now,
　　Receive His grace, His love and power.
No more a captive, to every sin,
　　For now Christ gives, His Spirit within.
He'll enable you, to hear His Word,
　　To trust in Him, your God and Lord.
Oh, hear The Word of The Lord, today,
　　He will save, do not delay!
Call out to Him, receive His grace,
　　Then you will look, and see His face.

You'll see it in the ones, He sends,
　　To heal your hearts, and spirits mend.
Align yourself with The Lord, this day,
　　For He is The Life, The Truth, The Way;
He'll make of you, a vessel pure,
　　Your calling and election sure.

When King David asked of Me,
　　I gave to him, My strategies,
And when he used, My strategies,
　　He defeated all, his enemies.
He realized the power I gave,
　　And thanked and worshipped, sang and praised!
He praised My Name, and what I'd done,
　　He gave the glory, to The One,
The only One, with power to save,
　　The One who conquered, death and grave.

So take a lesson from My Word,
　　And then your lives, will be assured.
You'll walk in the light, I have given you,
　　And by My Spirit, you'll choose what's true.
For when you call on, Christ as Lord,
　　Repent and all, your sin abhor,
His blood will cleanse, from every stain,
　　Forever His, you will remain!

CHRIST - THE GREAT HIGH PRIEST
Inspired by Hebrews 7:15 - Hebrews Chapter 10

Christ Jesus, You're our great High Priest,
    By death, You paid for our release,
Your blood poured out, became the price,
    To redeem our souls, from sin and vice.
You became High Priest, by Your sacrifice,
    The will of God, to pay sins price.
By God's own oath, You're the only Priest,
    Who can set our souls, and spirits free.

Now You sit, at The Father's right hand,
    The place of honour, from there to command.
For all authority, God's given to You,
    You paid the price, our sins to remove.
Now You plead, for the souls of men,
    As our Great Intercessor, again and again.

Oh what can we say, to this wondrous grace,
    The grace You give, to behold Your face?
For when we see, Your great pure love,
    We are shown the love, of God above!
Christ, You've revealed, by all you have done,
    The love of God, to all who come;
Who come by faith, of Your Spirit given,
    To lead them to, Your courts in heaven.

So help us show, by deeds of love,
    The love that comes, from God above.
So all may know, and all may see,
    That You Lord Christ, redeem, set free,
All who confess they've sinned, to You,
    Then ask, receive, a life brand new!

CHOSEN BY THE LORD
Inspired by Malachi 2:5-7

I chose you as My priests to stand,
    To stand for Me throughout the land;
To stand for righteousness and truth,
    To stand and preach and live what's true!
For men need truth, to know The Way,
    The Way that leads to God today.
I AM The Way, The Truth, The Life,
    The only way to eternal life.
So stand in awe and reverence Me,
    Pass on the truth, you've learned from Me.
Do not lie or steal or cheat,
    Walk with Me, I'll give good meat;
My Word gives meat, to strengthen men,
    That alters lives, that frees from sin.
Guard the knowledge, I give to you,
    Then keep these truths, pure and true.

When you speak, the words I give,
    Men's hearts will turn to Me, and live.
So give instruction, from My Word,
    So that My voice, is clearly heard.
For when My Word, and Truth are given,
    Men's hearts are stirred, for life and heaven.
The lives we live, on earth prepare,
    Our lives for what, God offers there.
There in heaven, where He abides,
    There to live, right by His side.
So fix your eyes on My goal for you,
    Do not waiver, speak what's true.
Speak My Word, in faith and love,
    Lead men to My courts above;
For My purpose and plan is to save all men,
    To bring them home, when I come again.

FILL YOUR MIND
Inspired by Psalm 119:11, 43, 50, 81, 105, 130, 140, & 160,

Fill your mind on what is true,
    My Words, for they are life to you,
To you and all you speak them to,
    I'll give them power to will and do;
To do the will of God above,
    To walk My walk, in faith and love.

This is why I came and died,
    Then rose again to break the lies!
The lies that kept the world in sin,
    Were lies the devil used to win,
But when I broke the chains of hell,
    The gates of death, I broke as well.

Now all who come to Me for life,
    Receive My power over sin and strife.
When they confess to Me they've sinned,
    And receive the life I give to them,
Their hearts are filled with hope and cheer.
    They're no more captive to their fears.

This godly hope from God above.
    Now fills their lives with faith and love.
For He who calls is Faithful True,
    And what He says, He'll surely do.
So, speak My Word, bring forth the truth,
    Then men can know what's really true!

<u>WHAT YOU SOW!</u> - Inspired by 2nd Samuel 12 & 13.

What you sow is what you reap,
  So do not slumber, do not sleep,
    Be on your guard, by night or day,
      For then your feet, will never stray.
The paths of sin, lead to death and hell,
  But the paths of God, will make you well.
    So choose this day, God's holy path,
      Flee from sin, and all it's wrath.
Choose the path, that leads to peace,
  For God will watch, and always keep,
    His children, in His precious arms,
      To shield and save, from deadly harm.
And though sometimes, the path seems dark,
  He'll take you through, you'll never park;
    You'll walk right through, held by God's hand,
      He'll guide you to, His Promised Land.
This land, God has prepared for you,
  Requires faith, and grace to do,
    The plans of peace, and joy and love,
      To bring His children, home above.
So do not fear, when the way seems hard,
  Trust in The Lord, His hand will guard,
    He'll guard and keep you, in each place,
      Will bring you to, His holy place.
Then in this place, you'll know His hand,
  Has kept and held you, firm to stand.
    So stand therefore, forget the past,
      Face the future, in hope at last,,
Knowing your God, will see you through,
  Knowing His plan, is best for you.
    In your weakness, He'll be your strength,
      For He gives His joy, with eternity's length,
And since eternity, cannot be measured,
  This joy with strength, will be your treasure!

THE PRICE - Inspired by Isaiah 52 & 53

You died for all, so all could be saved,
You died to ransom, from hell and the grave.
Oh what can we say, to such awesome love,
What gift to give thanks, to our God up above?

By Your awful death, You broke my chains,
By Your Resurrection Life, I live again.
I rise from the dust, where sin had me bound,
I rise and rejoice, for Your mercy I've found.

I walk in freedom, by Your death on the cross,
I walk in Your life, delivered from loss.
Your life Oh Christ, was the offering for sin,
The pure sacrifice, to bring us within,
To Your arms of grace, and Your mercy outpoured,
To receive Your love, Oh Holy Lord.

So help me to see, through Your loving eyes,
The souls of men, for whom You died.
Let my life now show, by word and deed,
That You Lord Christ, are all we need.

For in You Lord, is mercy and grace,
You paid the price, our sins to erase.
Now because of what, You did for all,
We can believe, and hear Your call.

Your call resounds now to all men:
"Come in, believe, and live again.
Leave off the world, and it's hold on you,
I've paid the price, to ransom you.
No more a slave, I broke your chains,
Rise up My child, and live again!"

LOVE ONE ANOTHER
Inspired by 2ⁿᵈ John, 3ʳᵈ John & Luke 9

Love one another, as I have loved you,
    Hear and do, what I've spoken to you,
For love is doing, what God commands,
        Giving from heart, and mind and hands.
        What do we have, that isn't from God?
        Our life and our breath, both come from God.
So hear the Word, of the Lord today,
    Hear and do, His Word and pray,
Pray to Your Father, in heaven for grace,
        The grace that you need, all fear to erase.
For He who gives food, to the birds of the air,
        Provides for His own, who trust in His care.
For He who gave us, His only Son,
        To redeem us from death, our souls has won..
He broke the chains, that held us fast,
    He set us free, from sin and past.

So lift your heads, to God above,
    To see and gaze, on The Son of Love.
See The Christ, at The Father's right Hand,
        See the power, that comes from command.
For He who gave, His life for all,
        Says, Come to Me, come one, come all.
Come to the Water of Life, and drink,
        Come and partake, so your souls won't sink.
Come up to where I AM, by grace,
        Come up and look, upon My face.
See what I see, then do what I do,
        I've given My Spirit, to choose what is true.
If you will listen, to My still small voice,
        And make My will, your perfect choice,
The provision you need, you then shall see.
        The provision to set, My children free.

WHERE DO YOU REST? - Inspired by Matthew 8:20

Foxes have holes, and birds have nests,
    But The Son of Man, had no place to rest.
He had not come, to establish a home.
        He came from heaven, to establish God's throne;
        A place in the hearts, of all human flesh,
        A place where His Spirit, could dwell and find rest.

So now by His Spirit, we are guided each day,
    To live for His kingdom, to watch and to pray;
    Watch the face, of our Precious Lord,
    Then pray according, to His Holy Word.
We must see the world, as God sees them,
    Then reach in compassion, for the souls of men.
    It is not by our words, that men are saved,
    It's by taking their hands, to show them the way.
Let us lead them to, The God who is love,
    Showing God's mercy, and grace from above.
    For only His grace, is sufficient for thee,
    Only His mercy, redeems and sets free.

His Spirit alone, can give faith to men,
    To come to The Lord, to begin again;
    Born of The Spirit, to a brand new life,
    Our souls set free, from sin and from strife.
Now we can live, in love and in peace,
    To receive His grace, our souls release.
    So strive not for things, they will all pass away,
    Reach out for men's souls, and show them The Way.
Live for God, in all that you do,
    Think God's thoughts, then do what is true.
    Then you will be, that holy place,
    Where God can live, by love and grace;

A home which He can call His own,
    A Holy Place, a Holy Throne!

HOLY SPIRIT, LEAD ME

Holy Spirit lead me, in the way I should go,
   Order my steps, so your path I will know.
My choices were made, by feelings sometimes,
   And these choices led, in paths less sublime.

So help me to hear, in my spirit, Your voice,
   To make Father's will, my absolute choice;
For then I will hear, and in hearing will do,
   The plans You have purposed, the plans You foreknew.

Before the beginning of earth, You had planned,
   That we would be holy, be chosen to stand,
As the bearers of truth, that Christ is The Way,
   The way to the heart, of The Father always.

You adopted us in, You made us Your own,
   Your blood You poured out, our sins to atone.
So now our hearts, and our voices we raise,
   To sing of Your glory, to speak forth Your praise.

For all of the wonderful kindness, You've shown,
   For giving us life, for making Your throne,
In our hearts to abide, we ask You to rule,
   Our will, our emotions, so we won't be fools.

Make us Your disciples, by word and by deed,
   Fill us Dear Lord, with Your incorruptible seed.
Cause The Seed of Your Word, to sprout and to grow,
   Then rise up in fullness, so all men can know,
The truth, that You, redeem from all strife,
   That You alone, are The Giver of Life!
You alone give the peace, that ever abides,
   In You alone, can our spirits reside.

IN YOUR PRESENCE

In Your presence Oh Lord, is mercy and peace,
    Joy unending, and love which won't cease.
So I lift up my voice, to You Lord this day,
    I thank You and praise You, for making The Way.

Now I can come boldly, before Father's throne,
    Now I can let all, my prayers be made known.
I thank You that when, I come in Your Name,
    That You Lord Jesus, have removed all the blame.

I ask You now Holy Father, Dear God,
    Give me Your power, so all men may laud,
Jesus, The Lord, as their Saviour and Friend,
    Jesus as Healer, and Redeemer who mends.

You mend all our hearts, You restore all our minds,
    You pour out Your love, and Your mercy, so kind.
Then when they see, the Light of Your Love
    They can choose to believe, in You God above.

Lord when my life ends, and I stand before You,
    Lord God, may my life, be an offering to You,
Of a life committed, to bring to all men,
    The message of Christ, as Redeemer and Friend.

Without You Lord God, my life has no meaning,
    Without You, life's senseless, no hope or redeeming;
But in You, is all I have ever dreamed of,
    In You is perfection, Salvation and Love!

LIVING STONES
Inspired by\ 1ˢᵗ Peter 2:4-10 and Malachi 3:17

Present yourselves to Me, as living stones,
    Ready to be set, in place to be honed,
Cemented by love, to each sister and brother,
    United in love, like a father and mother.
Watch out for My children, watch and then pray,
    Then speak out the words, that I want you to say.
Tear down each word, and work that destroys,
    So what I want done, can be strengthened, alloyed.
An alloy has all, the strength that it needs,
    To accomplish much more, to meet the need.
So let Me join you, to gather, to form,
    My children, My bride, the world to transform.

Then when the world sees, My church walking as one,
    Redeemed and in love, displaying My Son,
They will know by the love, that is shown unto them,
    That Christ Jesus is, their Redeemer from sin.
This Saviour redeems, from all that destroys,
    He makes of each life, precious treasures, not toys.
For toys will amuse, for but a short time,
    But treasures are valued, by My power sublime.

Jewels are not formed, without pressure and heat,
    They are not as common, as dust on the street
They are formed away, from every man's sight,
    They are formed by My hand, to bring into light.
The beauty, the grace, that My hand has wrought,
    The lives of My children, those My Son has bought.
These children of Mine, are My precious jewels,
    The ones who allowed, My fire, My fuel,
To burn off the trash, and the rubble of sin,
    That held them to harmful, desires within..
These are the jewels, I will place in My crown,
    The souls who have lifted My Name in renown!

LISTEN CLEARLY - Inspired by Isaiah 59 & 60

Listen clearly, Oh children of God,
　　Listen to the voice, of His Holy Word.
His arm is not shortened, His hand still can heal,
　　He gives of His Spirit, to all who will kneel.

Let us kneel from our hearts, and kneel with our minds,
　　Let us kneel by The Spirit, to The One Who's sublime.
Let us kneel and request, from our Father above,
　　His mercy, forgiveness, compassion and love.

Forgive us Oh Lord, for all we have done,
　　Forgive us and cleanse, by The Blood of Your Son,
Only You have the power, to cleanse us from sin,
　　To banish the evil, that lurks deep within.

The sins of our spirits, are greater by far,
　　Then the deeds that are done, by the light of the stars.
But You see all, Oh Righteous God,
　　You see all the paths, that our feet have trod.

Mercy and trouble, and violence proclaim,
　　That without You, we're lost in evil and shame!
Deliverance from sin, is far from us,
　　If we choose the darkness, the sin and the lust.

So Lord we ask You, to show us our sin,
　　Then wash us clean, from the evil within.
You are The Redeemer, who has come from above,
　　To make us brand new, alive with Your love.

You saw that our sins, had blinded our eyes,
　　That our lives and our future, were compromised;
By evil and sin, by death and the grave,
　　For that is the future, for all the unsaved.

Then in Your great mercy, You ransomed our souls,
    Your death on the cross, paid our price to be whole.
You broke all the chains, that had us bound,
    You gave us Your life, Your grace did abound.

You wrote Your words, on our hearts and our minds,
    A covenant by The Spirit, of God to define;
The way of salvation, and the faith to receive,
    The gift of Your grace, to all who believe.

When we turn from our sins, Lord God to embrace,
    Your grace and Your love, our sins You erase.
Your righteousness, peace and joy now are ours,
    Who receive and welcome You, God as ours.

Now we can worship, now we can praise,
    Now we can live for You, all of our days.
Then when death, becomes the door,
    We can enter Your life, forevermore!

There we'll behold, Your loving face,
    There we will worship, by Your great grace.
For we could not, have turned from our sin,
    Unless Your love, came to us within.

Enable our hearts, and our minds now to kneel,
    Before You Oh God, our hearts to seal;
Seal us Holy Spirit, so ever we'll praise,
    The Lord, our Redeemer, The Ancient of Days!

TO THE ENDS OF THE EARTH
Inspired by 1st. Thessalonians

To the ends of the earth, Your Word to proclaim,
To the ends of the earth, Your Name to acclaim.
For it is only by faith, in Your Precious Name,
The Name above all, that we're rescued and saved.

Jesus, The Christ, The Anointed of God,
You came to redeem, to restore us to God!
For we were not able, to save ourselves,
From sin and perversion, we were headed for hell..

All our good works, were but filthy rags,
They couldn't redeem us, they caused us to lag,
Behind all that God, had destined for all,
To redeem us from sin, that caused us to fall.

So God sent His Son, as our Redeemer to pay,
The price for our sins, on the cross that day.
Christ became sin, and by His death He won,
The salvation for all who believe, not some!

The whole human race, He redeemed that day,
His stripes healed our wounds, His blood made the way,
For all to come boldly, to receive His grace,
So all could behold, His love, His face.

Therein is revealed, by The Spirit of God,
A love that transforms, and redeems all to God.
For Christ is The Way, The Truth and The Life,
And it is only by faith, we enter His life.

His life brings purity, love and peace,
His life brings joy, and souls release.
A release to walk the way Christ walked,
A release to speak, the way He talked.

THE WORDS OF CHRIST

The words of Christ, bring hope to men
His words have power, to redeem from sin.
When we believe, the words He speaks,
His Spirit will strengthen, where we are weak.

We'll do His will, whatever the cost,
To share His love, with the broken and lost.
Then we can be, Christ's hands and feet,
To share His love, with all we meet.

For after He rose, from the grave that day,
And before He arose, to heaven to stay,
He gave this command, to all who believe,
Go and make disciples, of those who receive.

If they'll receive by faith, the work I have done,
To ransom their souls, to redeem everyone,
Teach them to observe, and obey My commands,
Then they can fulfill, all that love demands.

Always love The Lord God, with all of your hearts,
And then love your neighbours, right from the start.
For when we love with the love, He has given to men,
We'll take many with us, when He comes again.

Christ is coming again, to claim as His own,
To present all the saved, to His Father alone,
So let us believe, and trust Him always,
Then He'll take us with Him, to heaven That Day!

What a day of joy, and rejoicing that will be,
When we join with all saints, our Saviour to see,
We will cast our crowns, at His holy feet,
For He is The One, we have longed to meet!

GOD KNOWS WHO ARE HIS! - Inspired by Nahum 1:7

Oh Lord You know, the ones who are yours,
    The ones who trust in Your Name,
For You are The Lord, The God over all,
    Only You are forever the same.
Your goodness and greatness, give witness to all,
    To all who live on the earth,
To all who hear, and answer Your call,
    You give new life and new birth.
So we give of ourselves, asking mercy and grace,
    And forgiveness from You alone,
We ask to behold, Your beautiful face,
    For by You our sins are atoned.
When we behold You, our lives are changed,
    For in Your likeness we see,
All of Your glory, all of Your power,
    The love that can make us like Thee.

We ask that You give us, humility,
    The kind that knows when to bow,
For only You Lord, can redeem and make free,
    So to You we make this vow;
To hear when You speak, and do what You say,
    To follow The Spirit's call,
For only You Lord, can teach us to pray
    Then receive the faith to give all.
Conform us Oh Lord, to Your holy will,
    Your plans and purpose to be,
For then we can hear, Your voice pure and still,
    Saying, child come unto Me.
We give You our lives, for meaning assured,
    Our spirits to change by Your power,
Then we'll walk before You, our salvation procured,
    We'll stand by Your Spirit, not cower.

WHAT DOES THE LORD REQUIRE? - Inspired by Micah 6:8

What does The Lord, require of you,
    Oh child to be faithful and true?
This is the good, that our God wants done,
    To walk like The Christ, pure and new.
Do what is right, act justly to all,
    Always, show mercy and grace,
Call to all men, to receive The Lord,
    To seek His will, and His face.
Call out in meekness, for your life Christ restored,
    Never let pride enter in,
Call out with the love, that to you was outpoured,
    Christ saved you, when you were in sin.
It is only by grace, that we all are saved,
    By the grace and the love, that Christ showed,
He came down from heaven, His life He gave,
    To lift off of us sins load.

So leave off the past, and strive for the new.
    The life, Christ paid for with blood,
Purpose to live, for The Lord and His will,
    He lifted our souls, from the flood.
Live and abide, in The Lord every day,
    Let His Spirit anoint you, afresh,
For when you purpose, to live His way,
    You'll live by The Spirit, not flesh.
The Blood of Christ, will cleanse you afresh,
    He'll wash you, whiter than snow,
For love covers sin, never stands to condemn,
    All those by grace, God's atoned.
Let love be your anchor, your foundation stone,
    For then, by the grace you've received,
You'll stand strong and steady, by faith alone.
    You'll walk in faith, and believe!

PERSISTENT PRAYER - Inspired by Luke 18:1-8

Jesus told this story one day,
    So His disciples would know how to pray.
He told them this story, so they would persist,
    Knowing God always hears, when we pray.

A widow in a city, came before a judge,
    Who did not fear The Lord,
Protect and defend, my righteous cause,
    But her request, he just ignored.
The woman however, would not be put off,
    Till her need was met, she kept on,
Until the judge wanted, her voice to be stilled,
    He ruled, and righted the wrong!

Then Jesus said, learn a lesson today,
    God isn't unjust, but true.
But, pray in faith, knowing God is good,
    His justice, will come for you.
Continue in faith, until His answer is seen,
    For He rules for His own, who believe.
You'll not be put off, for God is loving and true,
    Only trust, and you will receive.

God is your Father, when Jesus is Lord,
    He's The Lord, of all of your life,
He'll hear every prayer, if you open your heart,
    He'll remove, all the worry and strife..
At the end of this story, Jesus asked His men,
    If when He returned, He'd find faith,
The faith that persists, when all round seems dark,
    That cuts off each doubt, like a lathe!

Will He find faith in us, who have answered His call?
    Will He find faith in us, who believe?
The question implies, that a test is for sure,
    To try all who want to receive.
So, don't give up, when you offer your prayer,
    Pray with faith, knowing God always cares,
The God who made heaven, and earth by His Word,
    Will answer the faith, that declares!.

Though heaven and earth, will all pass away,
    The Word of God, will remain,
The Lord can be trusted, He is holy and true,
    His Blood, has cleansed every stain.
So ask not for justice, when you pray your prayer,
    Ask for His mercy and love;
To care for the ones, who are blinded and lost,
    Who know not, The Saviour above!.

Ask for His power, to love and restore,
    To show to all men, The Christ,
For He is the Door, to salvation and life,
    The Lord Jesus Christ, paid our price.
Only in Christ, is salvation assured,
    Only by faith, in God's Word.
So if all around you seems dark and drear,
    Call out, for salvation assured!.

Christ will brighten the path, you walk each day,
    By the light, of His Holy Word,
If you walk in His light, you will never stray.
    Just believe in The Word, you have heard.
So to answer this question, that Jesus put forth,
    Say, yes I'll believe, I will trust,
I will trust by The Spirit, You have given to me,
    For You are Holy and Just!.

HOW DO WE GIVE? - Inspired by Luke 21:1-4

As Jesus sat in the temple one day,
 He watched as the rich came to pay.
They gave only what was required of them,
 The offerings from the hearts of men.
Then a widow came by and gave all she had,
 And even though it was small,
Jesus noticed and spoke, this word to His men,
 This poor widow gave more than all.
They gave but a portion, of all they possessed,
 She gave to answer God's call.
She trusted that God would meet every need,
 Her needs, whether great or small.

So when you bring, your offering to God,
 In your heart, do you give what God lauds?
Do you give because its required of you,
 Or give, because it's the law.
Do you give out of love, to The One who saved you,
 Who ransomed, redeemed, and restored?
Who lived not by bread, to bring us to life,
 But by love, His blood He outpoured!
So just as Christ gave, out of love for all men,
 Give by the love He has given.
Don't give by compulsion, or duty or greed,
 Give like The One, sent from heaven!

Give to the work, that sets up God's throne,
 The throne for God's Holy Rule, .
Give from your heart, to the place God has set,
 To establish your life, to be schooled.
Then learn by His Spirit, to think and to walk
 To live in His perfect way,
Then give with the love, that He's given to us
 For then our hearts will not stray!

HOLY! HOLY! HOLY! - Inspired by Luke 23 and 24

Holy, Holy, Holy Lord! God in heaven we bow before,
    Your holy throne, to worship You,
    With hearts of love to sing to You!
You alone, are The God who reigns,
    You broke the bonds, You loosed my chains.
    You came to earth, out of Your great love,
    You came, You gave, Your Precious Blood.
You didn't stay, wrapped up in that grave,
    You rose again, on that first day,
    You rose and appeared, to those You loved,
    You rose to show, God's power above!
You rose to give, to men the proof,
    That death cannot, hold back The Truth!
    You defeated death, that very day,
    And life from God, became The Way!
Now we can triumph, when we believe,
    When with our hearts and souls, receive,
    The gift of life, in Christ The Lord,
    The gift You gave, by Your blood outpoured!
For only in trusting, Your power to save,
    Are we redeemed, from hell and grave.

So help us live in the faith You've given,
    Holy Spirit of God make us ready for heaven.
    Make us a temple, for The Living Christ,
    For He became, our sacrifice!
Make us a temple, where Christ can dwell,
    A temple that topples, the realms of hell;
    A temple made pure, by Christ's Blood alone
    A temple where God, can rule enthroned!
Now we're purchased, redeemed, set apart to serve,
    To all everywhere, God's Living Word.
    Your Word Oh Lord, has the power to give,
    The life and breath so we may live,
The only life that has reward, The life committed to Christ The Lord!

THE GIFT OF GRACE - Inspired by Romans 4-6

The grace of God has been given, as a gift to bring back all men;
To redeem and make us His children, to restore our souls again.
No more are we slaves to sin, for Jesus has paid the price,
We're free by the love He has given, His life, His sacrifice!

Then what do we do, with the grace God gives,
Do we use it as license, to sin or to live?
The choice is ours, for we're no longer slaves,
Our lives Christ bought back, from death and the grave.

Christ Jesus defeated, the devil and his plan,
When He gave His life, for the saving of man,
Now we can arise, from the dust where we laid,
Rise to God's glory, by the price Jesus paid.

Sin is no longer, our master to bind,
Our souls unto death, and our minds to be blind;
For Christ Jesus came, and paid the full price,
Redeemed us from death, from hell and from vice.

So choose now today, by the grace we've been given,
Choose now to walk, on the pathway to heaven;
Ask for forgiveness, and mercy from God,
Ask in The Name, of The Christ whom we laud.

Our Saviour is waiting, with arms open wide,
To welcome His chosen, beloved, His bride;
To present to The Father, the ones He redeemed
To present us To God, The One we esteem.

What a welcome awaits, as we enter now,
To the family of God, as we make our vow,
To live in the love, and the grace God bestows,
To live for our Lord, held tender, held close!

OPEN MY EYES - Inspired by Luke 24

Open my eyes, so that I may see,
    Open my eyes, as I bow before Thee.
You alone, have the power to reveal,
    The truths You impart, to restore and heal.
You are the healer, of all of our hearts,
    Your life paid the price, so we can take part,
In the life You bestow, to the children of men,
    The life You impart, to be born again.
So take us and make us, alive and brand new,
    As we offer our lives, to be made whole and true.
Make us true to the witness, that You have revealed,
    True to the call, by Your Spirit who seals,
Our souls for redemption, by Your Precious Blood,
    The revelation from God, for our greater good.
Oh Restorer of souls, revive us again,
    So that we may show, Your love to all men.

Help us show by word, and by deed how You save,
    And deliver from death, and hell and the grave.
Cause us to live, in that perfect place,
    The place prepared, to receive Your grace;
For it is by Your grace, and grace alone,
    That we approach, Your holy throne.
Our works cannot, secure and seal,
    Only Your Blood, can save and heal.
Only Your Blood, redeems our souls,
    Only Your Blood, can make us whole
Lord, make us whole, and ready to live,
    In the love and the grace, by the power You give,
Send us Your Spirit, once again we pray,
    Inspire our hearts, to speak forth today,
The Words of life, by The Spirit given,
    The Words of God, that lead to heaven!

<u>BLESSED</u> - Inspired by Jeremiah 16 & 17

Blessed are those, who trust in The Lord,
  Who have made The Lord, their one strong cord,
To tie them to, the plans of God,
  To keep them on, the path Christ trod.
For only then, is peace assured,
  Only then, is life procured,
Then they'll flourish, like well watered trees,
  For Almighty God, supplies their needs.
Like a spring of water, that never runs dry,
  Are the lives of men, who always try,
To live according, to the Word of God,
  Directed solely, by The Spirit of God.

When we listen and abide, loving God's ways,
  Our paths are made clear, for all of our days.
Then when the way seems ever so dark,
  God leads us through, we will not park.
He'll lead us through, to The Promised Land,
  He'll not forsake, He'll take our hands;
And when His hand, holds ours in love,
  We'll feel the power, from God above,
The power to sit, or walk, or stand,
  Always upheld, by God's right hand.

We'll not be bothered, by heat or drought,
  We're planted by the stream, that never dries out.
So come my friend, to The Water of Life,
  His name is Jesus, He gave His life,
To redeem, set free, make new again,
  All those who believe, and trust in Him.
So confess your sins, knowing He saves,
  You will rise with Him, who rose from the grave.
Christ Jesus is, The God we serve,
  He always keeps, His Holy Word!

TO GROW IN GRACE - Inspired by Luke 1:80A

To grow in grace, by the Spirit of God,
  Walk in the faith, of The Christ of God;
    Then you will know, what real love is,
      Then you will hear, His voice and live!
John came preaching, in the wilderness,
  A message to turn, to the righteousness.
    That comes from trusting, Christ alone,
      Instead of works, which they have done!
Those who trusted, in their own works,
  Who refused to hear, The Word and shirked,
    The message to, confess their sins,
      Remained unchanged, no life within.
By their works, they were condemned,
  For in their pride, they rejected Him.
    They refused the grace, that God provides.
    To enter life, where Christ abides.
When we confess, our sins each day,
  To the only God, who has made a way,
    We're made brand new, by His Precious Blood,
    His Blood has saved, from sin's dread flood.
Sin had been, a flood to drown,
  All those God made, to wear a crown:
    A crown of life, and righteousness,
      A crown of peace, and blessedness.
So humble yourself, before The Lord,
  Hear His voice, obey His Word,
    Receive His grace, by confessing your sin,
      Receive His grace, and enter in,
To the life He purchased, with His own Blood,
  The life He gives, to make us good.
    Only in Christ, are you freed from strife!
    Only in Christ, can you find true life!

CHRIST THE LIGHT - Inspired by John Chapter 6

Do you seek the truth for you? Do you know The One who is true?
    Christ is The Way, The Truth and The Life,
        The only One, who frees from strife!

Striving causes discontent, it takes the lies the devil sent,
    And makes them seem, so pure and right,
        That men choose darkness, instead of light!
Only God's Light can lift the veil, of sin and death that do assail,
    Only God's Light can break the chains,
        That would bind our souls, to the devil's reign.

So come to Christ, He is The Light,
    He breaks the darkness of the night.
The Light of God, He came to earth,
    To give to all new life, new birth!

Don't walk in the light, of your own fire,
    For only God's light, lifts from the mire,
Of sin and fear, of doubt and shame,
    Of hell and death, your soul to claim.

Come to Christ, He'll set you free,
    To walk in love and liberty.
His liberty gives strength and power,
    To hear and heed His voice this hour.

This is the time to hear God's voice,
    The time to make His will your choice.
Then you will see His open door,
    The door to life forevermore.

You'll see with eyes of faith and love,
    The God you serve, The God above.
You'll see Him in His love and power,
    You'll see His grace and might this hour.

WHAT IS LIFE WITHOUT GOD'S LIGHT?

What is life, without God's Light?
    But worthless wandering, no life in sight.
Now when you come, to The Pure Clean Light,
    The Christ of God, He gives His might,
To walk and live, with pure clear goals,
    To speak His Word,, to transform souls.

So take the light, He has given you,
    And share with those, He brings to you.
This is why, He came and died:
    To bring men to His pure, clear side.
There they'll receive, the grace He gives,
    There they'll believe, and then can live,
By the power that raised Christ, from the dead,
    The power to live, for God instead.

A simple prayer, is all it takes,
    To receive His life, and then forsake,
The world, with all it's sin and death,
    To receive His life, The Spirit's breath!
Then as we pass from death to life,
    We're received by God, like a bride, a wife!

Say Jesus, I confess my sin,
    Make me whole, and alive again.
You paid the price, to set me free,
    I choose your life, for eternity,
I cannot cleanse myself, I know,
    I trust You Lord, for grace to grow,
By The Spirit, You have given me,
    To set my soul, and spirit free.
Thank you Lord, for hearing me,
    Thank You Lord, for saving me!

FOR MOTHERS

A mother is a treasured friend,
   Who loves her own, and all God sends.
She listens to, their joys and fears,
   To love and care, through all the years..
She hears their cries, even through the night,
   Then rises quick, to meet their plight.
She watches, as they grow up tall,
   She prays to God, who hears her call.

God watches, keeps her children near,
   For He's The God, who takes all fear.
He replaces it, with faith and trust,
   In Christ who saves, removes sin's dust.
Christ takes away, the grime of sin,
   Then by His blood, cleanses within,
He gives the hurting heart, new cheer,
   For He removes, all death and fear.

Christ is the source, of faith and hope,
   He gives the strength, to always cope,
With every need, that does arise,
   He is always there, to hear each cry;
For the love you give, comes from your Lord
   It comes from heaven's, endless store.
So if sometimes, your way seems hard,
   Bring Him your praise, like spikenard.

Now when you give, your thanks and praise,
   Your problems, lift like morning haze,
That disappears, when the sun comes out,
   Christ gives the faith, that removes the doubt.
So on this day to honour you,
   Dear Mother trust The Lord to prove,
That He will take, your every prayer,
   And hold your children, in His care.

<u>PRAYER</u> - Inspired by John Chapters 7 & 8

Do I do the will, of my Father in heaven?
  Do I let Him purge out, all of sin's leaven?
A little leaven is all it takes, to go to the soul and contaminate!
  Where I have tolerated, sin in my soul,
  I ask You to cleanse, and make me whole.
Let Your Word bring light, into every dark place,
  Where sin would hide, to deceive and disgrace.
Take my thoughts and my will, and make then Yours,
  Cleanse me and heal me, from the sin I abhor.
Write Your Word clear, upon my heart,
  So from Your presence, I'll never depart..
Only Your blood, can make me whole,
  Can purify and cleanse my soul.
Holy Spirit apply, The Blood of Christ,
For only His Blood and sacrifice,
  Are pure enough, to cleanse and redeem.
  Only His Blood, can make me clean.

Apply it to my spirit, my body, my mind,
  So I can abide in my Lord, The True Vine!
I want to honour and worship, and praise Him always,
  With joy and thanksgiving, for all of my days.
Just as You, Jesus, did The Father's will,
  Help me to do Your will, and be still.
You said to be still, and know You are God,
  Be still in Your Presence, and give God laud.
You are my Shepherd, and I am Your sheep,
  Help me to love, and never to bleat!
So when men revile, or put me down,
  Help me forgive, without a frown.
May I give the grace, You've given me
  For then we all, can be set free.
So Lord I pray, anoint me now,
  With grace and faith, to live this vow!

JESUS HEALS A BLIND MAN - Inspired by John 9 & 10

One day as Jesus was walking along,
    He saw a blind man, who needed a song;
A song of deliverance, from the state he was in,
    A song of praise, to Christ from within!
"Why is he blind, the disciples inquired?"
    "Was it sin of the parents, or the son they sired'?"
"He was born blind," the Lord Jesus said,
    So the power of God, can be seen instead!
"I AM The Light of the world" Jesus said,
    I came to give sight, to raise the dead!

The Lord made mud, as He spat on the ground,
    Put the mud on the eyes, of the blind man He found;
Sent him off to Siloam, to wash himself clean,
    Came back seeing clearly, his sight now redeemed!
The people then took him, to the Pharisees,
    To confirm the healing, for now he could see.
Once again Jesus healed, on the Sabbath to show,
    That the Sabbath was given, God's person to know.

For God is pure love, and His mercy He shows,
    To all who will hear, His words and bestow,
The love and mercy, He has given to all,
    Who hear His word, and obey His call.
Even when the Pharisees, put the man on trial,
    He kept saying the truth, wouldn't offer denial;
For He had experienced, the power of God,
    All he could do, was give glory to God!
He spoke the truth, of what he knew then,
    He gave a pure witness, to the souls of men,
That Jesus The Christ, is Messiah for all,
    Who will seek His grace, and answer His call!

So if you think, that you can see,
   Do not be like the Pharisees!
If God says to you, go and wash,
   Do His will, whatever the cost!
Doing God's will, brings blessings untold,
   His blessings redeem, and preserve your soul.
Now if you claim, that you can see,
   Refuse God's call to come, be clean,
If you reject His loving call,
   Your guilt remains, and you will fall!

So come to Christ, He died for you,
   He came, He paid, the price for you!
He came to set, the captives free,
   To bring all men, to liberty:
The liberty, to choose His grace,
   To be washed clean, to see His face!
In His dear face, you'll see His love,
   The love of God, from heaven above!
For the love of God, is shown to all,
   Who hear His voice, and heed His call!

"Come unto Me, and I will bless,
   With peace and joy, and righteousness!
All those who come, I will preserve,
   I'll keep them by, My Holy Word!"
So hear His truth, obey His voice,
   And make His will, your own by choice.
Then He will lead, to pastures green,
   Your life refreshed, by His pure stream!
No more a sinner, lost, forlorn,
   You're now His child, redeemed, reborn!

WHAT IS YOUR NEED? - Inspired by John 11

Are you weary or worn or sad?
    Come to The Master, to be made glad!
Come to The One, who can save your soul,
    Come to The One, who can make you whole!
He is The Way, The Truth and The Life,
    He'll set you free, from death and strife!

A man named Lazarus, was very ill,
    So his sisters sent for Jesus, their need to fulfill
To heal their brother, and make him whole,
    But Jesus delayed coming, to save more souls!
On the fourth day, after Lazarus died,
    Jesus came to Bethany, to stand by their side.

He stood, He listened, He wept, and He heard,
    For the power of His Father, would be unfurled,
To release His life, so men could know
    That Christ Jesus came, God's glory to show!
Jesus told the people, to roll away the stone,
    From the cave entrance, so the opening would show!

Jesus said, "Father I thank You, for hearing me,
    I speak this out loud, so the people can see,
That You have anointed, and equipped me to be,
    Their Messiah and Redeemer, and believe in Me.
Then Jesus shouted: "Lazarus, come out,"
    And out He came, without a doubt!

He was wrapped in the clothes, they buried him in,
    So Jesus said: "Loose him," from what bound him.
Many believed, in The Lord that day,
    For they saw the results, when Jesus prayed!
God wanted all, everywhere to know,
    That His power is there, and in Christ is bestowed!

His power is there now, for all who believe,
    Who choose to trust, in The Christ and receive,
To receive The Christ, as Saviour and Lord,
    He'll bring your lives, into one accord.
He'll anoint you with power, from His Spirit to do,
    The greater works, He designed for you!

By the death and resurrection, of Jesus, The Christ,
    All men can be saved, for Christ paid the price,
By giving His life, as an offering to all,
    He now gives the faith, to answer His call.
Come unto Me, all you weary and sad,
    I will save your souls, I'll make you glad!

Now even though weeping, may come in the night,
    Joy comes in the morning, to bring you delight.
So fear not My child, I hear The Lord say,
    I'll make you a path, My clear chosen way.
You'll not trip or stumble, or fall by the side,
    I'll save you and keep you, right by My side.

"When you live in Me, and I in you,
    The greater works, you then shall do."
These words Jesus said, before the cross,
    To those who'd believe, who would count the cost,
For The Father God, must be glorified,
    And Jesus is standing, right by His side!

He is watching to see, His children reach out,
    To heal and to save, to remove all the doubt!
To bring in the lost, the hurt and the lame,
    To bring them to Jesus, the One who will save,
There you'll enjoy, His Presence always,
    There you'll receive, His love everyday!

WHAT DOES IT MEAN TO WASH THE FEET?
Inspired by John 13

What does it mean, to wash the feet,
  To wash the feet, of those we meet?
As a lesson to the men, Christ had chosen to teach,
  He showed by example, on how to reach
The hearts and minds, of those He loved,
  To lead them to, His courts above!

After the supper, Jesus rose from the table,
  Filled a basin with water, to show He was able
To humble Himself, He took a servant's towel,
  Then bent to wash, their feet right now.
When He came to Peter, to wash his feet,
  Peter asked, Lord why should You, perform this deed!

He didn't know Jesus, was showing them,
  That if you would lead, you must first serve men.
Jesus said to Peter, "If I don't wash you,
  You'll never be part, of what I have for you!:
Then Peter said, "Lord, wash all of me,"
  But Jesus said, "No, only your feet I will clean."

His disciples could not, understand why He,
  Would perform for them, a servants deed.
Jesus washed the feet, of all of His men,
  Even Judas, who would betray Him to men!
They would beat Him, and mock Him and crucify Him,
  Jesus suffered this all, to pay for our sin!

This was the full, extent of His love,
  To be our Redeemer, from heaven above.
Jesus said, after washing their feet, "now you're clean,
  But not everyone," for He knew the unclean,
The one who had chosen, to betray by greed,
  His Saviour and Lord, by his dreadful deed.

After Judas had left, to do his deed,
 Jesus turned to the rest, to explain their need,
To trust in what, He would say and had said,
 So they'd know with a hope, that He'd rise from the dead!
The time has come, for God's glory He said,
 The time for God's glory, to be seen instead.

He told them to love, each other always,
 To love like He, had loved them each day.
He said by their love, the world would know,
 That they were His own, by the love that they showed.
So the next time you see, one who needs to be clean,
 Take a towel like a servant, like The One who redeems.

A servant is not greater, than the Master, Christ said,
 So serve one another, so all can be led,
By humility of heart, and reason to show,
 The love of The Father, to all here below!
Show the love and forgiveness, God has shown to you,
 For then they will see, God's love is true!

A BRUISED REED - Inspired by Isaiah 42:3

A bruised reed The Lord won't break, or smouldering wick put out,
For He's The Lord, He won't forsake, His children if they doubt.

He will not cry or shout aloud, to make His voice be heard,
He'll bring forth love and justice now, to all who heed His Word.

He will not fail or become weak, be crushed or in despair,
For God's Own Son came down to earth, to show His love and care.

So trust The Lord, The God who saves, He hears your every prayer,
His love and mercy reaches out, to prove that He is there.

So Praise The Lord and wait for Him, for He will come again,
His Spirit will give faith to you, to stand before all men.

IN THE LAST DAYS

In the last days, The Lord God said,
    In the last days, I will raise the dead!
Those who were dead, in their trespass and sin,
    I'll raise from the dead, make alive again.
No more will they live, for the world and it's ways,
    They'll live for The Lord, by His Spirit always.

When Holy Spirit comes, upon all men,
    Their souls are released, to worship again.
They'll worship The Lord, in Spirit and truth,
    With meekness they'll worship, like faithful Ruth.
She trusted the word of Naomi, that day,
    Then laid at the feet, of her master to say,
Cover me with, the hem of your robe,
    Come and keep me, by your word.

A greater than Boaz is here revealed,
    The Saviour, The Christ, our salvation has sealed.
He has sealed it with, His Precious Blood,
    We're washed and cleansed, from sin's dread flood.
Death couldn't hold, the Lord Jesus Christ,
    Couldn't keep His soul, in the grave like a vise!
The Holy, Sinless Son of God,
    Redeemed by His Blood, the lives He bought!

Now risen He sits, at The Father's right hand,
    To rule, intercede, and to command.
He sits in honour, until His enemies become,
    A footstool for all, who choose to come,
To The Risen Christ, for His saving grace,
    The Messiah, The Lord, to behold His Face
So come to The Lord, do not delay,
    Today's your salvation, today is the day!

THE BOOK OF LIFE - Based on Revelation 20:12

When the books are opened, will your name be there?
It will if you will give your heart, and pray this simple prayer:

Have mercy, Oh Lord, save me from sin,
Make me Your child, come dwell within,
Give me the faith, to stand, be strong.
Away from the stain, of sin and of wrong.
Give me the sight, to see Your doors,
So I can enter, and receive Your more.
What you give Lord, brings peace and rest,
Brings joy and hope, and blessedness.
Thank You Lord, for forgiving my sin,
Thank you Lord, for abiding within!

HOLY SPIRIT TOUCH ME NOW - Inspired by John 19-21

Holy Spirit of The Living God, come now and touch my soul,
Holy Spirit of The Living God, renew and make me whole.
Holy Spirit of The Living God, I need Your cleansing power,
Holy Spirit of The Living God, make known Your will this hour.

I cannot do this on my own, I need Your power Oh, Lord,
So all can know Your love Oh Lord, Your life and blood outpoured.
Blood and water flowed from Your side, so we can now abide,
In You Dear Lord, for only You, can keep me by Your side!

Oh Precious Saviour, Holy Lord, pour out Your Spirit once more,
Come to our city, nation, world, so men can know You Lord!
For only when they know You, and bow their knees and hearts,
Will they experience all you have, to give a brand new start!

Help us forgive as You forgive, to love as You love us,
For we would be the children Lord, Your children You can trust!
Prepare us now to preach Your Word, in truth and in Your power,
So men can know that You are God, each day and every hour!

ON THE DAY OF PENTECOST - Inspired by Acts 1 & 2

On the day of Pentecost,
    Holy Spirit came to save the lost,
He came in power, to anoint the few,
    The ones who waited, for His power to infuse.
Jesus had told them, to wait and pray,
    For His Spirit to come, and anoint this way.
Without His Anointing, their preaching would lack,
    The power to heal, the power to attack,
The lies that nailed, The Lord to the cross,
    The lies that said, that all was lost.
So they waited and prayed, one hundred and twenty of them,
    For The Spirit to come, and empower them.
When the day of Pentecost, was fully come,
    A rushing wind touched all, not some,
For tongues of fire, came on each head
    Of the one hundred and twenty, who waited instead!

They waited and obeyed, their Risen Lord,
    And now Holy Spirit, was being outpoured,
To equip, to preach, to all men, that The Christ,
    Was their only Saviour, who paid their price!
Christ Jesus paid the price, on Calvary,
    When He became sin, to set us free..
The disciples spoke, in the speech of all men,
    So all could then, understand they'd sinned.
They spoke so all, would know and hear,
    The truth of Christ's, redemption clear.
Holy Spirit equipped their tongues, to speak,
    To all who came, whether Jews or Greeks;
That Jesus Christ, is the only way,
    To receive salvation, to believe and pray,
To the Only Father, and God of all,
    Who sent His Son, as Saviour for all!
So come today, for Holy Spirit calls,
    All of mankind, to come, give their all!

COME TO THE CHRIST

Oh come to The Christ, The Anointed One,
    Come to The Lord, The Holy One,
Come in faith and hope and prayer,
    Come to The Lord, bring every care.
Now when you come, and confess your sin,
    He gives new life, and dwells within.
He'll direct your spirit, and guide your way,
    So you can choose, to watch and pray.
You'll watch and see, what God is doing,
    You'll pray and see, His Spirit moving.
God's Holy Spirit, is here today,
    Here in power, to equip this day.
He'll fill all those, who thirst for more,
    To lead to faith, in Christ, God's Door,
By faith in Christ, we enter heaven above,
    There to behold, our God of love.

Come quickly now, when God's Spirit calls,
    Come quickly now, receive the all,
The all of what, Christ has for you,
    So your hearts can sing, The Word that's true.
Let's sing with joy, and praise to God,
    Sing with faith, God's name to laud;
Sing and worship, praise and adore,
    The Holy King, our Mighty Lord!
Let's join with all, the saints to raise,
    Our hearts in one, accord to praise,
The Mighty God, The El Shaddai,
    Who hears our voice, our song, our cry.
Bow down before, your Awesome Lord,
    Then bring your hearts, into one accord.
This is the day, The Lord has made,
    Rejoice Dear Child, The Price is Paid!!

SPEAK WHAT I SPEAK AND DO WHAT I DO
Inspired by John 12

Speak what I speak, and do what I do,
    Then the will of My Father, will be done in you.
For out of the abundance, I have given you,
    You will do for others, what I've done for you.
The will of The Lord, is to always give,
    To give in love, and always forgive.
Whatever you give, is given to you,
    Blessings abundant, and grace to choose;
The will of The Father, above your own,
    For His will is perfect, and He's on The Throne!
So whatever you do, and wherever you go,
    Know He's chosen you, to make His will known.

This is the will, of The Lord God on high,
    That men should believe, in Christ Jesus who died.
But Christ rose again, by the Power of The Spirit,
    Rose to give life, to those who inherit;
Inherit by faith, in Christ Jesus alone,
    A life that's eternal; God's glory to show!

So if you are wondering, where should I be?
    Or what is the will, of The Father for me?
Open His Word, and get to know Him,
    The Master, Redeemer, The Saviour from sin!
He'll remove the veil, that blinds our eyes,
    The veil that the devil, used with his lies.
Christ alone is The Life, Truth and Way,
    He'll show you His path, every new day.
His mercies are new, His plans will succeed,
    When you seek for His grace, to meet every need.
It is not by your works, which you have done,
    But only by faith in The Christ, God's Son!

I AWAIT YOUR WORD

Holy Spirit, I sit, awaiting Your Word,
The Word that brings life, and salvation assured.
For You are The Author, and Giver of Life,
Your breath is what quickens, from death unto life!

Then listen and write, what I say unto you,
    Listen and hear, for My words are true,
Believe on The Lord, and what He has done,
    For He paid the price, your salvation He won!
The blood that He shed, was the price that He paid,
    To secure your salvation, to make the way.
So come to The Father, covered by Christ's robe,
    The Robe of His Righteousness, by which you are clothed!
You have no righteousness, on your own,
    Your every good deed, could never atone,
    Only by believing and receiving, The Christ,
    By trusting in Him, and His sacrifice,
Can you be made righteous, and pure and whole,
    Can you be made holy, to save your soul!

Your soul is the place, where decisions are made,
    So choose The Lord now, to hear and obey.
When you choose Christ, you choose life this day,
    When you choose Christ, He prepares your way;
The way to freedom, to fulfill God's plans,
    For the plans of The Lord, bring blessing to man.
Oh child of Mine, hear the words that I say,
    Listen and hear, really hear, then obey,
For I have a life, of blessing for you,
    And when you are blessed, you bless others too.
My blessings are abundant, and meant to share,
    The love and the care, from your God who is there.
He will hear every thought, He will speak and correct,
    For by Spirit and Word, your paths He'll direct!

LIVE THE TRUTH - Based on Acts 3 & 4

I have a work for you to do, To live the truth I've shown to you.
What I reveal becomes the seed, to plant in truth to meet the need.
My truth will open up the door, that leads to life forevermore.

As Peter and John, used Jesus name,
    The Name by which, all men are saved,
        The lame man leaped, and praised The Lord,
            For He'd been healed, by The Living Word!
God's Word became flesh, and dwelt among us,
    This Word was Jesus, The Righteous, The Just,
        The Pure and Spotless, Son of God,
            The Light of The World, The Christ of God!
Now in His Name, all can be saved,
    Can be redeemed, from hell and grave,
        Are saved to serve, and saved to live,
            Are saved to love, and then forgive!
Now when you choose, to live this way,
    Your needs are met, as prayers are prayed,
        According to, God's perfect will,
            To see The Lord's Name, lifted still!
At the moment we lift, His Name above,
    All other names, He shows His love,
        And mercy, to the children of men,
            To heal their hurts, and be born again!
They are not born, by the plan of men,
    But by His Spirit, are born again,
        To live a life, of joy and peace,
            For He has paid, their soul's release.

Come Holy Spirit, do this in me, so I can live this life so free,
Free from all that steals and kills, free from all life's deadly ills.
Free to worship You, Oh Lord, to join the saints in one accord,
Around Your Throne Oh God on High, to ever live and never die!

BELIEVE ON THE LORD - Inspired by Acts 16:31

Believe on The Lord, and you shall be saved,
Believe on The Lord, for the price has been paid.
Believe on The Lord, and be born again,
By The Holy Spirit, to live again!

Not for yourself, but for God above,
To spread the news, that God is Love!
The purest form, of love is Christ,
The Son of God, our sacrifice,

We could never, save ourselves,
Our lives were doomed, to death and hell.
But Jesus came, and gave His life,
He shed His Blood, to pay the price.

He ransomed us, and saved our souls,
To make us pure, alive and whole!
Oh Holy God,, what can we say,
To give our praise, and thanks today?

We give our lives, our thoughts, our plans,
For You to use, at your command.
Be pleased Oh Lord, to take us now,
To seal us, as we make this vow.

Lord Jesus, we present our lives,
Transform us, so we'll never strive,
To do Your will, by our own power,
But let Your Spirit, rule each hour!

NO POVERTY - Inspired by Acts 4

No poverty was there, among the throng,
Of those who chose, The Christ to belong,
For the people of God, chose to share,
Whatever they had, because they cared.

Wherever they saw that one was in need,
They reached and gave, they planted a seed;
A seed of good, for all were a part,
Of The Father's Blessing, The Father's heart!

The Apostles gave witness, to The Living Lord,
For the resurrection, of Christ The Lord,
Had proved to them, God's words were true,
And what He says, is what He'll do.

When questioned, by the priests one day,
After being jailed, for using The Name,
The Name of Jesus Christ, to heal,
They showed, God's healing power was real!

They declared that only, Christ's power can save,
They were warned by the priests, never use That Name!
The disciples were beaten, but that did not deter,
Them from using The Name, of The Lord to cure.

They spoke with more boldness, and said to all,
We'll obey our God, for He gave us His all!
When Peter and John, were released that day,
They went to their brothers, in Christ and prayed.

In one accord, they lifted their voice,
To Praise The Lord, for The Spirit's choice,
For He gave them boldness, to share and speak,
The Word of God, to the strong and weak.

They shared The Word, Holy Spirit had given,
To David, the King, about the rulers of men.
He spoke of Messiah, God's purpose to show,
That all that was done, was God's will to bestow!

They joined then in worship, and praise to The Lord,
Then asked for more boldness, to preach His Word,
To confirm His Word, with miracles too,
To show all men, that Jesus is true!

After they prayed, the place shook with power,
Holy Spirit filled them all, that very hour.
To lift Jesus Name, above every name,
So all can hear, and all can be saved!

He filled them afresh, to preach God's Word,
With boldness and power, so all could be sure,
That Jesus The Christ, is Messiah and Lord,
For hearts to be brought, into one accord.

Now with one heart, they shared all they had,
And so no one suffered, or had any lack.
The Apostles gave witness, with strength and with power,
God's great grace and favour, rested on them each hour.

Those who owned land, sold it and gave,
These funds to the apostles, to help and to save.
Joseph from Cyprus, also did like the rest,
So they called him Barnabas, he encouraged the best.

He too brought the money, from the land he had sold,
To give to the Apostles, for the young and the old.
Let us take a lesson, from God's Word today,
To give and to preach, and always to pray!

LORD WE NEED WISDOM - Inspired by Acts 6 & 7

Lord we need, Your wisdom now,
   To hear Your voice, fulfill our vows,
      For we delight, in serving You,
         To live a life, that's pure and true!
Be The Shepherd, of our souls,
   So we can hear, and see and know,
      Your voice, Your will, Your sovereign plan,
         To free all men, from the devil's hand!
You are The Door, to all that is true,
   You open up, the way to choose,
      To choose the life, of God above,
         To choose to walk, in faith and love.

Holy Spirit open, up our eyes,
   To see Your truth, and leave the lies,
      To walk the path, that Jesus did,
         While on this earth, so we can live;
Live for God, in all we do,
   Live the way, He taught us to.
      For the love of God, was shown to all,
         When Christ redeemed us, from the fall,
By being led, unto the cross,
   To bleed and die, for all the lost.
      He showed His love, by what He did,
         He gave His life, so we could live.

Oh Jesus, no one took Your life from you,
   You laid it down, so we could choose,
      To live for God, in all we do,
         To live a life, that pleases You.
So by the power that raised You, Christ,
   From death to life, to pay our price,
      Raise us once more, by that same power,
         So we can hear Your voice this hour.
We want to hear and then obey, Your voice, so we will never stray!

GOD'S OPEN DOOR

You know the way, you are to go,
    I've opened this door, so you can show,
The love I've given, to bless and give,
    My life to all, so they can live.
So live a life, that's free from care,
    Knowing that I AM always there,
There to hear, your every prayer,
    There to share, the yoke you bear.
My yoke is easy, and My burden is light,
    And I give to all, new life, new sight.
To all who trust, in Me and My power,
    Will have My peace, this very hour!

My peace is not, like the world gives,
My peace comes in, to those I forgive,
This peace passes all, that is know to men,
This peace restores, gives hope again!
So share the love, I have given you,
Serve your brothers, what I've served you.

I provided a table, in the wilderness,
    So all could partake, of My blessedness.
Now you are coming, into the place,
    I've prepared for you, to show My grace.
My grace and mercy, and love outpoured,
    I give so all, can be restored.
What I have chosen, before time began,
    Is a life redeemed, by The Holy Lamb.
The Lamb of God, Christ Jesus The Lord,
    To bring all men, into one accord,
With God as Father, by The Spirit's Power,
    To live in faith, in God each hour!

GOD'S INVITATION - Inspired by Revelation 3:20

The hour is now, the hour is late,
I AM standing and waiting right at the gate,
Waiting to see, if you'll open the door,
To allow Me to enter, to give you My more:
The more of life, that I have for you,
To live the life, I've prepared for you!

Oh Lord, Dear Lord, come in I pray,
Come in Dear Lord, this very day.
Make me Your child, in every way,
So I can hear, Your voice always;
And then in faith, and hope prepare,
To meet You Lord, in praise and prayer.

This is what, I have longed to hear,
Your invitation, pure and clear,
To receive My love, My joy, My grace,
To hold you in, My warm embrace.
I have so much, to share with you,
Of all The Father, has for you.

Then come into my heart, I pray,
Come in Dear Lord, this very day.
Take my hand, and lead me on,
To where You know, that I belong.
Take me into, Your Holy Place,
Let me behold, Your loving face!

DO YOU WANT TO SEE GOD? - Inspired by Matthew 5:8

Do you want, to see My face,
    Behold My Glory, and My Grace?
Then spend much time, alone with Me,
    So that your eyes, can really see;
Oh, see with your spirit, not just your mind,
    See what I AM doing, to heal the blind.
Those who don't know Me, cannot really see,
    The life I've prepared, to set them free.
They're caught up in, their daily chores,
    Always striving, for more and more.
They think that more, will give them peace,
    The peace that gives, their souls release.
The peace I give, is so much more,
    The peace I give, opens up the door,
To a rest from all, that hinders man,
    To experience My Grace, My Love, My Plan.

So come to Me, for the salve that heals,
    The salve for your eyes, that will reveal,
The life the Spirit, is leading you to,
    To bring all men, to saving truth!
I AM, The Way, The Truth, The Life,
    Without My life, you've only strife.
So choose this day, the life I give,
    Choose Me this day, and really live;
Live in hope and peace and love,
    Live in faith, from God above.
Live to show, My love to all,
    Live in grace, to conquer all!
Only My Grace, is sufficient for you,
    Only My Grace, will see you through.
My grace is made perfect, when you are weak,
    My grace will restore, if it is Me you seek!

HEAVENLY FATHER I WELCOME YOU

Heavenly Father, I welcome You,
    To do the work, only You can do;
To make of me, Your holy child,
    Your precious temple, undefiled.
Root out of me, what leads to sin,
    Root out and cleanse, from deep within.
I want all those, who know me Lord,
    To see in me, one You've restored;
To be the one, You have called to do,
    The work assigned, to make all new!

You sent Your Son, Your Only Son,
    To bring us life, to make us one;
One with You, in hope and peace,
    One to know, Your love released.
One to witness, and to share,
    Your Holy Love, Your Grace prepared.
From the beginning, You knew we 'd fall,
    But even then, You conquered all,
By sending Jesus, as The Christ,
    The Anointed One, our sacrifice!

He paid the price, of sin and death,
    Then gave to us, new life, new breath.
The Breath of Your Spirit, imparted Your Life,
    And gave us the faith, to see past the strife.
All that sin can bring is death,
    No life, no love, no heart, no breath.
But, in Your Awesome Holy Love,
    You sent us Jesus, from above,
To restore our souls, with life and peace,
    With love and joy, to never cease,
To praise You Lord, our God on high,
    To live by faith, and never die!

THE TEMPLE OF GOD - Inspired by 1 Corinthians 6:19-20

What is the temple of God really like?
    Is it timber, and stone, and glass, all alight?
What is the temple of God, to you friend?
    A building, a church, and a place to attend?
We gather together, to worship and praise,
    But we are the temple, God's destined to raise.
He has destined for us, to be His living stones,
    A witness to make, His Glory made known.
Then we'll be a carrier, of God's glory to show,
    So all He has called, His love will know.
So wherever you go, whether near or far,
    Be the light that leads, to Christ like the star,
That led the wise men from the east to show,
    The way to Messiah, The Lord Christ to know!

Then just as they gave, their gifts unto Him,
    The gifts they had brought, to honour The King.
Present yourselves now, to The King of all kings,
    As a living sacrifice, a pure offering!
Give Him your all, for His all He gave you,
    To ransom your soul, to make you brand new.
He'll take what you give, and restore and renew,
    So you can partake, of His blessings for you,
The Lord our God, will give and forgive
    His grace and His mercy, so all then can live,
Who turn unto Him, in faith and in love,
    To be their Redeemer, their Saviour above.
Christ Jesus now stands, at The Father's right hand,
    To make intercession, for all fallen man.
He stands as The Pure, Holy Sacrifice,
    The only atonement, that would ever suffice,
To pay our redemption, to save our souls,
    So turn to Him now, to make your life whole.

HELP ME TO BE AND HELP ME TO DO

Help me to be, a believer in You,
    Then help me to do, what is pure and true,
With a heart that is willing, to give of my all,
    Without hesitation, to answer Your call!
Help me to hear, and to understand,
    Your will and Your purpose, Your call and Your plan.
It is You that I love, my Lord and my King,
    To You I bow down, to You I sing.
Oh cause a new song, to be birthed now I pray,
    A song to bring joy, to Your heart God this day.
Let this song of worship, rejoice Your heart,
    A song of thanksgiving, for making me part,
Of your family on earth, and those up in heaven,
    All those that You've cleansed, from all of sin's leaven.

Your grace is abundant, it's full and it's free,
Your grace You poured out, to give liberty;
Liberty to walk, in the light You have given,
Liberty to lead, and to guide men to heaven.

Help us fix our eyes, on the heavenly goal,
    With Your light to illumine, our body and soul.
Your light to our spirit, blesses and heals,
    With resurrection power, that saves and that seals.
Oh Lord, light the path, that I walk on today,
    So that those who follow, won't be led astray.
Your light inspires, our visions and dreams,
    It gives us the faith, to see and believe.
For You have not called us, to mediocrity,
    But to hear Your dear voice, then to do and to be,
All the good You have planned, before the earth was formed,
    To give us a life, a life that's reborn;
Reborn now to live, in the light of Your love,
    Reborn to rejoice, in You Lord up above!

CHRIST OUR LIGHT - Inspired by John 8:12

When it seems, that there is no end in sight,
　　And every path, seems dark, not bright,
Look to The Lord, He will see you through,
　　His hand of love, will lead you too.
He will lead through the valleys, and to mountains high,
　　He will give you His power, which never dies.
For once you have given, your life to Him,
　　Have forsaken the ways, of death and sin,
A new life awaits, a life of pure peace,
　　A life of joy, where strength is released!.
This strength comes not, from the will of man,
　　By working out, but by following God's plan.

He levels the paths, so you can walk free,
　　He clears the stones, that block you and me.
Stones of bitterness, anger and hurt,
　　Are removed when we turn, from sin's awful dirt.
When we turn to Christ, in repentance and faith,
　　He takes what we give, and cuts off like a lathe,
All that would hinder, and harm our souls,
　　He removes and transforms, redeems and makes whole.

Now we can walk, in the light of His love,
　　Spreading the news, from our God up above,
That Christ has redeemed, all men from their sin,
　　As they confess their sin, and turn to Him.
So if you want Christ's life within,
　　Pray this prayer to be cleansed by Him:

　　Oh Precious Lord Jesus, forgive me I pray,
　　For walking and living my own stubborn way
　　Make me Your temple, pure and clean,
　　Your child forever, restored and redeemed,
　　No more a slave, to the ways of sin,
　　But Your child Oh Lord, without and within!

THE HEART OF THE GOOD SHEPHERD
Inspired by Matthew 18:12- 14 & John 10:10-18

The Good Shepherd left, the ninety and nine,
To seek out the one, who had left Him to climb,
Away to see, the world for himself,
Away to experience the world, and it's wealth.

So, seek out the lost, the disillusioned and hurt,
The wounded, defeated, by the devil besmirched.
From a distance what was offered, looked golden and fine,
But was only deceptive, for under the shine,
Was a grime that entered, to consume their souls,
To eat away and destroy what was whole!
You have a word, that will heal the soul,
That will bring life and light, that will make them whole,

For Christ Jesus came, paid the price, the whole cost,
To redeem all the fallen, the hurt and the lost.
Ask Holy Spirit, to lead you today,
To the one or the ones, who need Jesus this day.
Show them His love, by your words and your deeds,
Reach out and touch, with His love for their needs.
Christ's love is, a never ending supply,
To give His assurance, to heal their hearts cry.

Be ready, dear child, to hear The Lord's voice,
When He calls you to do, His will by your choice.
He'll make a way, He'll prepare the path,
To save men's souls, and to ransom from wrath.
For the wrath of God, is against the devil and sin,
These are the destroyers, that take God's children from Him,
So rescue the perishing, reach for the lost,.
Reach out in His Name, don't count the cost!

What Jesus did, He did out of love,
When He came and He died to bring men up above.
Hell was not made, for the souls of men,
But to punish the devil, and those with him!

So let Holy Spirit, lead you today,
As you listen and sing, as you watch and you pray.
He will show you the ones, to especially touch,
To reveal God's love, for He loves us so much.
His love will heal, His love will make new,
His love will restore, His power will do,
All that is needed, to forgive and restore,
All that is needed, to show men God's more!

The more that God gives, increases each day,
As we seek His face, as we kneel and pray.
He'll give you a download, of His perfect love,
He'll seat you beside Him, in heaven above.
There you'll behold, the world from His eyes,
Then you'll walk in His truth, that never dies.
So sit in the heavenly places with Him,
Then walk in His ways, to redeem men from sin.

Stand in the power, that God gives to you,
Stand and behold, Christ's redemption is true.
You do not stand, by your strength alone,
You stand by the power, of God on His throne.
So put on the armour, God's given to you,
Put on His armour, and you'll stand for what's true.
You will walk in the light, of His love each day,
You will bring His light, into darkness today!

Not by your power, and not by your might,
But by Holy Spirit, who pours out The Light!

LISTEN

Listen now dear friend I pray,
    As I share these words today,
Christ alone, is The Way to God,
    He came, He paid, our price with blood.
His Blood alone, pure, undefiled,
    Was shed for all, that sin defiled!

Sin had marred us, made us cursed,
    But the death of Christ, redeemed, reversed,
The awful penalty, for sin,
    He took the fall, we enter in,
To all that God, had planned for us,
    Now we're His children, if we trust,
In Christ as Saviour, King and Lord,
    Our lives redeemed, released, restored!

Oh what an awesome gift is this,
    To have His life, a life of bliss;
A life of blessing, health and peace,
    A life with joys, that never cease.
His joy will give us, strength and power,
    To live His life, in every hour.
So do not wait, He's at the gate,
    Call out to Him, don't hesitate.

Say Jesus, Come and make me clean,
    Restore my soul, my life redeem,
Make me Your child, in every way,
    So I can walk, Your path each day:
Walk in faith, and hope and love,
To share Your love, Oh God above!

MY WAYS - Inspired by Psalm 37:34

My ways for you, are not grievous or hard,
    For you have given your life, as spikenard;
As an offering to anoint, My feet and My hands,
    In the lives of My children, to bless many lands.
So take from My hands, what I've given to bless,
    Take it and use it, for My righteousness,
And when My righteousness, is known to all.
    My glory will come, My glory will fall;
On all who desire, to seek My face,
    Who seek My glory, and My grace.
There will be no lack, for all will see,
    My power manifested, as you live in Me.

Christ's wondrous salvation, is there for all,
    Who hear His voice and heed His call.
So speak forth His words, they are words of life,
    They will bring men deliverance, from fear and all strife.
Then peace like a river, will overflow,
    To refresh every heart, restore every soul.
God's peace alone, passes all understanding,
    The world cannot give it, because it's not standing,
For the truth of God, in Christ Jesus as Lord,
    For the truth of The Word, that brings men aboard,
To the ship of faith, that restores the soul,
    The faith that saves, and makes everyone whole.

This faith comes to all, who call on His Name,
    The Name of Christ Jesus, The One who became,
The pure and holy sacrifice, the only price that would suffice,
    To purchase men, from death and hell,
    To save their souls, to make them well.
So call to Christ, and He will give,
    New life, new hope and a reason to live.
Then you will experience, the joy of The Lord,
    With the strength that it gives, by hope restored!

<u>GOD'S PROVISION</u> - Inspired by Daniel Chapter 2

Provision shall come, as a result of My grace,
So seek My will, and seek My face.
The wisdom you seek, you'll find in My Word,
My Spirit reveals, My Blessing assured.
So give out of that, which I've given to you,
Whether natural or spiritual, for I'll see you through.

I have always provided, for all that you need,
When you gave out of love, when you sowed your seed.
You have never suffered, want or lack,
For you've sought My hand, to keep you on track.
So give with abandon, and give in love,
Give with the heart, of your Father above!

God gave us His Son, knowing He had the power,
To live and to die, to be raised then in honour;
To sit and to stand, at His Father's right hand,
Till the plans of His Father, were accomplished as planned.
So trust in The lord, as your source and supply,
For all you have need of, to live and not die.

Trust in His Word, for He's faithful and true,
And what He has said, is what He will do!
He will meet every need, to keep you on course,
He'll supply from His goodness, for He is your source.
You can never exhaust, His abundant gifts,
If you'll give with His love, the love that lifts.

Come then Holy Spirit, and quicken this word,
To our hearts and our minds, for salvation assured.
We will trust The Lord God, and seek His Kingdom first,
Then thank Him and praise Him, for quenching our thirst,
With The Living Water, that comes from You Lord,
For You are our life, our one, strong cord!

GOD'S GOOD PLANS - Inspired by Romans 1

Do not worry and do not fret,
For I have never left you yet,
My plans for you are clear and true,
What I have destined, I'll surely do!

So place your hand in Mine, My child,
Be at peace, let no worry defile.
Your dreams and hopes, aspirations too,
For the dreams I have planted, will always come true.

The key to this confident faith in Me,
Is to always trust that I can see,
Your future and, the good I've planned,
So be at peace, I understand!

REDEEMER, SAVIOUR, LOVER, FRIEND!

Redeemer, Saviour, Lover, Friend,
I will love You to the end.
When my life on earth is o'er,
Take me to that heavenly shore,
Where I will join with all the saints,
To praise and worship, without restraint!
For who is a God like unto You, full of grace and mercy too?
Who can cleanse and make me whole?
Who can wash my spirit, soul?
Only You can justify,
Only You can purify!
Only You have power to change,
Only You can rearrange.
So take me Lord and do in me, all that you need to set me free:
Free to love you all my days, free to worship, free to praise!

PEAISE BELONGS TO THE LORD - Inspired by Romans 3

Let Your Name be praised Oh Lord, we pray,
On this and every single day.
For You saw us, in our fallen state,
You saw and did not hesitate,
To rescue us, from sin's dread power,
You saved us in, that very hour.

When You came and gave, Your life for ours,
You paid in full, You broke the power,
That sin and death, had o'er our lives,
You came, You gave, You sacrificed:
Your very self, to set us free,
So we could walk, in liberty!

Oh Thank You Lord, for what You've done,
Thank You Lord, for paying the sum,
Of all the sins, of all mankind,
So we could see, and not be blind;
See The Father's, love in Christ,
Believe and receive, His sacrifice!

No more a slave, to sin and death,
We're made brand new, by The Spirit's breath.
So now we come, before Your throne,
We bow our knees, to You alone.
You alone, deserve all praise,
You, we will worship all our days!

GO NOW MY CHILD - Inspired by Romans 3:30

Go now My child, leave Babylon,
  The price is paid, the battle won.
Leave your bonds and slavery,
  Christ paid your price at Calvary.
Leave everything, that leads to sin,
  Christ paid the price, your soul to win!
So purify, your hearts and lives,
  Come to The Christ, who sanctifies!
It is not by deeds, that you have done,
  But by your faith in Christ, God's Son.
He alone, has the power to save,
  He gave His life, then rose from the grave!
Death couldn't hold, our Dear Lord down,
  He has the power, He wears the crown:
The crown of life, and righteousness,
  He stands by His Father, in Holiness!

These attributes, we can have in Him,
  When we let Him come, and live within;
Within our hearts and lives, to give,
  New life to us, so we can live;
Live in the peace, and the faith He gives,
  Live in the love, and power to forgive.

When we forgive as we've been forgiven,
  He sets us free, from all sin's leaven,
No more corrupted, by sin's power,
  We're saved to serve, this very hour.
Saved to serve, with the love Christ gives,
  Saved to really, truly live!
Rules won't do it, you can't keep them,
  You'll break each one, you'll always sin.
So don't trust in your goodness or in your power,
  Trust in Christ Jesus this very hour!

NOT BY DEEDS - Inspired by Romans 4 & 5

It is not by deeds which we have done,
That we're accepted, that we can come,
Before the throne of God to pray,
Before the throne to hear Him say:
Welcome child, don't hesitate!
Welcome child, come and partake,
Of all that Christ has won for you,
Come believe, He died for you!

We're saved by faith and not by works,
So let's press in and never shirk,
To come before our Lord each day,
To sing and worship, hear and pray.
In order to enjoy relationship,
We need to commune so we won't slip.,
Into ways that lead to death,
But let His Spirit give us breath!

When His Spirit breathes on us we'll see,
All God's plans, for you and me.
Christ has prepared for those who choose,
To hear, believe and never lose,
The good, the grace, that He bestows,
Of all who come, their God to know!

Oh Holy God, we come right now,
We come to hear Your voice, then vow,
With hearts and hands and life to choose,
Your life, Oh God so we won't lose,
The destiny, You've planned for us,
A life of blessing as we trust,
In Christ as Saviour, Lord and Friend,
Redeemer, Lover, to the end

TO FULFILL MY WORK - Inspired by Romans 6.7. & 8

To fulfill My work, and fulfill My plans,
    Submit to My Spirit, for then you will stand,
Strong in the truth, I have given to you,
    Steadfast and faithful, to My call on you!
No man can walk, in perfection to atone,
    Only by faith, in Christ Jesus alone!
He is The One, who purchased us back,
    From sin and from death, to experience no lack.
The thief had come, to steal and to kill,
    But God had a plan, to destroy his will!

Christ Jesus became, The Pure Sacrifice,
    His blood and His life, alone could suffice!
Christ Jesus was perfect, in every way,
    Son of God, Son of Man, to prepare our way;
The way to God, by faith in His cross,
    Christ Jesus redeemed us, from all that we lost!

Now when Holy Spirit, calls us to faith,
    In the Christ of God, who conquered the grave,
Listen and hear, what He's saying to you,
    Listen real close, for His word is true!
Then take the step, that will give you life,
    A life that is free, from sin and from strife!
Cast all your care, on Jesus The Lord,
    Ask him to be, your Saviour, your Lord!
Then when you give Him, first place in your heart,
    His peace and His love, will never depart.
They will guide you and keep you, all of your days,
    From all that would hinder, His path for your way.
In His Holy Path, is blessing and peace,
    In His Holy Path, your joys never cease.
Christ is The Author, of all that is pure,
    His life and His light, will make your life sure!

<u>INCREASE MY CAPACITY</u> - Inspired by Romans 9, 10, & 11

Increase my capacity, Oh Lord this day,
    Increase my capacity, to watch and pray.
Increase my capacity, to worship You,
    To worship You, in Spirit and Truth!
For Whom have I, in heaven but Thee,
    And none on earth, can satisfy me.
My flesh and my heart, cry out for You,
    Oh make me Your own, alive and true!
Make me true to the plans, You have planned for me,
    True to the vision, imparted to me.
It is only by, Your Almighty power,
    That I can stand, and do this hour,
The work assigned, the tasks laid out,
    To do Your will, and never doubt!
So come inside, afresh today,
    Oh Spirit of The Lord, I pray,
Clean out what stains, and what defiles,
    So that my life, can be worthwhile.

Oh Holy Father, hear my prayer, I cast on You, my every care.
    I'll trust You Lord, for strength and power,
To do, what I must do this hour.
    Help me to live, with a grateful heart,
For every blessing, You impart.
    Then when I feel, so weak and tired,
Cause Your Word, to impart, inspire;
    The faith, to always seek Your grace,
For by Your grace, I see Your face!
    There in Your face, is mercy found,
Your grace and love, which know no bounds
    In all that You, have planned for me,
I'll walk by faith, and trust in Thee!
    For only what, is done for You,
Can bring Your blessing, make me new.

WHAT CAN WE SAY? - Inspired by Romans 11

What can we say, to Your grace Oh God?
    How do we respond, to such awesome love?
For when we were dead, in our trespass and sin,
    You reached out in love, to bring us within!
Now we have freedom, to hear and to choose,
    New life forever, for we have been loosed;
From all of the sin, that held us bound,
    Our chains You have cut, Your life we've found!
Your life is love, and mercy and grace,
    Now forgiven and cleansed, we behold Your face!
Oh wonderful Lord, Oh Awesome God,
    We bow and we worship, to give You all laud!

But then we arise, and stand to our feet,
    To show You the honour, at The Mercy Seat!
For here was the place, Christ offered His blood,
    To pay for our ransom, to save from the flood.
Our sins had tried, to snuff out our lives,
    But Lord Jesus Christ, redeemed by His life.

So now we can come, in faith with our prayers,
    Knowing, Oh Lord, that You hear and You care.
Your love is eternal, Your grace knows no bounds,
    Your mercy and goodness, have made our lives sound!
No more have we reason, to trip or to fall,
    Your Spirit is in us, to answer Your call.

So guide us today, Holy Spirit we pray,
    Guide us and teach us, Your Word to obey.
Then we can reach out, to the hurting and lost,
    Reach our in God's love, for Christ paid the cost.
Christ's blood and His life, He has given for us,
    His seal of redemption, has sanctified us!
Oh Lord, we thank You, with all of our hearts,
    We thank You for saving us all, not just part!

DO UNTO OTHERS - Inspired by Romans 14

Do unto others, as you want done for you,
    Judge not your brother, for you'll be judged too!
The measure you use, will be used for you,
    So do unto others, as you want done for you!
Let love be the highest, goal for your life,
    The love of your Lord, manifested in life!
The love of God cleanses, and heals and restores,
    The love of God gives, and receives evermore.

Don't let what you do, be a stumbling block,
    But let your life lead, to The Solid Rock.
It is only by faith, in Christ Jesus as Lord,
    That we live and we move, have eternal reward.
So on this new day, as you prepare to walk,
    Walk in a way, that matches your talk.
Show by your deeds, that the words that you speak,
    Are words that give life, and strength to the weak!

Let faith be your shield, to quench every dart,
    Let Christ be The One, who rules in your heart.
For out of your heart, come the words that you speak,
    So give of salvation, and hope for the meek.
Then blessed you will be, in all that you do,
    When you let His love guide you, to do what is true.
For everything comes, by God's awesome power,
    Everything exists, for His glory and honour!

How wonderful God, is Your knowledge of me,
    Cause me to know You, then really see,
How great are Your riches, wisdom and knowledge,
    Your Spirit and Word, have become our college.
So teach us and train us, to walk in Your power,
    To love You and serve You, in every hour.
By reaching and teaching, in word and in deed,
    The ones You have died for, Your Holy seed!

FOR JERUSALEM'S SAKE - Inspired by Daniel 9:1-19

For Jerusalem's sake, Oh Lord, I pray,
    Have mercy, Oh Lord, on Your people this day,
Cause them to hear, in their spirits, Oh Lord,
    Your Word in it's fullness, so in one accord,
They will turn from trusting, in their own foolish ways,
    Then turn to You Lord, from deception and pray!
What deceives looks and sounds, like a beautiful light,
    But hinders their hearts, and blinds their sight!
So reveal Yourself, in mercy, I pray,
    Reveal Yourself to, Your people today.
Give to them true, and repentant hearts,
    To see Christ Jesus, who did His part,
When He came and lived, and died for all men,
    Then rose to redeem, and cancel all sin.
Cause us all to become, that one new man,
    The man to show forth, God's love and God's plan.

Make us one Lord God, united to tell,
    The world of The Saviour, who saves men from hell.
Christ Jesus is Saviour, for the souls of all men,
    His blood paid the price, to redeem us from sin.
So Lord God I pray, remove all the walls,
    Of division that separates, so we can call
With one clear voice, Your call of love,
    The call to be saved, from Your Spirit above!.
For we are not saved, by the works which we've done,
    We are saved by faith, in The Christ, God's Son!
Forgive us Oh Lord, from trusting our deeds,
    For we could not save us, but You saw our need.
You came and redeemed us, You ransomed our souls,
    Your life showed the way, Your blood makes us whole.
So now we can live, by Your grace and Your power,
    Now we can live, by Your mercy this hour;
In faith and in hope, for You made the way,
    Our lives You redeemed, our price You paid!

GOD'S MEASURE OF WEALTH
Inspired by Romans 15 & 16

Live to please others, not just yourself,
    For then you'll experience, God's measure of wealth.
Do what helps others, to know The Lord,
    For then you and they, will reap God's reward.

Christ Jesus came, not to please Himself,
    But gave His life free, to impart us God's wealth.
For those who will call, on Christ's Name to be saved,
    All those He redeemed, from death and the grave,
Will receive of the blessings, the wealth God bestows,
    For then each will know, even as they are known!
To be known by God, as His own dear child,
    This is the wealth, that is truly worthwhile.
So let this mind also, be in you who love,
    The Lord your God, in heaven above.
Live in harmony, forgiving each other,
    Each with the attitude, of Christ toward the other.
Then all can join, in an anthem of praise,
    To The Lord God Almighty, The Ancient of Days!

Accept one another, as Christ accepted you,
    Then God will be glorified, in all that you do.
Jesus came as a servant, to redeem the lives of all men,
    He came with God's purpose, to reinstate again,
The ones God chose, and made for His own,
    The ones He is calling, to come away home.
So let's love and forgive, and serve all men,
    With the love our Lord showed, when He died for our sins.
We sinned and were sentenced, to death and the grave,
    But praise be to God, our life Jesus saved!
So let us acknowledge, and repent of our sin,
    Let's call on Christ Jesus, and then enter in,
To the incredible wealth, His grace has bestowed,
    The treasure that's greater, than finest gold!

LOVE WITHOUT LIMITS - Inspired by 1st Corinthians: 1

Oh Wonderful Saviour, Redeemer and Friend,
    Whose love has no limits, whose mercy no end,
What can we say, to such awesome love,
    How do we respond, Oh God above?

So we come before You, with our thanks and our praise,
    To reverence and worship You, Ancient of Days!
You made the way, when we were dead and lost,
    To redeem us and save us, You paid the cost.
You sent Your Dear Son, as Messiah and Lord,
    To restore and redeem, bring into accord,
Our hearts to Your own, by Your perfect love,
    The Blood of Christ paid, to bring us above!
Now we can sit with You, in heavenly places,
    By Your loving gift, beholding Your graces.
You make us partakers, to deliver from shame,
    All those who believe, in Your Holy Name!
Now all who are lost, like we once were,
    Can have their election, and calling sure.

For it is only by grace, that we all are saved,
    From hell and damnation, from sin and grave!
Oh God, You are Love, that redeems and bestows,
    The faith to reach out, to hear and to know,
That salvation is offered, to each person on earth,
    Who will call on Christ Jesus, by faith for new birth!
Help us never to boast, in what we have done,
    But clearly declare, how salvation was won:
That The Lord Jesus Christ, by His death on the cross,
    Redeemed us and set us, free from all loss.
Only in Christ, are we saved and set free,
    By His resurrection power, we have liberty;
Not license to do, whatever we will,
    But the liberty to walk, and to do God's will!

DECIDE - Inspired by 1ˢᵗ Corinthians:2

Decide to focus, on The Lord Jesus Christ,
For only His blood, and His death do suffice,
To bring us before, our Father above,
To receive of His mercy, His grace, and His love.
Let Holy Spirit, control what you do,
Let His Words with His power, flow out from you,
For then Jesus Christ, will be glorified,
And the power of God, will be magnified!
Then the faith of men, will not rest on your words,
But on the power of God, for salvation assured.

No eye has seen, or ear has heard,
No mind has imagined, the power of God's Word!
But if we believe, let His Spirit flow,
Then we will see, and hear and know,
The wonderful wisdom, and love of God,
As revealed by His Spirit, The Breath of God!
Now as God's Spirit reveals God's plans,
Our souls are set free, from the devil's demands.
Now we can walk, in the grace Christ has given,
Now we can lead others, to God up in heaven.

Heaven is real and hell is too,
So let us decide, to speak only what's true!
May our purpose in life, be to live for The Lord,
So all who see us, will not stumble but soar,
On the wings of faith, in Christ's blessedness,
Ready to receive, His righteousness,
As a robe to cover, to cleanse and restore,
To His life, as His child, forevermore,
With God as our Father, by faith in The Christ,
Our Saviour, Redeemer, our pure sacrifice!

WORK TOGETHER - Inspired by 1ˢᵗ Corinthians: 3

Work together, as partners, as a team,
For we are Christ's body, the ones He's redeemed.
Put envy and anger, and jealousy away,
For these works of the flesh, only cause you to stray,
Away from the plans, and purposes of God,
Plans for goodness and blessing, while on earth we trod.
Only God's grace, saved from hell and the grave,
It is only by grace, that we have been saved.

If we put our dreams, and desires first,
We neglect The Lord, who gave us new birth!
This birth was conceived, By God's Spirit, not man,
This birth empowers, and equips for God's plan.
So decide to have now, a bond servant's heart
For then you'll receive, what our God will impart.
God gave us His Son, to ransom our souls,
So give of His life, to restore and make whole!

God's life when imparted, bring blessing and peace,
His plans will bring healing, and souls release.
Now we can have, Christ's mind always,
We can know His voice, by His Spirit and pray,
Then listen for what, He's designed you to do,
And pray for His power, to do what is true.
For it is not by the strength, of our own hands,
But by Holy Spirit, that we'll sit, walk or stand!

So let us prefer, one another in love,
In the power God's given, from heaven above,
Let us honour each other, as more than ourselves,
Forgiving and blessing, while on earth we do dwell,
For then Jesus Christ, will be magnified,
Then Jesus' Name, will be lifted high.
Now when His Name, is lifted up high
His love will draw, all men to His side!

SERVANT OR CHILD, WHICH ARE YOU?

A servant or a child, how are you named?
Are you a servant of God, His Name to proclaim?
Then have the mind, of The Lord Jesus Christ,
Who left heaven's realm, to be our sacrifice;
To pay in full, the penalty of sin,
To redeem us, and save us to enter in,
To the realm of His Spirit, by His new birth,
Then bring forth His Kingdom, to all here on earth!

God first makes us, His child and His heir,
Then by Holy Spirit, He equips and prepares,
Our hearts to hear, and respond to His call,
To give Him our hearts, our lives and our all.
Then we can choose, from a heart of love,
A heart that's sold out, to our God up above,
To become a servant, of The Most High God
To seek His will, and give Him laud!

Let's prepare men's hearts, by being the link,
By all we say, or do or think,
To tell them of, Christ Jesus, The Lord,
The only way, for His blood was poured,
On God's Mercy Seat, to save our souls,
To ransom, provide, protect and make whole.
So don't judge, or brag, or complain of another,
But love one another as sisters and brothers.

Love is the key, that ransoms, sets free,
God's love pouring out, from you and from me.
Let His love propel us, into the world,
Let His love compel us, to preach His Word.
To all who are dying, who hurt and are lost,
Tell them of Christ Jesus, who paid the whole cost.
Then lead them by love, the love shown to you,
For then they will know, that your God is true!

236

ALL WE HAVE

All we have is from You, Oh Lord,
So bring our hearts into one accord.
Help us put away, all vanity and pride,
Then choose to live, by Your Precious Side!
For who have we, in heaven but Thee,
There is none on earth, can compare to Thee!
So help me Lord God, not to covet wealth,
But to give You my all, my very self,
As a jar of ointment, to anoint Your feet,
For You paid my price, at God's Mercy Seat!

I love You Lord, what more can I say,
Make me Your bond servant, this very day,
To hear and do, what You command,
To speak Your words, of life to man.
Only You, are The Author of Life,
Only You free us, from sin and strife.
Only You, have the power to save,
From hell and death, from sin and grave.!
So help me Lord God, to always bless,
To respond in love, and gentleness.

To all who would speak, an unkind word,
Give us Your grace, to forgive and then gird
Our minds and theirs, by responding in love,
So they then can see You, Father above!
Your goodness and grace, reach out to all men,
To restore, and redeem, to cancel our sin.
So Lord my God, have mercy on me,
Help me to show mercy, so all can see,
Your life, with its love, hope, and liberty,
That You give to all, who receive and believe!

THE TEMPLE - Inspired by 1ˢᵗ Corinthians 6:19 & 20

Lord Jesus Christ, we humbly pray,
   Forgive our sins, this very day.

Make us the temple, where You can live,
   A place from where, Your heart can give
      The words and deeds, that free all men
         To hear, The Saviour's voice again!
Remove the veil, that blinds their eyes,
   So they can see, the devil's lies,
      Then run to You, and get Your peace,
         The peace that brings, their soul's release.

For when we seek You and Your grace,
   You take us in Your heart's embrace.
      You show us love, like we've never known,
         You bring us to Your Father's throne!
What can we say, to such great love?
   Words can't express to You God above,
      The enormity of what we feel,
         Within our hearts that You have healed!
For now You have given us, brand new hearts,
   With tenderness and love that starts,
      A flow of life, and faith and grace,
         Of love that seeks, Your will, Your face!

So Holy Lord, to You we give,
   Our lives, our wills, so we can live,
      A life of love and grace and peace,
         To bring to all their soul's release.
Then with all saints we'll join to raise,
   Our hearts, our lives, in total praise.
      For You, Oh Lord, are God of all,,
         To You we kneel, to hear You call;
The call that says: Come unto Me,
   Come now, My child, I'll set you free!

LORD GIVE ME WORDS - Inspired by 1st Corinthians 10:13

Lord give me the words, that I must write,
   To give men faith, within the fight,
      Then see the power, that God does wield,
         By The Spirit of grace, and glory revealed.
For by Your Word, we have power to stand,,
   And by Your Word, we'll take the land.
      We'll preach Your Word, with glory and grace,
         So all can see, Your loving face.
Then when we see, the love that's there,
   Our soul is at peace, we release our care.
      By casting it all, onto You Dear Lord,
         Our hearts are brought, into one accord.
No more do we have, the worry and care,
   For You, Oh Lord, hear every prayer,
      That's offered to You, in faith and trust,
         For You, Oh Lord, are pure and just!

Now we can know, with faith assured,
   That You, Lord God, hear every word,
      And when we pray, Your Word to You,
         You answer with, Your will that's true.
Then in that truth, we walk in light,
   With power to see, with purer sight,
      What You are doing, Lord God above,
         What You want done, by Your awesome love!
For Your love conquers, and cleans each stain,
   So sin cannot, defile or remain.
      You keep temptation, from becoming too strong,
         Your faithfulness keeps us, all day long.
You give the power, to refuse the sin,
   You show us the way, to live within,
      Your grace and glory, and power to refuse,
         Your mercy has cleansed, we will not lose,
But triumph over all, that would hinder our way,
   Victorious to stand, in every day!

WHY DIVISION? - Inspired by 1ˢᵗ Corinthians 3

Why are there divisions, within God's Church?
　　For by these divisions, God's Name is besmirched!!
His Name is love, That's Who He is,
　　And if we don't love, are we really His?
Love prefers another, above oneself,
　　Love covers offence, love dies to self.

When our Dear Lord Jesus, came down to earth,
　　To be born as a man, in a lowly birth,
He left the honour, and glory of heaven,
　　To be our Saviour, from all sin's leaven!
He did not consider, His former estate,
　　He came to deliver, from sin and hate!
He showed us The Father, by what He said,
　　Then backed it up, by what He did.
He did what He saw, His Father do,
　　So men could be changed, restored, renewed.
Now consider The Lord, in all you do,
　　And do unto others, what He's done for you.

Love with compassion, mercy and grace,
　　Love in a way, so men see Christ's face.
Forgive one another, as God forgave you,
　　Show goodness and kindness, and gentleness too.
For then the Name, that's above all names,
　　Will be honoured and glorified, and given the fame
That's due to The One, who paid the price,
　　Who redeemed our lives, by His sacrifice.
When you think of all, He has done for you,
　　Consider your thoughts, and actions too.
Do you speak and show love, to all you meet?
　　Are your thoughts and words, to help the weak?
Consider then, what Jesus would do,
　　For then your lives, will show Jesus too!

THE BODY OF CHRIST - Inspired by 1ˢᵗ Corinthians 12 &13

The body of Christ, what a wonderful gift,
    To be parts of each other, our spirits to lift.
For when one is down, the other lifts up,
    Or when one is thirsty, we offer a cup.
This cup is salvation, it is healing and health,
    It's a cup of remembrance, and thanks for the wealth
That is ours when we honour, Christ Jesus as Lord,
    For then we are fastened, with love's strong cord.
We are fitted and fashioned, to be a body of grace,
    A body of love, beholding God's face.
What an awesome privilege, dear ones, is ours,
    To behold our God, who made all, even stars.

He made everything else, that is perfect and good,
    So we could partake, of all that we should.
Then we can show, what our Lord provides,
    So none will go hungry, so all can have life.
For in God's abundant, mercy and love,
    He gave us His gifts, from heaven above;
Gifts to enrich, and gifts to restore,
    His body, His children, to life evermore.

So whatever the gifts, God has given to you,
    Use them to bless, and give others too,
All that The Lord, brings into your life,
    Bless with the love, that frees from all strife.
God's love is the greatest, gift of them all,
    And then when you love, you answer His call,
To give of yourself, in love to each other,
    Now this is how we, are to love one another!
Jesus Christ calls us, His family and friends,
    So let us show love, and the mercy that mends.
Our Head in this body, is Jesus The Lord
    So let us all live then, in one accord!

THE BREAD OF HEAVEN - Inspired by John 6

The bread of heaven, came down to earth,
    To give men life, new hope, new birth.
He came to give, His life for man,
    For this was what, The Father planned.
He knew we could, not save ourselves,
    Our lives were stained, with sin and self.
We hungered not, for the things of God,
    But only hungered, for this earthly sod!
We knew there had to be more to life,
    But all we saw was sin and strife.
Then the Spirit of God, opened our eyes,
    To know, to see, and to realize,
That God The Father, sent His Son,
    To redeem, restore, to make us one;
One with Him so we could raise,
    Our hands and hearts, to give Him praise.

Now when we praise, The Lord, The King,
    His presence comes, our voices sing.
Now we are freed, from sin and vice,
    Free to receive, The Lord's advice.
So come to Christ, The Living Bread,
    For then your spirits, will be fed,
You'll hunger not, nor thirst again,
    When you come to Him, your life to mend.
God then restores, and gives to all,
    The grace to hear, and heed His call.
So let His Word, be part of you,
    And let His power, empower you.
Christ alone, has the words that give,
    Eternal life, so we can live;
Live with eternity, in our hearts
    Live by His Spirit, to never depart,
Away from Our Lord, The Redeemer, The Christ,
    For He purchased us back, by His sacrifice!

THE THINGS OF GOD

What can a man give, in exchange for his soul?
What can restore, renew and make whole?
Only The Blood of Jesus redeems,
Only His Blood cleanses and frees!

Oh hear The Word of The Lord, my friend,
Turn to The Lord, for you can depend
On every word, that proceeds from His mouth,
He will give you His faith, that removes every doubt!

You'll look at the world, with brand new eyes,
You'll see the ones, for whom Christ died!
You'll see by His Spirit, His love for all men,
You will know that His plan, was to restore again
The hearts of all, to His Father above,
So they could experience, the depth of His love!.

For all who experience, His holy love,
Will receive revelation, from heaven above.
For the things of God, are revealed to men,
Who seek to know, His will, His plan.
So come to God quickly, in Jesus Name,
Come to The Lord, His life to attain.

The world will hold you, no more in its grasp,
For you will receive, God's love that lasts!
Only God is eternal, is good and pure,
He will make your election, and calling sure.

He alone, has the power to save,
To redeem from hell, from death and grave.
Christ Jesus has conquered, these all for you,
So give Him your life, He is The Truth!!

GOD'S DOOR - Inspired by 1ˢᵗ Corinthians 16:9

What is the door, God has opened for you?
What is the door, that you're to walk through?
Is it a door, of life and peace?
A door to bring, your soul's release?
Christ is The Door, and the only way,
He will save your soul, this very day!

So enter in to the life He gives, enter in so your soul can live.
Walk in faith & hope & love, walk with The Spirit of God above.
He'll give His power, to conquer all sin,
He'll give you the peace, to abide within
The heart of The Father, where true love is found,
The heart of The Father, where mercy abounds.

Oh lay your head, next to The Father's heart,
He'll bring sweet comfort, you will never depart.
For the love of God, is so awesome and pure,
And the ways He leads, are plain and sure!
You will not stumble, when He holds your hand,
For in earth and heaven, all is at His command.

He will not hold you, against your will,
His heart is love, and He'll always fill
Your life and heart, with joy and peace.
If you give Him your life, and never cease
To let Him hold and cradle you,
His love and His grace, He will ever renew.

So when opposition, comes against you,
And against the door, that you're to walk through,
Ask for God's Spirit, to make the way,
He waits for your call, each and every day.
He will be your teacher, to save from the fools,
If you will invite, His Presence to rule!

Holy Spirit will teach you, the ways of God,
He'll clear the distortion, of those who mock God!
He will give you the power, to know and to do,
His will and His way, and His knowledge to prove
That the ways of God, are holy and true,
His ways are mercy, and love and truth!

Let Jesus The Christ, and His Spirit guide,
To love and forgive, when you're mocked and reviled.
For the power that comes, when you forgive men,
Will free them and you, from the power of sin.
Grace will flow free, to the forgiven, now freed,
Grace will be poured out, to redeem you and me.

What an awesome gift, this grace from God,
To empower our lives, while here we trod.
By grace we'll accomplish, the perfection we seek,
If we only acknowledge, to God that we're weak.
Then He will provide, He's just waiting to hear,
The cries of His children, the ones He holds dear.

God comes to our aid, as only He can,
For He has endowed us, with power to stand,
To face all the problems, that would try and defeat,
The plans He has purposed, our needs for to meet.
So let us call out, to our God up above,
For the grace He gives, to be perfect in love!

God's love will conquer, will erase every fear,
God's love will enable, to strengthen and cheer,
God's love will empower, to face every test,
God's love will endure, will bring what is best.
So stand still and see, the salvation of God,
Watch Him protect, with His Shepherd's Rod!

WEEP NO MORE - Inspired by Matthew 6:33

Weep no more, for what is past, is past,
    But seek for the treasures, of God that last.
Seek for His kingdom and righteousness,
    Then your life will be filled with blessedness.
The blessing of God enriches and seals,
    The hearts of men, to what His Spirit reveals.

Dear child, come close and hear The Word,
    The Word by which, salvation is assured,
Come now, draw close, then hear Jesus heart,
    So you will never, allow one part
Of all you are, come away from Him,
    For He has cleansed us, from all our sin.

The Righteous One, became sin for all,
    So we could hear Him, when He calls:
Come unto Me, all weary and sad,
    I will make your hearts, and spirits glad.
No more will you wander, forlorn and lost,
    I have called you by name, I have paid the cost!

Sin had a penalty, and death was the price,
    But The Blood of Christ Jesus, alone could suffice!
His blood was pure, for He did no sin,
    He paid the price, so we could come in.
He purged and cleansed, and then He made new,
    All those who come, for His living truth!

Christ is The Way, The Truth and The Life,
    Only in Him, are you freed from all strife.
Striving for things, will only cause pain,
    But peace can be yours, in Jesus' domain!
The peace He gives, passes all understanding,
    For the peace Christ gives, never has ending!

Christ's peace comes, from The Father above,
 And it comes to our hearts, in a baptism of love.
This love transforms, renews and refines,
 This love restores sight, to all who are blind.
This love leads the way, to seek out the lost,
 To release and redeem, from sin's awful cost!

Dear child, choose Christ, don't put it off,
 His love made the way, His blood paid the cost.
Damnation was never, God's plan for His seed,
 That's why He sent Jesus, so we could be free,
From all of the devil's, deception and lies,
 For he knows his end, he knows his demise!

So choose to love God, in all that you do,
 Then let His love speak, and reach out to make new
All of the ones, for whom Jesus died,
 So they can come now, and by His mercy find,
The true only way, of living is here,
 It comes by the love, of our Saviour so dear.

He'll not force His way, into your heart my friend,
 For he wants us to come, in free will to Him.
Not by coercion, but in response to His love,
 So all can come up, to His Father above.
There we will experience, joy without end,
 There every sorrow, and tear He will mend!

When Christ comes again, with His heavenly host,
 To gather to Him, all those who love most,
He will divide, as a shepherd His sheep,
 From the goats that only, would bellow and bleat.
So let us love God, with all of our hearts,
 Then love each other, as His Spirit imparts!

Please read the first letter of John!

WHAT IS YOUR NEED?

What do you do, about the state you are in,
    Do you murmur or complain, or talk to Him?
Only Jesus The Christ, can meet your need,
    Only He is God's Son, The Redeeming Seed!
He is The One, who came down to earth,
    He is The One, who by His birth, became for us,
God's redemptive plan, to bring all men to Him again!

    So what is your need, Oh child of Mine,
    What can I do, so you can shine?
    Shine with My glory, before all men,
    Shine to bring hope and release from sin!

Dear Father, I come to Your throne of grace,
    And ask for the grace, to behold Your face.
For when I come, before Your throne,
    To worship You, and You alone,
My fears and troubles, all pass away,
    Your love gives faith, that will not sway.
Now all that would trouble, body and soul,
    All that pains and wounds, to control,
You wipe away, with Your power and grace,
    So I once again, can behold Your face!

Father God now, I come to You,
    To make me whole, and make me true,
Heal and deliver, Lord, I pray,
    So I can walk, Your way today;
Full of joy, to give me strength,
    Full of power, to add the length, of hours I need
To accomplish the tasks, this Oh Lord, is what I ask.
    Thank You Lord, for all you have done,
Thank you for giving me, grace in Your Son!

CHRIST - MY SACRIFICE!

I thank You Lord God, for all You have done,
    I thank You Lord God, for sending Your Son,
My Lord and Saviour, Jesus, The Christ,
    For You Dear Saviour, paid my price.
Christ Jesus, The Pure, The Undefiled,
    It was You we mocked, we cursed, we defiled,
For by our sins, we were part of that crowd,
    And by our sins, we too cried aloud,
That The Christ of God, should be crucified,
    We didn't know, it was for us He died!!

Then You, Holy Spirit, brought us to faith,
    We were dead in our sins, our sorrow and pain.
What awesome love, Oh Saviour divine,
    That You should die, for me and mine,
And for all the people, on this big wide earth,
    To give us life, and a brand new birth!
What joy and peace, what love You have given,
    When we accept, Your life from heaven.
A brand new way, is opened up now,
    As we embrace, Your life right now!

Now we can see, with brand new eyes,
    The hope, by which we realize
And then partake, of the grace You give,
    The grace that makes, our souls to live.
For it is by Your grace, alone we're saved,
    Only by grace, can we behave,
As children of God, in truth and love,
    To show to all, our God above.
For it is only by deeds, which are done through You,
    That men are led to You, God of Truth!

Please read John 14:6

LET MY LOVE SHINE - Inspired by Matthew 5:14-16

There are some things, that you must do,
    To let My love, shine out through you;
Deeds of kindness, done in love,,
    To show to all, My face, My love!
For this is what, the world needs,
    So plant My love, like holy seed.
Even today, show forth My light,
    So all can see, with brand new sight
My love for them, by what you do,
    My love, that is forever true.

This world and all it offers men,
    Is temporal, and leads to sin.
Sin leads to death, and then to hell,
    But that is not, where My life dwells!
My plan is life, forevermore,
    I AM The Way, I AM The Door.
By Me, if all will enter in,
    Forgiveness comes, to free from sin.
So ask My Spirit, to lead The way,
    In how you speak, and how you pray,
For by your words, you are justified,
    And by My power, you are sanctified.

You are set apart, for holy use,
    To be a temple, that I choose.
Ask now for grace, to fill your day,
    The grace to seek My will and pray,
For all I have is yours if you,
    Will use these gifts for others too.
Go out today and share My love,
    So men may see their God above,
See Him in all you say and do,
    To lead them to The Living Truth!

GOD'S WONDROUS GIFT - Inspired by 2nd. Corinthians 9:15

We thank You God, for Your Dear Son,
    For by His deeds, our lives He won,
And by His sacrifice of love,
    He made us fit for heaven above!
So now Oh Lord, to You I pray,
    Extend Your grace, to me today,
So I can show to others too,
    The grace and love, poured out from You!
Help me to act like Jesus did,
    So men can see the way to live;
Not through force, to make the way,
    But by Your love, so we won't stray.

Let all we do, proclaim Your Word,
    So those who trust, can be assured,
That when we trust, in Christ as Lord,
    We'll walk in faith, and then we'll soar,
To heights of love, in heaven's bliss,
    To see Your face, receive the kiss,
Of love You give, to all who come,
    To honour You, and kiss The Son!

For all we are, and all we have,
    Comes from Your throne, and by Your hand.
Help me to never, hoard Your gifts,
    But share with all, the love that lifts.
For You saw us in, our helpless state,
    Then sent Your Son, to save by grace,
All who would change, the way they think,
    Turn from their sin, then come and drink,
The Water of Life, that satisfies,
    That always flows, to justify
The souls of all, who come to You,
    For eternal life, Salvation true

MY PSALM TO GOD - Inspired by Matthew 13:45 & 46

Holy Lord and God of all,
   To You we come, to You we bow,
      In adoration and in praise,
         To You Lord God, Ancient of Days!
You alone, are The One we love,
   We love You first, Oh God above!
      We thank You for, Your faithfulness,
         Your grace, Your truth, Your righteousness.
By The Blood of Jesus Christ, Your Son,
   You've made us Yours, forever one;
      One with You, by grace and power,
      One to stand, with You each hour.
For it is by Your power, and Yours alone,
   That we can come, before Your throne,
      There to receive, the love we need,
      To show to all, their God in deed.
For when Christ Jesus, came to earth,
   Was born of man, by virgin birth,
      Then lived and died, to save our souls,
      He made our wounded spirits whole!
Christ showed Your love, Oh God to all,
   By words and deeds, to save from fall,
      All men and women, boys and girls,
      The grace to choose, The Precious Pearl!
This is God's Pearl, the Pearl of great price,
   Salvation by trusting, Christ's sacrifice.
      No more condemned, to sin and hell,
      But turning to The Lord to dwell,
      With Christ alone in righteousness,
Then giving to all, through blessedness,
   The message true, the message given,
      The power to live, then go to heaven,
      There with Christ, to ever abide,
      There to live, by His Dear Side!

BOASTING - Inspired by 2nd Corinthians 12 & Isaiah 64:6

Boasting is all such foolishness,
    For who can take pride, in their righteousness?
All our righteousness, is as filthy rags,
    So who are we, to boast or brag?
The righteousness, of Christ alone,
    Provides for us, before God's throne!
He stands to plead, our case in heaven,
    For He alone, dealt with sin's leaven!

He cancelled the debt of sin, that damned,
    Our hearts and souls, to the devil's plan.
So focus on what, The Lord has done,
    Seek His kingdom, the total sum,
Of all He has prepared for you,
    To see His love, so pure and true.
His love shines out, to all mankind,
    To heal and save, restore our minds,
To what God planned originally,
    To be His friend eternally.

Sin will darken, will confuse our minds,
    But faith in Christ removes what blinds,
And shows us who, we are in Him,
    His child forever, freed from sin.
So come to Jesus and be saved,
    From death and hell, from sin and grave.
For who is like, our Precious Lord,
    Who has saved us, from the sword,
Of all the devil, planned for man,
    To steal from him, God's love, God's plan?
Christ alone, deserves our lives,
    He paid with blood, by sacrifice!
He bore our sins, our pain, our loss,
    When He saved us upon that cross!

NO ONE CAN DO WHAT GOD HAS DONE
Inspired by Ephesians 2:8-10

No one can do, what God has done,
    Christ Jesus paid, the total sum,
Of all God's justice, did require,
    Christ paid the price, went through our fire!
Destroyed hell's gates, by Spirit's breath,
    He took the keys, of sin and death,
For death couldn't hold, our Saviour down,
    He rose again, He wears the crown!

Now Christ stands, at The Father's right hand,
    There to defend, the souls of all men.
At the instant the devil, brings accusation,
    Upon us to Father, for His condemnation,
The Lord Jesus then, provides the reply,
    I paid their debt,, they'll live and not die!
The price to forgive, the price to make whole,
    The Lord Jesus paid, with His blood for our souls.

So do not tarry, waste time, or delay,
    Come to The Saviour, come and pray;
Confess your sins, and your foolishness,
    The pride that keeps, from His blessedness.
Receive the salvation, He purchased for you,
    Receive of His goodness, so you then can do,
The will of The Father, in heaven to bless,
    His children with goodness, forgiveness, and rest!

New sight will come, as you call out,
    His love will heal, no more will you doubt.
His Spirit will come, and live in you,
    To give you a life, and a love that's true!
And then with all, the saints You'll raise,
    Your voice to Him, in joyful praise!

STAND FOR THE TRUTH - Inspired by 2nd Corinthians 13

Stand for the truth, whatever the cost,
    Rescue the perishing, care for the lost.
Let the works of Christ, be seen through you,
    So all can see, that God is true!
God is true to His Word, His love He shows,
    To all who call on Him to know,
The saving grace, by Christ that gave,
    Our freedom from death, hell and grave.

Let the power of Christ, rule in your hearts,
    So from His ways, you'll not depart,
For He alone, is The Way to God,
    He alone, is The Truth of God!
He alone, gives the God kind of life,
    The life that frees, from sin and strife!
So let His Word, abide in you,
    So that His love, shines out from you,
For it's only love, that wins the war,
    His love will open, every door.
His love will cover, all our sin,
    The love of Christ, our souls to win.

So walk in love, and faith and power,
    Walk in His grace, this very hour.
Walk in the faith, that He will do,
    All that He said, to bring you through!
In that faith, is strength and hope,
    A life that lives, to more than cope,
A life that overcomes, all odds,
    So we can stand, before our God;
Dressed in Christ's Robes of Righteousness,
    Faultless to stand in holiness,
As sons and daughters, of The King of kings,
    To raise our praise, to Christ and sing!

THE WORD OF GOD - Inspired by Psalm 118 &119

Let The Word of God, dwell richly in you,
For then His light, will shine through you;
Shine to brighten, every dark way,
Shine to lead, those gone astray,
Back to the arms, of their loving Lord,
To be held and cherished, by love's strong cord!

The love of The Lord, is stronger by far,
Then the power of sin, that can only mar,
The plans and purposes, God has for man,
To set them free, from death and sin.

So let God take, your hand in His,
Taste His life, receive His kiss;
Then you will know, what real love is,
When you make the choice, to be only His.

This life is but, a passing stage,
To prepare us for, God's brand new age,
When we will reign, with Him on high,
Reign and live, and never die!

So Blessed Lord, hear now my prayer,
Make me Your friend, so you can share,
The way You want, my life to go,
So I can lead, to The God who knows!

I want Lord God, to bring with me,
The souls of those, You died to free,
From what the devil, had in store,
To steal from them, Your blessed more.
Help me to show, by word and deed,
That You Lord God, are all we need!

IN THE SPIRIT - Inspired by Revelation Chapter 1

John was in the Spirit, on The Lord's Day,
    When Jesus Christ, appeared to him to say:
        Write down now, what I say to you,
            What you will see, and send it to
The churches, so they will hear and know,
    Who they must hear, so they can show;
        The way to God, the way to live,
            To lead men to The One who forgives!
For the time is coming and coming soon,
    When there will be no sun, or even a moon.
        The earth will be lit, by The Glorious One,
            The God of all gods, The Holy One!!

Christ Jesus is coming, on the clouds of heaven,
    And all will weep, who chose sin's leaven.
        They will see The One, whom they had killed,
            Arriving in power, God's will to fulfill.
Then they will mourn, for not believing in Him,
    For not repenting, of all their sin.

So church, I say, as one with you,
    Let's be a lamp stand, with The Light that's true.
        Let us lift the Light, of God up high,
            So men can choose, to live, not die.
Let us live in the light, of God who loves,
    Who died for all, to bring above,
        The souls of all, He died to save,
            To ransom from death, hell and grave!
Let us realize, that we're only the stand,
    That holds The Light, to light all men,
        To The Light of the world, The Christ of God,
            So all can worship, all give laud,
To The Only Wise God, and King and Lord,
    For He is our joy, our eternal reward!

THE CORNERSTONE - Inspired by Zechariah 10:1-6

Judah means praise, and praise is just,
>And true and holy, for those who trust,
In the Living God, who gives them life,
>Who redeems, makes whole, removes all strife.
For who but God, can redeem our souls?
>Who but God, can strengthen, make whole?
He is the Good Shepherd, He guards His sheep,
>He never slumbers, He never sleeps
There is no other, god like Him,
>Who redeems our souls, sets free from sin!

Let us ask Him then, for the rain that brings life
>The former and latter, to cleanse from all strife..
Let us ask Him for mercy, and forgive us our sins,
>For trusting ourselves, not trusting in Him.
Then let us all praise, His Holy Name,
>And with all His saints, proclaim His fame.
God is mighty and just, He is holy and pure,
>The Blood of His Christ, makes our calling sure!
By giving His Holy Spirit to us,
>He has made us His church, glorious!

So lets take His glorious, message to all,
>To give them the grace, to walk and not fall.
To strengthen the hands, that seem to fall down,
>So they can be strong, to help others along.
Let us give to all, a hand to lift up,
>So they can partake, of Christ's loving cup.
The cup that He offers, is salvation and grace,
>The cup that He gives, will bless and will raise,
To the heights of God's heaven, where we will know,
>The Great God of Love, and His grace bestowed.

AWESOME GRACE - Inspired by Colossians 1

Oh what can we say, to Your awesome grace,
    This grace that helps us, see Your face;
For in Your face, is the perfect love,
    The love of God, from heaven above.
What words can express, our thanks and our praise,
    What words to extol You, Oh, Ancient of Days!
Lord we ask for Your wisdom, and glorious power,
    To live for You Lord, in this day and this hour;
To live in the light, that You shed on our way,
    To love You Oh Lord, when we sing or we pray.

We ask for Your mighty, enabling grace,
    To show to the world, Your love and Your face.
For when they behold, Your compassionate way,
    They will know and repent, and trust You this day.
They will ask You Oh Lord, to save them from sin,
    To be their Redeemer, to come live within.
Then joy of all joys, will be given to them,
    When they know they're forgiven, set free from all sin.
So help us proclaim, by word and by deed,
    Your love and Your mercy, to meet every need.

When we look at this world, and all of it's ways,
    We see that their need, is salvation today.
We ask You, Oh Lord, then to open the door,
    For us to show forth, Your love evermore,
So that we can tell, to those You bring near,
    Of the Love of our Saviour, The One we hold dear.
For You are the essence, of all that is good,
    By Your blood we are purchased, for our greater good.
You made us Your friends, by Your death on the cross,
    So we could be free, from all sin, death and loss.
Make us holy and blameless, by Your Spirit's power,
    To live for You always, this day and this hour!

<u>LET GOD BE PRAISED</u> - Inspired by Romans 3:4

Let God be praised, and every man a liar,
 If he thinks he can make it, by his own fire!
Only the fire of God, can make clean,
 Only God's fire, can cleanse and redeem.
God's fire will free us, from sins dread ropes.
 That would bind our hearts, and drown our hopes..
For when the fire of God, burns free,
 Our souls are redeemed, into liberty.
The liberty God gives, redeems and makes whole,
 His liberty gives freedom, to body and soul.

Then when our souls, have been revived,
 Our hearts and minds, can choose The Vine.
This Vine is Christ, The Perfect One,
 This Vine is Christ, God's Only Son!
He came, He lived, He died for man,
 He rose victorious, conquered sin!
Now when we live, and abide in Him,
 We're free from death, and hell and sin.
No more a prisoner, of fear or hate,
 His child we are, to enter His gate!

Christ is The Gate, that leads to life,
 Eternal life, that is freed from strife.
No longer slaves, but sons we are,
 To live for Him, and travel far,
To places we have never known,
 Then stand before The Father's throne!
There we will worship and adore,
 The Christ, our Saviour, evermore.
So don't delay, put out your fire,
 Come to The Lord, and get His fire.
He'll only burn, what traps your soul,
 He'll purify, redeem, make whole!!

REDEEM MY SOUL - Inspired by Psalm 62 and Romans 8:23

Redeem my soul, Oh Lord, I pray,,
   So I may choose, to walk Your way,
      Filled with Your Spirit, and by Your Grace,
         To stand in wonder, behold Your Face!
In Your face is love revealed, and in Your face, I see, I 'm sealed,
   By the greatest love, that I could know,
      By The Holy Lover, of my soul!

Oh cause me now Oh Lord, I pray,
   To seek You Lord, this very day,
      With all I am, so I can know,
         The joy and peace, that You bestow.
Now in Your joy, I find new strength,
   And by your peace, my life has length;
      The length of days, to do Your will,
         That by Your grace, Your will fulfill.

In Your will, dimensions decrease, when You create, all limits cease!

Oh Wonderful, Holy, Awesome Lord,
   Stretch out our tent pegs, by Your Word,
      Increase our faith, by knowledge given,
         The revelation, from God in heaven.
Then we can enter, Your domain,
   And free from sins restraints, remain
      A child of yours, by Spirit empowered,
Your child Oh Lord, each day and hour;
   Dressed in Your robes of righteousness,
      Faultless to stand in holiness,
Before the throne of God above, there to worship, there to love:
   The God of all gods, The King of all kings.
      Our Father, Creator, to praise and to sing!

AWAKE MY SOUL - Inspired by Psalm 57:7-11

Awake from your sleep, to seek My face,
    Awake My child, to mercy and grace,
Awake to the sound, of My still small voice,
    Awake to the tune, that makes spirits rejoice.
For then you will know, even as you are known,
    Then you will read, My truth and be shown.
For when you awake, to hear My voice,
    When you make, My will, your choice,
These words of Mine, will be shown to you,
    My words will give strength, in all you do.

The entrance of My Word, gives light and life,
    My Word gives direction, and frees from strife!
Striving is foolish, and harms your soul,
    So sit like Mary, and be made whole.
Mary sat at My feet, to listen and hear,
    My words from My lips, that warm and that cheer.
So allow your heart, and your spirit be still,
    Then quiet your mind, and listen at will..
For when you purpose, to hear My heart,
    Your fears will subside, your sorrow depart.
You'll know with assurance, that My plans for you,
    Are plans that complete, make whole and make true.

What I have decreed, I will bring to pass,
    My Word gives the power, to stand and stand fast.
So when arrows of doubt, or fear assail you,
    Take the shield of faith, to protect what is true;
These words I have given, into your heart,
    Will give you the strength to stand, not depart.
My Spirit will quicken, will equip and will guide,
    My Spirit will lead, will help, will abide.
He will give you the power, that transcends this earth,
    He will show you My face, and you'll know your worth!

IN YOUR PRESENCE - Inspired by Psalm 16:11

Let my soul be refreshed, and my spirit redeemed,
By Your Presence Oh Lord, by the light that streams,
From Your holy face, to illumine make free,
By Your Holy Grace, that cleanses my stream.

Oh Light of the World, You're the joy of my heart,
Oh Light of the World, You bring a fresh start;
For as the day dawns, Your mercies are new,
Your faithfulness comes, my soul is renewed.

Let joy be the watchword, today Dear Lord,
Let joy be my strength, to live in accord,
With all that Your Spirit, directs me to do,
So what You want done, will be done, pure and true!

For You are the Light, of my life every day,
You hear and you answer, every prayer that I pray.
You know all my thoughts, my hopes and my dreams,
Even when afar off, You know and make clean.

You purify all, by Your precious blood,
By Your Spirit, You lift us all up, from the flood,
Of all that would hinder, would tear and would drown,
The joy that comes, from lifting Your crown!

You Lord Jesus Christ, are The King of all kings,
You bore the cross, You felt the sting,
Of the cruel lash, that paid the price,
You became Lord Jesus, our pure sacrifice.

Your life granted us, a redemption that's true,
With healing and strength, and a life that is new.
Your life gives us life, to live in each hour,
A life that is born, by The Spirit's power.

SPEAK LIKE THE LORD - Inspired by 1ˢᵗ Timothy 5

Never speak harshly, to an older man,
But speak with respect, to honour each man.
Talk to each other, like brother to brother,
And respect all women, like sisters and mothers.

For we are all part, of God's family,
And He wants us to live, in purity;
Let us live in godly, responsibility,
With love and respect, in unity.

Let us work for others, as though for God,
With strength of heart, and hands to laud,
The God of all gods, who gives us the strength,
And joy that gives, our days the length,
To accomplish all, we are to do,
So that our lives, show service true.

For if we desire, to live for The Lord,
Our hearts must be, in one accord,
Ready and willing, and able each day,
To live for God, in what we do and say.

Let us back our words, by our good deeds,
So the Word of God, can truly feed,
The hungry and the thirsty, souls,
The hearts that need, to be made whole.

Christ Jesus is The Word, made real,
So let us share, with holy zeal,
The love of Christ, who our lives did save,
From sin and death, from hell and grave.

Holy Spirit, lead us we pray, to those who need God's love today,
Showing Christ, to every man, For He is The Holy Spotless Lamb!

SIGNAL TO THE NATIONS - Inspired by Isaiah 47-49

Signal to the nations, Oh people of God,
  Show them the way, Your Saviour trod,
Show them by word, and show them by deed,
  That we are His children, His holy seed.
Words won't suffice, in the task we are given,
  Words alone will not lead, men into heaven.
Nevertheless when words, are backed by deeds,
  Holy Spirit will cause them, to see their need.
He will sow God's Word, into hearts that will hear,
  He will draw them in love, to The Saviour so dear.

He'll direct our steps, and order our thoughts,
  So we can walk, like our Saviour taught!
We will walk in paths, of love mercy and grace,
  Paths that reveal, God's favour, God's face!
Now what we behold, is what we will be,
  His children, His people for eternity;
Transformed by His Spirit, and washed in Christ's blood,
  We're lifted forever, from sin's awful flood.
We are saved for a purpose, we are saved for God's goals,
  Saved to live freely, to offer men's souls,
The gift of salvation, the gift to know Christ,
  Our Lord, our Redeemer, our Pure Sacrifice.

Drawn near by His Spirit, each heart then is changed,
  For when we will listen, our lives He'll arrange.
No longer a wanderer, or slave to our fears,
  No longer a sinner, but saved to bring cheer.
For now we're a message, a letter from God,
  To tell to all men, that The God that we laud,
Is The King of all kings, The Saviour of all men,
  The Author of Life, The Yea and Amen.
He's Alpha, Omega, The Beginning and End,
  Our God and our Father, Redeemer and Friend!!

GLEAN TO ESTEEM
Inspired by Jeremiah 2:13 & John 6:37 & 38

Oh Holy Omnipotent Wondrous God,
    Help us to give You, our thanks and applause!
Teach us to worship, in spirit and truth,
    And to glean with a purpose, like faithful Ruth.
Sometimes it seems, like all has been done,
    Like there's nothing new, under the sun;
But then we open, Your Holy Word,
    And the truths You reveal, make our calling sure!
Forever and always, Your Words give us light,
    They lighten and brighten, the darkest night.
Your Words are alive, and fresh and new,
    Then made alive by Your Spirit, our lives are renewed.
We are given new vision, new direction and hope,
    We are given the power, to walk and not grope.
When Your light shines, Your life brings forth,
    The will to choose, Your will as our source.

No more will we draw, from cisterns of ours,
    We will draw from Your river, the river of power.
Then in Your river, we are cleansed and renewed,
    So we can partake, of Your holy food.
Oh Jesus, You are The Bread of Life,
    Make me, Oh make me, Your bride and Your wife.
Draw me in close, right next to Your heart,
    Hold me real close, so I'll never depart.
Only Your gracious love, satisfies my soul,
    Your love alone, has redeemed, made me whole.
Only Your Blood, could cleanse and redeem,
    Only Your power, could heal, take the beam,
Of the pride and the sin, that hindered my sight,
    To see with Your eyes, all men in Your light,
And then to extend, the same mercy and grace,
That You gave me Oh Lord, when You showed me Your face!

AGAINST WHOM DO YOU ROAR?
Inspired by Psalm 2 and Ephesians 4:8

Against whom do you roar, Oh nations of the world?
    You protest, you fight, but against whom with your might?
You fight and you yell, to get your own way,
    You bicker and quarrel, like children to say;
That you want to walk, in the paths that you pick,
    You want to rely, on that broken stick!
For that is all, that the devil is now,
    A broken stick, that cannot drive or plow!
He pretends to be mighty, he's got a big mouth,
    But he speaks to destroy, and he's going south!

God in Christ Jesus, took his power away,
    When He rose from the dead, that glorious day.
Captivity, He took captive, disarmed Satan's powers,
    So now you can walk, in freedom this hour!
Now you're free to awake, each brand new day,
    To open your heart, and your mind to Christ's way.
Say, Oh Holy Spirit, please open my eyes,
    To see Who is holy, and make Him my prize.
For Christ is The One, who opened the door,
    To life everlasting, and truth evermore!

So put on the armour, The Lord God provides,
    Then stand at attention,, at The Saviour's side.
Stand for the right,, the defenceless, the poor,
    Stand for what makes, your election sure!
Stand as a light, to lighten the way,
    To Christ as The Saviour, by night or by day.
Pray to Your Father, in heaven above,
    Ask Him for His, Baptism of love.
Ask Him to pour out, His Spirit of Grace,
    For then you'll walk true, beholding His face!

HOLY SPIRIT CLOTHE ME - Inspired by Ephesians 6:10-18

Holy Spirit of God, clothe me I pray,
With the armour of God, so that I can stay,
Near to the heart, and the voice of my Lord,
Near to hear His Word, and then give forth
The message He wants, to set people free,
From the devil's deception, and tyranny.
Give us grace Holy Spirit, to walk like we talk,
So we will not cause men, to stumble or balk,
But live in the love, Christ purchased that day,
When He died on the cross, our sins for to pay!

Help me speak, Holy Spirit, to decree and declare,
The Word of The Lord, that He wants me to share.
Let the Sword of Your Word, separate soul and spirit,
So that we can live, a life that has merit.
For You gave to Your church, the gifts that we need,
To equip us in spirit, in truth and in deed.
Let faith be our shield, and God's Word our sword,
Let truth be our belt, to hold in one accord,
The ones for whom, Christ bled and died,
The ones He has called, to come by His side.

Let integrity and righteousness, be our breastplate,
And salvation the helmet, that protects at the gate
Of our mind and our heart, from all that defiles,
So we won't be fooled, by the devil's wiles.
Shod our feet with the strength, of the gospel of peace,
And the will to speak forth, so men are released.
Then cause us to pray, in every occasion,
For all that would need, Your life and salvation.
Keep us ever alert, equipped to withstand,
Every power that tries, to defeat Your great plan,
Then boldly proclaim, Your redeeming grace,
So all can be held, in Your loving embrace!

FAITH TO SEE - Inspired by Hebrews 11& Revelation 3:18

Holy Spirit, I pray, cause me to see,
    The Light and The Glory, that comes from Thee;
For then I will know, even as I am known,
    The power, the life, that comes from God's throne.
Anoint my eyes, with your eye salve this day,
    So that I can see, all men in Your way.
Help me see and then pray, Your will to be done,
    See by The Light, of God's Glory, God's Son!
Cause me then to walk, in faith by God's Light,
    To meet every challenge,, by day or by night.

So when lions roar, or the flames get high,
    Help me to trust You, if I live or I die!
For I place my trust, in You Holy Spirit,
    To make of my life, as one that has merit.
Bring to pass the plans, You have prepared for me,
    So all then can know, and all then can see,
That Christ alone, is The God who saves,
    Who triumphed over, hell and grave!
Who rose victorious, Who reigns above,
    Who stands to give, God's grace and love.

Oh give us grace, now Lord, I pray,
    To confess our sins, and repent each day.
Then we can know, the joy You give,
    When sin is cancelled, as You forgive.
Then walk in the strength, and the grace that's given,
    To lead all men, to The Light of heaven.
Only You, Lord God, can save each day,
    Only You, have the power, that makes a way,
For us to come, before Your face,
    To boldly stand, receive Your grace.
So I bow Oh Lord, with worship and praise,
    I bow and I worship You, Ancient of Days!

TAKE A SEAT - Inspired by Luke 9

When you take a seat, at The Lord's command,
    When you cease from your labours, and seek His hand,
You'll receive of His goodness, compassion and love,
    You'll receive of the blessing, from God up above.
When the ones who listened, to Jesus' words,
    Listened and heard, from His life-giving words,
He commissioned His disciples, to give them to eat,
    So they could be fed and strengthened, not weak.
Five loaves and two fishes, were all that they had,
    The lunch of a boy, who gave all he had.

They brought this to Jesus, not knowing that He,
    Would take what they brought, to make them then see,
What happens when we give, of all what we have,
    What happens when we give, what we have to God's hand!
For what we give without stinting, is blessed by God,
    Is multiplied richly, for He's a blessing God.
As Christ gave the blessing, on the fish and the bread,
    Then distributed generously, five thousand were fed;
Were fed from the hands, that were offered to serve,
    The Lord Jesus Christ, The Living Word!

So take the time, for The Living Word,
    Ponder His truths, for salvation assured.
You'll not suffer lack, for those who take heed,
    To what Jesus says, by word and by deed,
Will have His abundance, to share with all men,
    With have to give freely, again and again.
And what is leftover, will be more than enough,
    For meeting your needs, you won't have it tough.
Every need will be met, by God's Blessing, God's Hand,
    When you listen and do, all He says, His Commands.
Honour The Lord, seek His Kingdom first,
    You will hunger no more, you will never more thirst!

ARE YOU THE CALLED? - Inspired by Joel 2

Are you the called of God today?
　　Are you the called, then watch and pray!
Watch and see what God will do,
　　Watch and see, His Word come true!
For what He has said, is what He will do,,
　　He will make a way, and a path for you!
His path will lead you, right into His light,
　　His light will lighten, the darkest night.
Your sons will prophesy the truth,
　　Your daughters too, will speak what's true!
Old men will dream, young men will see,
　　The visions God gives, so they can see!

When we receive by faith, God's Son,
　　For that is when salvation comes,
As our Redeemer, Saviour, Friend,
　　We're given life, that never ends;
A life eternal, full and free,
　　A life that lives for God, not me.
Then when our focus, is placed on God,
　　When we let Him lead, while on earth we trod,
No fire will quench, our faith in Him,
　　For now His Spirit, lives within.

Holy Spirit will keep, will guide and protect,
　　The ones who choose, for God to direct.
For this is what, our God desires,
　　To save all men, from hellish fires.
The day of judgement, is close at hand,
　　The day when God, will judge all men.
So call to The Lord, do not delay,
　　Oh hear His voice, hear Him today,
He'll forgive your sin, He'll make you clean,
　　When you call to Christ, He will redeem!

THE VOICE OF CREATION
Inspired by Romans 8:22 & 23 and Psalm 108:1-5

I will awake to the dawn, Dear Lord,
To the sound of the birds praising You,
For all of creation will raise its voice,
To The One who gives life, The Truth!

Your voice awakens us each new day, awakens our hearts to sing,
For this is the reason why we were born, to make all heaven ring!

You called and redeemed us, You made us Your own,
To stand and to worship, before Your throne.
So we'll join with all angels, and the saints that adore,
To praise and to worship You, Lord evermore!

So quicken my heart, to praises brand new,
To sing with my spirit, and a heart You've made true.
To sing a new song, that brings joy to Your face,
A song that extols, Your mercy, Your grace.
All that we are, and we have is from You,
Every breath that we breathe, is a gift from You.
Forgive me for taking, for granted this grace,
The grace to behold, Your mercy, Your grace.

Help me to see, with eyes made brand new,
That all that I am, and I have is from You.
Then let a song, of thanksgiving come forth,
For the Blood that was shed, the Blood that You poured.

You saw us, Oh Lord, in our fallen estate,
Then poured in Your wine, and Your oil on the break,
To cleanse and to heal, all the sorrows and tears,
You redeemed us Oh Lord, from each wasted year.
So I thank you and praise You, Holy Spirit for this,
Your wonderful love, Your matchless bliss!

CALLED TO PRAY - Inspired by 1st Timothy 2:1-6

You've been called to come, to this holy place,
    Here to behold, My mercy, My grace,
Here to pray, for the ones who rule,
    Here to establish, My holy school.
My people must hear, the words that I say,
    To hear and to worship. to speak and to pray,
The words I want spoken, the words that give life,
    The words that bring healing, from sin and from strife.
So don't help the wicked, those who hate The Lord,
    For this brings God's anger, His terrible sword!
Purify the land, of its idols that kill,
    That poison the land, take from people their will.

Know you are here, to please The Lord in this place,
    You are here to seek God, His mercy, His grace,
You are here to intercede, for the hurting, the lost,
    To bind up the broken, whatever the cost.
Just as The Lord, reached out and saved you,
    Reach out in His Name, in all that you do.
Don't tolerate sin, in whatever its form,
    For that would destroy, the reason you're born.

So if you must judge, judge to please The Lord,
    With mercy and truth, and love outpoured;
Not with whitewash, for that would be sin,
    But with mercy and truth so men can see Him:
Jesus, The Saviour, the Redeemer, The Christ,
    The God who forgives, by Christ's sacrifice!
So let men behold Christ, in all that you do,
    So their lives can be changed, and their hope renewed.
Then they'll give of their lives, to the One God who saves,
    Who's redeemed them from death, from hell and the grave!
So pray, and believe, with all I have called,
    To petition, to plead, to restore, what's been lost!

<u>GOD RULES</u> - Inspired by Ezekiel 38 and 1ˢᵗ Thessalonians 5

Lord God, You rule over the affairs of men,,
    You see our folly, You see our sin.
        And yet in mercy, You reach out,
            To quell our fears, and remove our doubt.
You pour Your Spirit, upon all flesh,
    You rekindle hope, our spirits refresh.
        You open our eyes, with Your anointing true,
          So we can see, what we're to do.

Give us the words of life again,
    The words to speak, to revive all men;
        To call to repentance, and to reform,
          Our hearts, our lives, to be reborn.
Cause us to die, to our sinful desires,
    Then ignite us Lord God, with Your holy fire.
        With love and passion, not considering the cost.
        Give us zeal and ardour, to win the lost,

The cost of our souls, was paid that day,
    Our sins were laid, on Lord Jesus to pay.
        Jesus, The Christ, became sin for us,
          To save and deliver, from sins awful crust.
Sin's crust had blinded us, to our state,
    We could not see, our doom, our fate.
        But then Your Blood, washed away our sin,
         Your Spirit quickened us, to faith within.

We saw ourselves, in our wretched state,
    Then called to Christ Jesus, in repentance and faith.
        You spoke the words, You gave us life,
         We're born anew, now free from strife.

Now born anew we can praise Your Dear Name,
    Born to live holy, Your Name to proclaim!

CHRIST IS COMING - Inspired by Matthew 24

We see from Your Word, that You're coming again,
    Coming to judge, the souls of all men.
Coming to separate chaff, from the wheat,
    Coming to separate, bitter from sweet.
You will punish the evil, with flaming sword,
    To purge the earth, and then give Your reward,
To all who stood, by Your Spirit's power,
    For truth and righteousness, in that hour.
So cause us to always, live in Your light,
    As children of day, and not of the night.
Walking always, in faith and love,
    Walking to please, our Father above.

Then we won't be surprised, by Your coming, Dear Lord,
    For we'll be walking by faith, in Your Precious Word;
Confident always, of the salvation You gave,
    That rescued our souls, from hell and the grave.
Oh Holy Spirit, keep our eyes on the goal,
    On Jesus our Saviour, The Lover of souls,
Till we cast our crowns, at His holy feet,
    Then to rise with all, the saints to meet,
Our God and our Father, The Ruler of all,
    Who reached out in mercy, to answer our call.

He saved and redeemed us, to make us His own,
    So we could come boldly, before His throne,
There to worship, there to adore,
    The Lord our God, forevermore!
Who can compare, to our Lord and our King,
    Who cannot stand, without a song to sing?
For God alone, sits on The Throne,
    He is Lord and God alone!
So come all ye saints, let us worship and praise,
    Our Lord and Redeemer, The Saviour always!!

IS WORSHIP THE CENTRE OF YOUR LIFE?
Inspired by Ezekiel 37:28

Is worship the centre of your life, My friend?
    Do you want a life, that has no end?
Then worship God first, in all that You do,
    Give Him the praise, for He is Lord of you!
Your work can be worship, if done in Christ's Name,
    If you walk in His ways, His Name to proclaim.
If you honour Christ first, seek God's rule for your way,
    He will see that your path, is cleared and made straight.
Stay clear off broad roads, they lead only to hell,
    Pursue the narrow, for on it you'll dwell,
Close to God's hand, that leads you along,
    Close to His heart, to keep you strong!
The narrow way, has room for just two,
    Christ and you, in spirit and truth.

For each must come, to Christ on their own,
    For Him to present them, before Father's throne.
Each one must make, the decision to come,
    To respond to His Spirit, who calls each one.

So gather with those, who seek God's face,
    But purpose to commune with Him, face to face.
You seek, to know God more, and that is good,
    So seek for His fire, to rekindle the wood,
To burn off the ropes, of religion and sin,
    To burn all that hinders, so you can come in,
Into the place, where God's presence abides,
    There to receive, His embrace at His side;
There to experience, what it means to be loved,
    There to worship, The God that you love.
Burn off the dross, all that hinders my prayer,
    Oh burn it off Lord, so I can enter there!
Oh God, You are, The One I desire,
    So purge me now, with Your holy fire.

MY HEART'S DESIRE
Inspired by Psalm 38:9 & 1ˢᵗ Corinthians 14:39

Dear Lord I want to preach Your Word,
   So all can hear, and be assured,
That they are saved, to live and dwell,
   Free from the curse, of death and hell.
So Holy Spirit, equip me now,
   To hear and listen, make my vow,
To live for You, Your face to behold,
   So You can form me, in Your mold.
Cause me to be, a vessel for good,
   A vessel that is filled, without a hood.
A vessel that can, be used to pour out,
   The words that give life, to remove every doubt.

Give me a heart like Mary, to sit at Your feet,
   To listen and worship, then take my seat,
Here at the place, where Your presence is found,
   Here to abide, in Your love which abounds.
Then in the silence, help me hear Your voice,
   So I can make, Your will, my choice.
For in Your Presence, is sweet delight,
   Only there, is perfect light.

Then come My child alone, be still,
   Be still to hear, My perfect will.
Quiet your heart, so you can know,
   The peace that comes, what I bestow.
You'll never suffer, want or lack,
   For I'm The One, who protects your back.
Forget those things, which are behind,
   Then let My Spirit, renew Your mind.
You will walk the paths I have for you,
   Paths of love, and peace and truth!

HEAR AND PONDER - Inspired by John 10:16

Hear My voice, and ponder still,
   Let all your thoughts, be on My will;
      For then you life, will stay the course,
         You'll have no fear, no dread remorse!
If you'll allow, My Spirit in,
   To cleanse and make, you pure within,
      What blessedness, and peace you'll find,
         You'll hear and know, you'll not be blind.
So seek My salve, to anoint your eyes,
   Then you'll discern, the devil's lies,
      And with My power, you'll cancel sin,
      And by My blood, you'll enter in,
      To where My grace and love abound,
      To where My peace and joy are found.

So present yourself, to Me this day,
   In worship, prayer, and praise always.
      I will be found, as you call out,
         In faith, not fear, without a doubt!
Oh let Me make, your spirit pure,
   Then you will stand, your calling sure.
      You'll press ahead, and not give up,
      You'll offer to all, My cup to sup.
Then together you will know, even as you are known,
   The joys that come, from Father's throne.
      Sweet peace and comfort, joy and love,
      These gifts are there, as you come above.
So come in faith, to there possess,
   My grace and love, My righteousness.
      And let My Spirit, direct your thoughts,
      For by My Blood, your life was bought.
Now take back all, that the devil stole,
   Possess it now, receive My gold!
      Establish now, My kingdom rule,
      Your heart and mind and soul to school!

<u>YOU SHALL BE HOLY</u> - Inspired by Ezekiel 33

I have created you in, My image to bless,
    To speak My Word, in righteousness.
Not with pious platitudes,
    But with truth and purity, in servant hood.
You asked to be, My bond slave once,
    To hear My voice, to feel My touch,
But now I have, much more for you,
    Revelations to give, that are deep and true.
So come real close, come by My side,
    Listen now, and then abide.
I have much more, to say to you,
    Words to give, to bring forth truth.

My truth will pierce, each inward part,
    So from My side, you won't depart.
My truth will open, each new door,
    For you to serve Me, more and more.
So let My Word, have its effect,
    Let it divide, make true, correct,
For then you will, by word and deed,
    Fulfill My will, plant holy seed.

Oh Holy Spirit, fill me now,
    Help me to keep, my solemn vow,
A vow to always, speak Your Word,
    In truth to purify, make sure,
The words that You, want spoken to men,
    The words that will, convict of sin.
Then when men see, their fallen state,
    They'll turn to Christ, not hesitate,
To forsake the sin, that had them bound
    They'll choose the life, where grace abounds!

FORGIVE ME - Inspired by Proverbs 29:25

Forgive me for, the times when I,
    Was fearful, to correct the lies.
Grant me a boldness, to proclaim,
    The glory of, Your Holy Name!
I ask now Lord, for another chance,
    To share Your word, and then enhance
By word and deed, Your Name, Your Face,
    So all can come, receive Your grace.

For we could never, save ourselves,
    Only Your grace, provides true wealth;
The wealth of having, sins forgiven,
    The wealth to live, for God in heaven.
This is the wealth, no money can buy,
    For by Your wealth, I'll never die,
But live in life, eternal to hold,
    The life You give, more precious than gold.

So help me cast off, all that hinders now,
    Then present myself, as a living vow,
To let You do, Your will through me,
    In such a way, that men can see,
The Living Word, The Christ, The Lord,
    The One whose blood, for me was poured!

Draw near Oh Lord, teach us to pray,
    As we begin another day;
To pray Your will, on earth as in heaven,
    To remove all sin, all doubt, all leaven.
For what puffs up, is pride and sin,
    So burst our bubbles, so truth can win,
Then in Your truth, our lives are lit,
    And placed on high, like a candlestick!
To give forth light, the light that leads,
    To Christ who saves, God's Holy Seed!

MY SOUL'S DELIGHT - Inspired by Isaiah 64-66

Oh, be the one, in whom My soul delights,
    Flee from the darkness, and flee from the night.
Exhibit My glory, in all that you do,
    So all can see, that My Word is true!
You've come to this place, at this time, by My grace,
    You've come to serve Me, and to seek My face.
You've put your desires, and your plans on hold,
    To seek for what's true, more lasting than gold!
So then My dear child, rest in My embrace,
    Look up and behold, My measureless grace.
My grace will perfect you, bring joy and peace,
    My grace will enable, your soul's release.
For what is now in your soul, must be transformed,
    Must be cleansed and redeemed, away from the norm.

    Come away My beloved, up to where I AM,
    Come away to receive, My will and My plan.
    Come for the direction, My Spirit will give,
    Come up and receive, so your soul can live.

What comes from My hand, is more precious than gold,
    It's the eye salve to see, what I will unfold.
For I speak to My children, in visions and dreams,
    I speak in a way, so you'll seek what's concealed.
I want your passion, and your will to pursue,
    With wholehearted devotion, My words that ring true.
For only My Word, by My Spirit can lead,
    To the pastures and streams, where My children can feed.
So now in the quiet, and calm of this day,
    Listen and ponder, the words that I say.
Listen then wait, till I tell you to go,
    For then doors will open, and you will know,
That the plans I have for you, I will perfect,
    And what I want done, in you I will erect!

THIRTY SILVER COINS - Inspired by Matthew 27 & 28

Thirty silver coins, were all that were paid,
　　To betray The Lord Jesus, to Judas that day.
The price of a slave, was the given amount,
　　Thirty pieces of silver, was the total count.
When Judas realized, what he had done,
　　When he realized their intent, to murder God's Son,
He was filled with remorse, for his terrible deed,
　　Was filled with remorse, o'er his spirit of greed.
But remorse didn't lead, to repentance for him,
　　For repentance means turning, away from our sin;
Turning to the only, Redeemer, The Christ,
　　Jesus, The One, who paid The Price!.

We look at Judas, and the priests of that day,
　　We condemn them all, for their actions always,
But would we have been better, if we had been there?
　　It is only God's grace, that we know Him and care;
Care that the Lord Jesus, Our Saviour, The Christ,
　　Paid for our sins, by His sacrifice.
He became our sin, who knew no sin,
　　Carried our burdens, and our pains on Him.
For He died on the cross, that day to provide,
　　Our soul's salvation, and then to abide,
By His Spirit into, each and every soul,
　　Who call out His Name, to be cleansed and made whole.

For only the Holy, Precious Blood, of The Christ,
　　Has paid sin's cost, to redeem us from vice.
We were all dead, in our trespass and sin
　　Until The Lord Jesus, paid with His life to win.
To win from the devil, the souls of all men,
　　To take back the keys, so we could come in,
To the abundant life, He's prepared for us,
　　A life that has promise, that lifts from the dust!

Jesus Christ didn't stay, in the grave always,
   But rose from the dead, upon the third day.
So now as we believe, on The Lord Jesus Christ,
   Our lives can be changed, by His sacrifice!
The Blood that Christ shed, was offered to pay,
   Our ransom from death, and hell and decay.

So now that you know, there is freedom for you,
   What will you do? — Whom will you choose?
Will you choose to follow, in Judas' path,
   To experience all death, all hell and all wrath?
Or will you turn to The Saviour, The Lord Jesus Christ,
   The Anointed of God, The Pure Sacrifice?

Will you call out to Him, to forgive your sin?
   Will you answer His call, to repent and come in?
If you do, you'll experience, His matchless grace,
   That comes from seeing, the love on His face.
You will know the joy, of sins forgiven,
   You'll receive the peace, from God in heaven.

Oh the great peace and joy, that is ours,
   For now we can know, His love, each hour.
We'll know God, The Father, we'll know Christ, The Son,
   We'll know Holy Spirit, The Three in One!!
We'll know by faith, and grace bestowed,
   That Christ paid the price, to remove sin's load.

So now, what shall we say, to Him?
   To God, The Christ, our Redeemer from sin?
Let us say with our heart and our souls as well,
   Oh save me, Christ Jesus, right now where I dwell.
Reveal to me now, by Your Spirit's power,
   That I am your child, this moment, this hour.
Fill me with the joy, from sins forgiven,
   The joy that's my strength, to fit me for heaven!

LET CHRIST CARE - Inspired by 1st Peter 5:7

Let Christ displace worry, at the centre of your life,
  Let Him remove, all the sin and the strife.
Keep your eyes always fixed, on the heavenly goal,
  For there you will find, what refreshes your soul.
Don't fret or worry, cast your cares on The Lord,
  For He paid the price, He is The Door—
The door to a life, everlasting and free,
  The door to the more, He has planned us to see.

We haven't yet arrived, to the place where we,
  Have perfect sight, but we're straining to see,
With passion and purpose, to fulfill God's will,
  To keep on the right track, by His Spirit until,
We reach the perfection, He has for all men,
  Till we are presented, to God to win:
The Crown of Righteousness, prepared by Christ,
  To all who received, His sacrifice!!

So let's keep focused, on Jesus The Lord,
  Let's allow His love, to be the strong cord,
That binds our hearts, and our souls to Him,
  That keeps us pure, and free from sin.
For sin will entangle, and trip us up,
  It will take our eyes off, of Christ's will, His cup.
His cup holds provision, and the power to do,
  His will and His plan, to perfect in you,
His image in all, that is said and done,
  To reach the goal, to be like His Son!

Remember then child, where you belong,
  Remember who gave you, the life to be strong,
Remember The Lord, in all that you do,
  Remember, He's waiting, in heaven for you!
So if your cross, seems too much to bear,
  Cast your burdens on Him, knowing He always cares!

NO ONE IS LIKE OUR GOD! - Inspired by Isaiah 11 & 51,

Who is a god like unto our God, or a lord, like unto our Lord?
For all of the heavens and earth are His, to bring into one accord!
To establish His will in righteousness, to bring into perfect peace,
This is the will of God on High, whose mercies never cease!

So Holy Spirit, come to me now, and hear my earnest plea,
Make me a vessel, You can use, a soul restored, redeemed!
I am nothing Lord, without Your power, to lead and guide my way,
So take my hand, and give me strength, to seek Your will always.

Fill me afresh, as the day begins, cleanse me from secret sins,
For I desire Your fire, Oh Lord, to make me pure within.
Remove from me each hidden part, that hurts Your heart today,
Possess my soul and spirit Lord, Oh guide me in Your way!

Then Lord I ask, that You would lead me, to the ones who fear,
Who do not know, Your love or grace, who need Your love to cheer.
They do not know their value, they don't know why You came,
So help me show, by word and deed, the love that's in Your Name!

Your love and mercy, You pour out, to bring us to that place,
Where we behold You in Your power, Your Awesome Holy Face!
What we behold, we can become, for by Your love, we're free,
From all the devil tried to snuff, by sin and tyranny.

The Blood of Jesus washes us, from every sin and stain,
When we submit unto Your grace, to make us pure again!
So forgive our sins, Oh Lord I pray, forgive each one of us,
Make us Your children pure and clean, remove all sin and lust.

Cause us to walk Lord, in Your light, to leave the dark and vile,
So that with all Your children Lord, we'll go that extra mile!
Then when You come to earth again, to bring us home to God,
We'll bow with all the saints to praise, The Holy God we laud!

THINK ON THESE THINGS - Inspired by Philippians 4

What are the things that are holy to you?
What are the things that are lovely?
What are the things that are pure and true?
What are the things that are comely?

Ponder then My child, for My Word is true,
It shows you The Way. The Life and The Truth.
My Word will lead, by the way you should go,
It will lead to The One, who always knows.

My Spirit will quicken, My Word that is true,
He will show you the paths, that are good for you.
He will lead you right to, the pastures that feed,
To the place where you, will never have need!

That place is My Presence, a place to abide,
A Strong Rock to lean on. The shelter to hide.
Then from that place, of feeding and rest
You will rise and go out, for your soul is blest.

I will send you out, with My Living Word,
A word of peace, so your life is assured;
Assured of a place, of purpose and plan,
A place where you, can extend My hand.

For people must see, My Hand and My Face,
If ever they'll know, of My mercy and grace.
For in My hand, is pure mercy and love,
The love of My Father, from heaven above.

So as you walk out, in My world today,
Give forth of the words, Holy Spirit would say.
My Words, by My Spirit, will come with My power,
They'll transform and bless, those who hide and who cower!

In My Word, is The Living Bread,
And the power and will, to choose life instead!
So feed on My Word, for strength My child,
Feed on the good, the pure, undefiled.

Now your soul and your spirit, will be renewed,
By My Living Word, My Holy Food.
For you cannot give, if you do not have,
So ask for your eyes, My healing salve.

Then you will see, precious truths unfold,
The truths that enrich, your spirit to mold
Into My image, so that men can see,
My glory, My wisdom, that come forth from thee!

My glory will shine, to illumine the souls,
Of those I desire, to cleanse and make whole.
My glory will transform, will heal the hearts,
My glory transcends, renews every part.

For what My Glory reveals, is My holy love,
The love that transforms, from heaven above.
This love is best shown, by those I have changed,
The ones I've forgiven, their lives rearranged.

So be the ones, who carry My Light,
Who carry My Light, in the darkest night,
Into the places, where souls can be freed,
For I AM the answer, to everyone's need.

I pour in the wine, to cleanse and renew,
Then anoint with My oil, to heal and make true,
All of the good, I have destined for man,
Then give of My power, to evermore stand.
Stand in the faith, that I AM your God,
Stand for the truth, while on earth you trod!

<u>LET US GO TO GOD'S HOUSE</u> - Inspired by Zechariah 5-8

Come let us go, to the house of our God,
   Come let us rise, to His courts up above;
   Rise with worship, and praise on our lips,
      Rise up to The One, who strengthens, equips.
For what He has called us to do, we will do,
   We'll proclaim that His words, are alive and true,
   For He offers us peace, and life without end,
      If we will give Him, our lives to mend.

He takes what we give Him, though tattered and torn,
   Then fashions anew, our lives are reborn.
   Then as each new day dawns, we are alive,
      With a power to live our brand new lives.
His mercies are new, every morning to all,
   Who welcome His voice, who await His call,
   To receive His grace, to embrace His truth,
      Who truly repent, from all that's uncouth.

Now we can stand, for what's pure and what's right,
   Now we can walk, by day or by night,
   Without fear or dread, for we've tasted His grace,
      For now we have seen, the love on His face.
God, in Christ Jesus, has come by His Spirit,
   To grant us a life, that will never no limits.
   Now we can give, and forgive by His power,
      Now we can live, for our God every hour.

So let's trust Holy Spirit, to guide and direct,
   For then by His power, our homes He'll erect,
As places of love, where God can rule,
   As places of mercy, and grace then to school
   The ones that He brings, His love to embrace,
      The ones that He longs to heal by His grace.
Then when our lives, line up with His will,
   We will know His peace, our hearts will be stilled!

WHAT CAN YOU OFFER? - Inspired by Isaiah 66

What can you offer, your God and your King?
What is the substance, of what you can bring?
What can you give, so your soul can live?
What can you give, that won't pass through a sieve?

For all that we see, shall soon pass away,
All will be destroyed, by death and decay,
Only the eternal, forever shall last,
Only God's truth, can redeem our past!

So come to The Lord, as a sacrifice,
Present yourself to Him, to be cleansed from all vice.
Ask Him to burn off, all of your sin,
The lies and deceit, that would lurk within.

Only the pure, in heart shall see God,
Only the pure, can walk as Christ trod.
Nothing hindered, Jesus eyes to see,
What The Father wanted done, for you and for me.

So let us give of ourselves, afresh every day,
To our God who hears, every prayer that we pray;
Let us submit to, His Holy fuller's soap,
To cleanse us, so we can live in full hope.

The greatest salvation, every offered to man,
Is faith in Lord Jesus, who came by God's plan;
For even our faith, in Christ Jesus is God's gift,
The gift to believe, by Holy Spirit who uplifts.

He lifts hearts and minds, and our bodies as well,
To live in the place, where our Saviour dwells.
So let's always stay, near the heart of our Lord,
Ready to hear, and obey His pure word.

FAITH AND OBEDIENCE - Inspired by 1ˢᵗ John 5:1-5

By faith and obedience, our love is made pure,
By faith in Christ Jesus, our calling's made sure.
So Holy Spirit, I ask you today,
Create in me, a pure heart always.

Wash me clean, and show me how,
To live for Christ, to kneel and bow,
So I can stand, before Your throne,
Saved by faith, in You alone!

Dress me in robes, of Your Righteousness,
That come by the grace, of Christ's blamelessness.
For by His Precious Holy Blood,
I stand redeemed, cleansed from sin's flood.

For all the blessings, You have given to me,
I will stand in faith, and liberty,
And then declare, to all Your ways,
So they can know, and give You praise.

For all that I am, and I have is from You
And all I desire, is to always be true,
So those who hear me, pray or talk,
Will know the way, that they should walk.

Cause us to be true, in whatever we say,
True to Your Will, in the prayers that we pray,
True to uphold, Your Name above all,
True to say yes, when You issue Your call!

Help us preach Your Word, whatever the cost,
So men can be saved, and regain what was lost;
Communion with You, as Father to son,
Restored to walk freely, with Jesus, Your Son!

SIT AND WAIT - Inspired by Psalm 111 and Revelation 8 & 9

I sit and wait with pen in hand, ready to write at Your command,
Ready to hear, Your still small voice,
Ready to make, Your will my choice.

    Then write, what I will say to you,
    Let the words you write, be pure and true,
    For I have much, to say this day,
    So that your feet, will never stray.

Don't look to men, as your strength or source,
But seek My face, My will, My course.
Then as you do, I will make it plain,
My will for you, will not bring shame.
Instead I'll lead, to open doors,
Doors that lead, to foreign shores.
For the work I have, prepared for you,
Will lead men to, The Living Truth!

Only in Christ, is truth to be found,
Only in Christ, do mercies abound.
What is needed, this day and this hour,
Are the grace and the mercy, that come by My power.
For what can you give, that's not given to you?
How can you forgive, if your love is not true?
True love must be, at the foundation for then,
My grace and My mercy, can be shown unto men.

So look today, for God's ways to be shown,
Look for the way, to make His Name known.
And then with the power, He has given to you,
He will give His anointing, to make each word true.
With His truth comes the light, to see The Way,
The light of His love, to welcome the strays.
This is the day, for the strays to come home,
To receive God's grace, before God's throne!

291

FATHER, HELP ME - Inspired by Romans Chapter 8

Father help me to do, what You want done,
   So Your Name will be glorified, in Your Son!
      Help me to lift You Name, on high,
         So men may see You, and never die!
For The Name of Jesus, has the power to save,
   Only He redeems, from hell and grave.
      Only He can release, from sin and death,
         Only He can give men, life and breath.

So I thank You Lord and praise you too,
   For the work that You, have called me to do.
      The yoke You have chosen, for me to wear,
         Is not grievous or hard, for You put it there.
You have formed and made it, especially for me,
   So that I would put, my trust in Thee;
      To help me carry, my particular load,
         With grace and faith, not kicking the goad.

Cause me always to listen, for Your still small voice,
   Then ever to make, Your will, my choice.
      For only You, have saved my soul,
         You've given me grace, and made me whole.
Now I present myself to Thee,
   Use me to set, the captives free.
      By praise and prayer, help me use Your power,
         To see Your will, accomplished this hour.

May Your Name, Lord Jesus, be lifted high,
   As the only way, to never die,
      For You alone, are pure Truth and Life,
         You are The Way, that frees from strife.
By You we enter the perfect rest,
   Whereby our souls are truly blest.
      So help me to cease, from striving Lord,
         For then my faith, can truly soar!

EXPAND YOUR HOUSE WITH FAITH-Inspired by Isaiah 54

I will sing to You Lord, for though barren indeed,
    You saw me and granted to me, precious seed.
The seed of Your Word, established my soul,
    And gave me the grace, to live, be made whole.
So now in faith, by Your Spirit and Word,
    I'll expand my house, by Your Word assured.
I will not fear, I'll not suffer shame,
    For You have redeemed, and restored by Your Name!

You called me back, and made me Your own,
    Now I can come boldly, before Father's throne;
Boldly for help, in each time of need,
    Bold to receive, of Your Precious Seed.
Your Word is The Seed, that has life to give,
    Your Word is The Seed, that I must give,
To encourage the hearts, of the broken and lost,
    To receive Your salvation, that paid their cost.

This is the covenant, You made with man,
    That forgiveness is given, to redeem from sin,
To all who would call out, in faith to receive,
    Forgiveness from sin, and the will to believe.
So believe that Christ Jesus, paid with His life,
    Became sin for us, to redeem us from strife.
He'll fill you with love, like you've never known,
    Pure love in abundance, from Father God's throne!

So rejoice child of God, in what you've been given,
    Rejoice for Christ Jesus, made the way to heaven.
Rejoice for the faith, that's been given to you,
    Rejoice in God's Son, for His mercy on you.
Rejoice for your barrenness, is no more,
    For Christ has become, your open door:
A door to life, which knows no end,
    A life that knows Him, as Saviour and Friend!

YOUR RESPONSE TO THE CALL - Inspired by John 6 & 7

What do you do, when you hear God's Words,
The Words by which, your life is assured?
Do you hear and listen, and then obey,
Or do you take the wide, the easy way?
The choice is yours, will you stay and abide,
Will you stay right close, to The Saviour's side?
Does His Holy Word, seem hard to understand,
Does it seem too much, to take His hand?

Oh child of God, you will only live,
When you choose to hear, the words He gives,
When you choose to let, Christ take your hand,
And lead you to, His Promised Land.
This is the land, where God is King,
Where the rocks cry out, and nature sings!
This is the land, of pure delight,
Where sight is given, no dark, no night!

In God's land, is eternal day,
Where death and darkness, flee away,
Where sight is given, to what is true,
Where God reveals, His will for you!
You will walk with joy, in every step,
Held by His hand, by His Spirit kept.
No more a wanderer, seeking the way,
For now His love, keeps you always,
As a shield to watch, your heart and mind,
And a guard to protect you, from behind.

So come to The Lord, do not delay,
Forsake this world, it's evil ways,
Leave behind, what maims and kills,
Enter now dear child, to His perfect will!
Give your spirit and will, and life to Him,
Forsake your plans, and abide with Him!

THE LIGHT OF GOD - Inspired by John 1:1-12 and John 8:12

Your light is the light, that purifies,
That redeems, that restores, that clarifies.
Your light reveals, the devil's lies,
The lies that come, to traumatize.
For he cannot speak, a word that is true,
He only can muddle up, what is truth!
So when God's Word, doesn't seem real clear,
And when your path, seems dark and drear,
Look to The Lord, The Giver of Light,
He'll turn your darkness, give you sight.
He will point the way, to Father God,
He will show the path, your feet should trod!
Then He will take you, by your hand,
To set your feet, on rock not sand,
For troubles come, to all alike,
But for us who trust, He sheds His light.

Now in His light, we see His love,
We're lifted to, His courts above
No more a wanderer, blind and lost,
But His child redeemed, by His love, His cross.
We are held in His arms, by love and by grace,
Redeemed and restored, to behold His face.
There to be transformed, by what we behold,
Into vessels of worship, holy and bold!
No more a worm, in our sight or mans,
But His child forever, redeemed by The Lamb.
We're made perfect and complete, by His Precious Blood
Lifted up high, above the flood.
Forever to walk, with the saints in light,
Forever cleansed, made His bride in white.
No launderer's soap, could do the job,
We're cleansed by Christ, before our God!

TWO MEN - Inspired by 2nd Samuel 12

There were two men, in a certain town,
    One was rich, had great renown,
The other was poor, didn't have much fame,
    But gave his love, to a lamb without name.
He cradled that lamb, in his arms like a child,
    He loved that lamb, so meek, so mild.
Then a need arose, for the rich man,
    A guest arrived, and he needed a lamb.

Now, instead of taking, a lamb from his flock,
    He took the poor man's lamb, to the chopping block.
He prepared it and served it, to his guest,
    His greed was quenched, he had spoiled his nest!
As Nathan, the prophet, told this to the king,
    King David, the shepherd, whom God had made king,
He arose in anger, at the crime that was done,
    Said, who is that man? I'll punish that one!

Nathan replied, you are that man!
    You are the one, who took the lamb!
God had given you power, had made you king,
    You had more and more blessings, God's praises to sing!
But you wanted what wasn't, yours to hold,
    In your passion and pride, you forgot what was told.
What you did in secret, will be done before men,
    But because you've repented, God's forgiven your sin

Now the child you've conceived, shall surely die,
    For you've caused men to blaspheme, God Most High!
David fasted and prayed, when the child grew ill,
    But on the seventh day, God's word was fulfilled,
The child was taken, to God Most High,
    To live with The Lord, to nevermore die.
Then David knew Bathsheba again,
    She conceived, and gave birth to a son, once again.

Now God sent Nathan, with a word to the king,
    A message that caused, David's heart to sing,
Your son God will call, "Beloved of The Lord,"
    He will seek My wisdom, and love outpoured.
He will realize, of his need for Me,
    The need for My wisdom, to rule righteously!
He will build the temple, for My glory to dwell,
    But I'll let you provide, so it will be built well.
So take what I've given, and set it apart,
    To be used by your son, the son of My heart.

With truth and purity, before My throne,
    He will build a temple, where My Glory is shown.
I will come and abide, in that holy place,
    My Glory will fill, each and every space!
So weep no more, for what is past is past,
    Worship The Lord, with a love that lasts!
Look to Him now, for He is your source,
    The One who redeems and restyles your course.

Take the new path, God's prepared for you,
    Let your ceiling become, the floor for the new!
For a new generation, is arising now,
    Who have set their hearts, and made their vow.
Like Nazarenes of old, their hearts are fixed,
    On Christ, His kingdom, their goals not mixed!
For I have given to them, a heart to be true,
    For all I've commanded, for them to do.

My kingdom will come, on earth as in heaven,
    When My children ask Me, to remove sin's leaven.
For leaven puffs up, just like deadly pride,
    But it is only gas, no quality inside.
Let God reveal to you, what He wants done,
    For His Name and His praise, to be given His Son.
Then The Son of God, will be lifted up high,
    High above all, so that men will not die!

Christ died for our trespass, our guilt and our sin,
  So we could receive, God's forgiveness and then,
Live by the faith, that His Spirit gives,
  Live to proclaim, by our deeds, how to live.
Live in the love, that He showed when He died,
  For all of mankind, to bring to His side.
So let Holy Spirit, birth fresh faith in you,
  Let Him perfect, God's will in you.
He'll redeem and renew, your vision, your sight,
  You'll not walk in darkness, but walk in the light.

The light that God sheds, will open the door,
  To His mercy, His grace, His love evermore.
You are not a failure, you have only begun,
  For you are loved of The Lord, His daughter, His son!
So rise to your feet, come boldly before,
  Your God and your King, the One you adore,
He'll take you and hold you, right close to His side,
  Forever and always, to live and abide.
For God has a plan, to redeem and restore,
  And in His great plan, is grace evermore!

SHARE WHAT I GIVE

You have been given, these poems to share,
  To show My love, to show I care,
To lead all men, to My throne of grace,
  To hear My voice, and behold My face.
For when they see, My love for them,
  They'll leave their sin, be born again.
They'll experience the life, I give to them,
  A life that is free, from death and sin.
So share the words, I have given you,
  I'll meet your need, and provide for you,
All I require, is that you bless,
  The souls of men, to righteousness!

GOD'S PROTECTION - Inspired by Ephesians 6

Oh Lord, You light, the darkest night,
    You give me grace, to stand and fight,
With weapons made, of grace and truth,
    And love that offers, up the proof,
That Jesus Christ is Lord of all,
    Redeemer, Saviour from the fall!
Salvation's helmet, protects my head,
    My mind is free, from fear and read;
No more a sinner, lost, forlorn,
    I know I am yours, redeemed, reborn!
Now with this knowledge, comes Your shield,
    The faith to quench, what the devil wields.
For all he has, are lies that steal,
    The truth The Spirit, has revealed.
So use God's Word, like a sword to cut,
    The lies that keep you, in a rut.

Rise up in faith, and truth to use,
    God's Word against, the devil's tools.
Use every weapon, God gives to you,
    To stand, for righteousness and truth.
Apply God's Word, in every case,
    So you can run, to win the race.
Walk straight and true, like Jesus did,
    Give men the truth, so they won't slip,
Then pray for those, God's brought to you,
    Pray long and hard, don't cease to do,
His will in love, and faith to hold
    His Word above, all that's been told.
Deception comes, masquerading as light,
    To blind men's eyes, reduce their sight.
So pray and pray, and don't give up,
    Drink long and deep, of The Saviour's cup.
You will be refreshed, by what you receive,
    And from His side, you'll never leave!

SHUT THE MOUTHS - Inspired by 1st. Timothy 2:1-6

Shut the mouths, of those who claim,
    That they are right, but they defame,
        The ones that You, have chosen to rule,
            The ones You have placed, in power to school.
            For what is true, and moral and right,
            Must replace the sin, the dark, the night.
So cause us Oh Lord,, to ever be,
    Your church of truth, and purity,
        To stand in the gap for the souls of men,
            To pray for our leaders, again and again.
Cause us to be, a source of light,
    Your light to shine, through the darkest night,
        Ever willing, to lend a hand,
            To those who rule, across the land.
Help us to bless, what You want blessed,
    So we can live, in righteousness.
Cleanse us by, Your Blood, Your Power,
    Help us defeat, the lies that devour,
        The hearts and minds, of this nation of ours,
            So we can uphold, Your name each hour!
Help us by word and every deed, to be a source to all in need,
    To be Your hand, of mercy and grace,
        So men can see Your love, Your face.
Oh Lord, I pray, help me this day,
    To always walk, Your narrow way,
        Walk in the steps, that You have laid out,
            Walk in faith, and never doubt.
For Your hand is leading, us by Your light!
    To bring to men, new vision, new sight,
        Only You are The Way, The Truth and The Light,
            Only You can restore, redeem, make right!
So now we present, our lives to you,
    Cause us to see, and by Your Spirit do,
        The works that You, Oh Lord, want done,
            So The Father can be glorified, in The Son!

LISTEN MY CHILD - Inspired by Isaiah 1-6

Listen My child, to what I say,
    Listen well, and then obey.
Hear My Word, and take it to heart,
    My will to dwell, in every part.
For if you would be, My own dear child,
    To be like Jesus, meek and mild,
Then I must be, The Lord of all,
    Your ears must hear Me, when I call.

So read My Word, in such a way,
    That you can know, and hear and pray,
My will to be done, right here on earth,
    Like as in heaven, to bring to birth.
The reality, of Who I AM,
    So men can know, My will, My plan.
The Blood of Christ, has paid the cost,
    To save all men, from what they lost.

So bring men, to, My saving grace,
    For then I will, their sins erase.
Oh, child of mine, portray My love,
    To all to bring, to courts above,
All that I call, so they can know,
    The grace and mercy, I bestow.
Let mercy cover, judgement now,
    So men can see, My love and bow.

Then from that place of worship know,
    That I AM God, above and below.
I AM The God, who sees all things,
    The God who gives, a song to sing,
A song of love and life and peace,
    A song of praise, that brings release,
To every soul, of every man,
    Who gives his life, into My plan!

WHAT'S ON YOUR LIST? - Inspired by Matthew 6:33

You make a list, of what the body needs,
　　To be kept strong, to fulfill your deeds,
But with what do you fill, your spirit, your soul,
　　So they can be strong, to fulfill My goals?
I know that you need, to fill the natural,
　　But do not neglect, the spiritual!
It is by My Spirit, that you have life,
　　And it is by My Spirit, that you're freed from strife.
So first fill up, the important things,
　　Communion, reflection, My Word that sings
The truth, into your inward parts,
　　So you'll have much then, to impart.

Physical food, only lasts for awhile,
　　But spiritual food, builds all the while.
Line upon line, My Words build in you,
　　A temple of worship, a place of truth.
A deposit account, where you can draw from,
　　To meet the needs, of all, not just some.

So as you make, your list today,
　　Fill up your soul, on My Word, then pray;
For the sight to see, what is holy and pure,
　　For My Light to establish, for then you'll secure
My will, in what you do and say,
　　So men may trust, and then obey.
My perfect will, brings life and hope,
　　And joy which gives, the strength to cope,
For then your heart, will never stray,
　　You'll have the power, to walk each day,
In truth and love, and holiness,
　　Dressed in My Robes, of Righteousness!
Do not be preoccupied, with what you can get,
　　But fill up your mind, in response to God's gifts.

For what do you have, that has not been given,
    By The Father who loves you, your God up in heaven?
So seek first God's kingdom, in all that you do,
    Then you will receive, what is needed and true.
You will have such abundance, you won't have a care,
    For all His provision, is yours to share.
Therefore, give no attention, but learn to relax,
    And rest in the knowledge, God hears when you ask.
He'll meet every need, from His abundant supply,
    You'll not need to worry, or fuss or cry.
He will carry you through, by His strong right arm,
    Kept right and pure, away from all harm.

Therefore give your attention, to God right now,
    See what He's doing, and ask Him how,
You can enter, and then co-labour, with Him,
    To deliver the captives, caught up in their sin.
He will show you the way, that is best for you,
    Then give you His Spirit, to will and to do,
The works of righteousness, that lift up His Son,
    To be glorified, in all that is done.
When you lift up the Name, of Jesus, The Christ,
    So that men can see, of His love sacrifice,
They will turn from their sin, and receive God's grace,
    Then receive His forgiveness, all sin then erased.

Therefore focus on what, God has called you to do,
    Seek first His kingdom, in all that you do,
You'll experience the love, and the joy that He gives,
    Your soul will delight, in His life to live.
For you were conceived, by His love to fulfill,
    Good plans He's ordained, to accomplish His will,
That is where, true joy is found,
    That is where, pure love abounds!

<u>WHY?</u> - Inspired by Jeremiah 20-29 and Haggai 1

Why do the people, mock My Name?
    Why do they live, in sin and shame?
Why don't they tremble, at My Word?
    Why don't they want, salvation assured?
Oh people of God, hear now what I say,
    Listen and hear, take heed and obey.
Are you living for self, or living for Me?
    Is the temple you're building, to set men free?
Are the works you do, for the applause of men?
    If that's all you do, you are dreaming then!
You must be different, with lives set apart,
    Lives that live, to reflect My heart,
Lives that are pure, and holy and true,
    For then you'll, reflect My Glory to do
What I want done, so My kingdom can come,
    So My will can be established, for salvation to run
Like a river that freshens, wherever it goes,
    Like a well springing, up to quicken the soul.

Now if you desire, My Kingdom to come,
    Then come and receive, living water, not scum,
For the water I give, will be a well springing up,
    With more than enough, to fill your cup.
Then when you pour out, what you received from Me,
    I will give you My more, so you can really live free.
You'll be free from the world, and all of it's charms,
    Free from the evil, that kills and disarms.
The choices you make, will bring life or death,
    So choose My Spirit, to give you breath.
Breathe deep of the life, He imparts to you,
    Drink from the fountain, that He's offered to you.
Then you will be, My people indeed,
    Your lives will show forth, My glory like seed,
To plant in the hearts, of those who are lost,
    The message of love, that comes from Christ's cross!

THINK ON THESE THINGS - Inspired by Philippians 4

Father in heaven, forgive me I pray,
    For wanting to walk, in my own selfish way.
Help me to live, with a heart that is pure,
    To make my call, and election sure.
Help me to build, Your temple Lord,
    To foster Your peace, bring to one accord,
Your children, Your church, as a body to dwell,
    Together in love, to drink from Your well.

You Lord alone, are The Pure Living Drink,
    That cleanses our hearts, and our minds to think,
On the pure and the lovely, the excellent, true,
    Things worthy of praise, so that we can do,
The works you want done, in Your Holy Son's Name,
    The Name of Christ Jesus, so all can be saved.
Then cause me to live, with a thankful heart,
    For all that You do, all You bless and impart.

Help me to learn, and then live what I learn,
    The truths of a life, that I never could earn.
For all of the good, that is mine to hold,
    The treasures You give, more precious than gold,
I never could gain, by what I have done,
    I can only receive, by faith in Your Son.
So help me to live, in Your strength everyday,
    With joy and obedience, to do what You say.

The love that You give, always blesses my heart,
    And gives me the grace, to stand strong, and apart,
From the world and the sin, that would steal and would kill,
    Stand strong by Your power, to do Your will;
To love you Lord God, with all of my heart,
    Then love my neighbour, with the love You impart,
For then men will see, that Your love is made true,
    When they see that our lives, are directed by You!

FEED MY LAMBS - Inspired by John 20 & 21

Feed My lambs, The Master said,
    After He'd risen, from the dead,
Shepherd and feed My sheep, to know,
    The truths of God, for then they will grow.
They will grow in the knowledge, of My will,
    They will hear My voice, and listen still.
My Spirit will quicken them, to believe,
    And The Words I give, they will receive.

My Words must be planted, deep within,
    Then rise to free, your hearts from sin.
So let My Word, do it's perfect work,
    For then My ways, you will not shirk.
Like Mary you will wait, for My Presence to bless,
    Your life, your soul, with righteousness.
Then peace will come, as you open your soul,
    With blessedness, that makes you whole.

For what do you have, that I haven't given,
    Only I can prepare, your hearts for heaven,
Only I can give you, the words of life,
    Only I have redeemed you, from sin and strife.
So don't return home, like the disciples did,
    But wait like Mary, for My voice to bid,
To bid you come, to bid you hear,
    To bid you dwell, in My Presence dear.

For life as you know it, is passing away,
    So stay by My side, for then you'll not stray,
Away from My Presence, away from My Voice,
    But closer to make, My will your choice.
For as you come close, you will see what I see,
    As you come close, My Word you'll decree.
Then you'll know My heart, and what I want done,
    You'll lift up My Name, Glorify My Son!!

FEED MY SHEEP - Inspired by John 21:16 & 17

Help me Lord, to feed Your sheep,
  To tend Your lambs, their hearts to keep,
Close to Your precious bleeding side,
  There to be cleansed, there to abide.
Abiding in You, Lord, brings perfect peace,
  Abiding in You, brings our soul's release.
No more to abide, by religious rules,
  But to live in the way, that Holy Spirit schools.
As deep calls unto deep, I call,
  Hold me close, so I'll never fall,
Away from You, and Your presence dear,
  Away from Your will, that makes my way clear.
For then I will know, even as I am known,
  The way to lead all, to Your Heavenly Throne.
There we will kneel, to worship and praise,
  There to applaud You, Oh Ancient of Days!

Then when we behold, Your Holiness,
  We are changed by Your grace, and Your righteousness,
Changed from glory, to glory by faith,
  Changed to Your likeness, Your life to embrace.
From there we will know, what it is like to be held,
  Like a bride in Your arms, our spirits to meld,
Into one with Yours, for there we are blest,
  With peace and love, our souls then to rest.
No more will we strive, but rest and be still,
  Content to know, that we are kept in Your will.
Now we will bless, to make Your Name known,
  Walking to lead, Your flock to Your Throne,
There to behold The Shepherd, who keeps,
  Who watches with love, who never slumbers or sleeps.
Always and everywhere, You keep by Your side,
  Your lambs and Your sheep, to always abide,
There to experience Your peace, without measure,
  There to partake, of Your love as our treasure!

MY SOURCE OF STRENGTH - Inspired by 1ˢᵗ Thessalonians 5

Your Word, Oh Lord, is a lamp to my feet,
My source, my strength, my guide.
For when I need Your light to lead, it takes me to Your side.
From there I feel, Your strong embrace, Your hand encloses mine,
I look into Your holy face, and know that I am Thine.
So help me Lord, Your voice to hear, Oh Spirit make it clear,
For I would be a place where You,, can live and enter here.

Bring me each day to this place of peace,
This place, where my life You can rule,
A place of rest and blessedness, a refreshing holy pool.
Help me to drink at this Holy place, The water You give to me,
Then from this place of sweet embrace,
I'm cleansed, made whole, by Thee!
No more a wanderer in the night, but now Your child made clean,
For now You lead me into Your light, a soul, made free, redeemed!

GRACE TO FORGIVE - Inspired by Matthew 6:14 & 15

Help me Oh Lord to remember the grace,
    You gave, when You forgave me,
Then help me extend, that grace to all,
    So those I forgive, are set free.
For when we forgive, as we've been forgiven,
    Our souls are redeemed, made clean,
For the keys that locked, our souls by sins,
    Are unlocked, by Your grace that frees.
No more a prisoner, but free indeed,
    By the power of Jesus, redeemed,
Now we can give forth, Your precious seed,
    Your Word, that meets every need.
When Your Word comes in, Your light comes too,
    And now what was dark, is dispelled,
For You Lord Jesus, took the keys that day,
    When You triumphed, over death and hell!

<u>SETTING LIMITS</u> - Inspired by Colossians 3:1-4

Don't set limits on what God can do, don't set limits on Him,
Set your affections on God who is true,
He will strengthen and comfort you.
For where would you be without God's hand?
Where would you fit in?
How would you traverse this land, if His Spirit did not lead within?

For the still small voice, that guides your path,
The still small voice of God,
Will keep your heart from sin and wrath, will mark the path you trod.
If you will walk, in the light of God's Holy Word,
If you will walk, by His Presence within,
You will walk by faith, salvation assured,
Redeemed and set free from sin.

You could not do, all this on your own,
You could not do, without God,
You could not stand, before His throne,
Without trusting in The Christ of God!
So take the time to listen well, with ears anointed to hear.
Listen to what His Spirit says, for then, you will draw near.

You will receive the instructions, God wants to give,
To affect and change your world,
You will speak the words, so men can live,
No more their lives in a swirl.
For the entrance of God's Word, brings light and life,
His Word redeems, and heals,
No more a wanderer, lost in the night,
But saved by Christ's Blood, your sealed.

You are sealed by His Spirit, for eternal life,
Saved, set free, made whole,
Saved to encounter His Presence, His life
God's child, His own to hold!

DREAM HIS DREAMS - Inspired by Psalm 108:1-5

Help me dream dreams from You Master,
    Dreams that take me beyond,
The realms of my very small thinking,
    Away from the normal and fond.
Take me by faith, to a world unseen,
    Take me by faith, to Your Place,
Where I can behold, with eyes made clean,
    Your wonderful, beautiful face.
Then I will know, even as I am known,
    What a wonderful God, You are,
Then I would see, by the grace You have shown,
    What I have only beheld, from afar.

Your greatness is greater, than everything,
    You are greater, than sun, moon or stars,
For with a Word, You created all things,
    And then man to live close, not afar.
You created us in Your image to dwell,
    In communion and intimate love,
But then we sinned, and were destined for hell,
    Until Jesus came from heaven above.

He was made in our likeness, and born a man,
    But conceived by Your Spirit, to show,
How we could live by Your Spirit, Your plan,
    So all of the world, could know:
That The God who made them, loves them still,
    Your mercies are new every day,
That You will direct, in Your perfect will,
    If we will seek Your face, and pray.
If we will pray to You Father, in Jesus Name
    Then repent of our errors, our sins,
Ask for forgiveness, in Jesus' Name,
    Then You will abide and come in!

You will cleanse with Your blood, and by Your mercy erase,
    You'll redeem us, from all of our sin,
You will make us brand new, by Your mercy and grace,
    By Your Spirit, You will dwell within.
For we were dead, in our trespass and sins,
    We could never cleanse our lives, or begin,
To come to You Father, by deeds we had done,
    We could only be saved, through Your Son!

So we bow to Your greatness, Your awesome love,
    We bow before You, Mighty God,
We bow and we worship, before Your throne,
    We bow, give allegiance, Holy God
For who but You, could redeem our souls?
    Who, but You, could make us whole?
Who but You Lord, showed compassion and grace?
    Who but You Lord, cradled, embraced?

So hold me close to Your heart, I pray,
    Let Your presence enfold me, each new day,
For to experience, Your Presence, Your Holy Love,
    Is to experience, Your mercy, Your grace from above!
Oh, Holy Spirit, cause me to know,
    Your plans and Your purpose, for me here below.
Give me eyes to see, and ears to hear,
    What you want me to see, and the words that cheer.

Then cause me to show, to all men here below,
    The Jesus that died, so then they can know,
Can know and believe, by the faith You give,
    How to walk, How to dream, How to really live,
Live in the dreams, You have given to them,
    Live to believe, that You are coming again
Live by Your power, live in Your rest,
    By walking with Jesus, The Christ, The Best!

RAISE FROM THE DEAD - Inspired by Matthew 12

Holy Spirit, I pray, raise from the dead,
    The words that were spoken, or sung, or said,
Awaken our hearts, and our minds to receive,
    Your breath of life, Your holy seed.
Forgive us, where we have tolerated sin,
    For this toleration, brought death within.
But, a bruised reed, You will not break,,
    Nor a smouldering wick, will You forsake.
So we ask, Holy Spirit, please quicken our lives,
    By Your very breath, to destroy the lies,
That weakened our faith, destroyed our hope,
    That caused us to stumble, tremble and grope!
Bring us, we pray, into Your Holy Light,
    Where there is no darkness, or death, or night;
To that Holy Place, where we see Jesus, as Christ,
    The Anointed of God, The Pure Sacrifice!

Help us see Him afresh, in a way that is new,
    As The One who establishes, God's perfect rule;
Where love and forgiveness, rule every act,
    Where truth and right living, portray the fact:
That Jesus alone, is The King of all kings,
    That He is The Reason, all heaven sings!
Reveal to us now, Holy Spirit, we pray,
    The ways we can show, all others Your way.
Give us the words, that lead to The Christ,
    The words that bring honour, to The One True Light!
Christ Jesus, You alone, are The Light of The World,
    Only Your sacrifice, can redeem from the swirl,
The swirl of sin, that leads to the pit,
    The swirl of pride, that thinks we are it!
For only in Christ, is our salvation made sure,
    Only by receiving His Grace, are we pure.
Only His Blood, has cleansed our souls,
    Only His Pure Sacrifice, can make whole!

PRAY FOR ALL MEN - Inspired by 1st Timothy 2:1-6

You pray for The Hindus, The Muslims, The Jews,
    You pray for all men, so they'll cease to be fools,
You pray for the leaders, of churches and nations,
    You pray that they will come to Me, for their ration.
So keep on praying, don't quit the fight,
    Till all can be brought, right into My Light.

I AM coming again, for My Chosen, My Bride,
    To present to My Father, to stand by My Side.
But My Bride will not, be complete until,
    All men can hear, My Word and My Will.
My desire is for all, everywhere, to be saved,
    That all be redeemed, from hell and the grave.

Oh pray for My light, to shine in their hearts,
    And pray for My Word, to pervade, every part.
For darkness must go, when My Light comes in,
    And My Light must be shown, to eradicate sin.
So pray for My Light, to shine everywhere,
    Through My Church, My Bride, so all can share,
In My Life-Giving Presence, to vanquish hell,
    To destroy Satan's schemes, and devices as well.
This is the reason, why I came to earth,
    To restore and redeem, and give all, My new birth.
I paid with My Blood, to redeem every soul,
    To procure their salvation, to make everyone whole.

So don't give up, on your prayers this day,
    Let My Spirit direct, every word that you say,
Then you will hit every target, by what you decree,
    Then eyes will be opened, so that they can see,
The True God from heaven, their Saviour to be,
    Has come in His love, to redeem and set free!
Only His love, and His mercy, can cleanse,
    His Blood our salvation, our only defence!

REBUILD THE WALL - Inspired by Nehemiah and Colossians

Rebuild the wall, that's been broken down,
Rebuild so men, can see My crown,
For I would be, your King and Lord,
The God you worship, and adore.
Sin has broken down, your walls,
Has closed your ears, to hear My call,
But still My voice, calls out to you,
Rebuild, so you can know My truth.

My truth will set, your spirit free,
Free to walk, in liberty.
So seek My truth, so you won't fall,
Seek My truth, and give your all.
Then even if your all seems small,
And even if you don't feel tall,
Remember, I AM the God, who multiplies,
I AM The God, who never dies.

What is given to Me, with heart and hands,
For Me to use, at My command,
I strengthen, and equip to stand,
Forever by, My strong right hand.
For Christ, My Son, your Saviour too,
Stands by My right hand, to plead for you.
He knows the struggles, you are in,
He walked the walk, but without the sin!

My Spirit will, empower you,
To hear My voice, and do what's true,
This truth will be, the building block,
So you can build, on The Solid Rock!
This Rock is Christ, your foundation stone,
So trust in Him, and Him alone.
He'll bring you through, in every way,
So you can praise, His Name each day!

314

HEAR GOD'S WORD
Inspired by Matthew 6:14 & 15 & Mark 4:22-25

Hear My word, and don't delay,
    To listen, hear, and then obey,
        For what I want, for you will live,
            If you'll show mercy, and forgive.
So forgive as I have, forgiven you,
    And show the mercy, I have shown to you.
        Seek first My kingdom ways and then,
            My love can be, displayed to men.
How can they see, unless they are shown
    My Way, The Way, of truth alone.
        I AM The Way, The Truth, The life,
            I AM The Door, that leads to life.
The life I give, is so much more,
    Then men could ever, gain or store.
        What I give, is meant to share,
            For there's always much, to give, to care.

So give what I, have given to you,
    Give so all, can know The Truth;
        The truth that, God above is love,
            Who sent His Spirit, in the form of a dove,
To declare that Jesus, is His Beloved Son,
    The Anointed, The Christ, The Only One!
        By Christ, all men, can be set free,
            By trusting Him, for their liberty.
When they see their sin, and Christ's saving grace,
    They'll repent of all, their foolish ways,
        They'll return by trusting, in Christ's Blood,
            The Gift of Life, that saves from the flood.
Now they're made brand new, by His love and power,
    To walk in faith, and hope this hour.
        No more delays, for the time is now,
            To worship Christ, to kneel, to bow,
He Alone is the King of kings, The God of all, to Whom we sing!

REACH OUT AND RECEIVE - Inspired by 1ˢᵗ John 3

Reach out and receive, what God has done,
  Reach out and believe, in The Christ, God's Son!
Reach out to Him in faith to do,
  So Christ and His love, can be seen through you.
For what do you have, that has not been given?
  What good is in you, that wasn't from heaven?
Christ, our Redeemer, paid sin's awful cost,
  By shedding His blood, on that cruel cross!
So reach for The One, who gave you His life,
  Reach out to Christ Jesus, to remove all the strife.
Striving comes only, by trying to prove,
  That our way is best, but we're playing the fool!
God in His mercy, and wonderful love,
  Made the way for us all, to come up above.
Jesus, The Way, The Truth and The Life,
  Paid for our sins. by His Blood sacrifice.

Therefore, let's put into practice, the love that was given,
  Let's live like His children, as citizens of heaven.
For we've been transferred, from death unto life,
  We've been delivered, Christ has made us His wife.
No more are we outcast, and dead in our sins,
  But a Bride for our Christ, by His Spirit within.
So let's not just talk, about being like Christ,
  Let's show by our deeds, that we're truly His Bride.
Let's reach out and welcome, the ones He died for,
  Let's show by our love, that Christ is The Door;
The Door that leads, to Father God's throne,
  Where we can come boldly, by Christ's blood atoned.
Boldly to stand, in the faith Christ has given,
  And then to receive, with all in God's heaven,
The joy that comes, from knowing we are saved,
  To walk in His love, redeemed from the grave!

DON'T BELIEVE EVERYTHING YOU HEAR
Inspired by 1st John 4

Do not believe, everything you hear,
    But let God's Spirit, make it clear
He'll guide and lead, and comfort you,
    He'll make the way, to live in truth.
So check the ways, of those who talk,
    How do they live, How do they talk?
Do they openly confess, that Jesus is Lord?
    Do they walk in the love, of The Lord outpoured?
For those who refuse, to believe in the Christ,
    Have nothing of God, They're the antichrist!

So submit yourselves truly, to The Spirit of God,
    To walk in the light, of God's Word as it's taught,
By those who follow, Christ's doctrine and walk,
    Who show by their lives, that they have been bought;
Bought by The Blood, of Christ Jesus The Lord,
    Purchased and cleansed, into one accord,
In the faith that The Spirit of God, gives to men,
    When they repent of their sin, ask Christ to come in.
Then victory is theirs, over death and hell,
    For they have chosen, The Christ, and His love to dwell,
In their hearts by faith, in their hearts by love,
    The love of their Father, in heaven above.

So love not the world, and it's wicked ways,
    For the devil will use this, to lead you astray.
Be holy and pure, in all that you do,
    Let God's Spirit guide you, into all that is true.
Our destiny that God has planned, will not fail,
    If we let Him control, let His love prevail.
He will level the mountains, and fill every hole,
    He will make a plain path, He'll restore our souls,
He will lead us in paths, of His righteousness,
    He will grant us His life, His blessedness.

MY PLEDGE - Inspired by Psalms 1-27

I will stay with You God, as long as I live,
　　For You are The God, who hears and forgives.
You are The God, who lights my way,
　　You set me straight, so I won't stray.
Your Words are a light, unto my feet,
　　They guide my steps, Your Face to greet.

For by Your grace and mercy Lord,
　　You have washed and cleansed, prepared a sword,
To cut off all that maims and kills,
　　So that by faith, I will do Your will.
I know it's not works, which I have done,
　　That I can come, before Your Son,
But by His Blood, and His alone,
　　I stand before, Your Holy Throne.

So let me always realize,
　　That by Your Truth, I'll live, not die.
I'll live for what, You have called me for,
　　Live to lead men, to Your door.
For Christ alone is The Door to life,
　　Life everlasting, without the strife..
Oh cause my heart, to ever comprehend,
　　To ponder on, Your words that mend,
The tears and breaks, the wounds, the hurts,
　　That maim and kill, defile with dirt.

Help me to use, instead Your Words,
　　To heal men's hearts, their spirits gird,
So that with strength, and hope and faith,
　　In You Lord God, they'll never faint!
You'll lead them to, Your wells of life,
　　Refreshed, redeemed, restored from strife.
Then they'll see You Lord, as The God of Love,
　　Who has destined them, for heaven above!

<u>YOUR WORD</u> - Inspired by Ephesians 5:1 &2

Your Word is a lamp, that lightens my path,
    It gives me direction to see,
Your Word purifies, from what causes wrath,
    Delivers what's evil from me.
In Your Word, is light for my soul,
    A light that cleanses and heals,
Your Word, by Your Spirit, will make me whole,
    Your child, set apart, and sealed.
I am sealed for Your purpose, sealed for Your will,
    Sealed for Your holy goals,
Sealed by Your Spirit, and nurtured to fill,
    Your children, to make them whole!

Love from You Father, is what we need,
    Your love is the food that fills,
That satisfies, sanctifies, illumines Your seed,
    The Word that heals every ill.
We are Your people, we are called by Your Name,
    Your people, forever, Your own,
You gave up for us, Your Glory, Your Fame,
    To save us and take us all home.

Your Blood, You poured out, on Calvary's cross,
    Our sins, were the nails that held You,
That tortured Your body, to pay for our loss,
    To pay for the penalty due.
My heart is so full, I cannot express,
    What I feel in my heart today,
For without Your grace, and forgiveness Lord,
    My life would have passed away.
I stood before You, unclean and condemned,
    A sinner, lost and forlorn,
But now by Your wonderful mercy, I'm cleansed
    Your child, by Your Spirit reborn!

WHAT IS YOUR LIFE? - Inspired by Proverbs 23-25

What do you have, that hasn't been given?
    Consider, take heed, then pray.
Your very life, is a gift from heaven.
    Consider, then choose life today,
By the power of The Spirit, put away what defiles,
    Then reach, for the holy and pure,
For only what is pure, has the power to clean,
    Jesus' Blood, will provide the cure!
So come to The Lord, for His cleansing now,
    He'll save you, for you He esteems.
Come to The Lord, and make your vow,
    For He will restore, and redeem.

Only the love of God, in Christ,
    Is sufficient, to cleanse all our sin,
So ask for His Spirit, to equip and empower,
    Then you can, resist and win.
Oh make a covenant, child today,
    A promise that's, steadfast and sure,
A covenant ordained, by the Spirit of God,
    A promise, for salvation's cure!

Realize that without The Lord, you are lost,
    You can't purify yourself,
For what has been squandered, and wasted and tossed,
    The Lord has redeemed, by Himself!
True riches that come, from The Father above
    Will satisfy the hunger within,
Then what God has given, by His wonderful love,
    Will provide you, with power over sin.
You will not falter, or fail to stand,
    If you'll trust, in The Lord's Mighty Power,
You will stand and declare,, to all in the land,
    The God of all Grace, in each hour!

THE ANSWERS - Inspired by Isaiah 49:8-13

Let the answers you give, be gentle and kind,
    For then men can see, what has made them blind.
Your patience will pierce, their indifference,
    And the love that you give, will give them a sense,
Of what God has planned, for every soul,
    What God has provided, through Christ to make whole.
What comes forth, from your mouth should bless,
    All those God has called, unto righteousness.
But be careful as well, to not bless what God hates,
    Be wise and discerning, to close every gate,
That leads to sin, and what brings a curse,
    For these things will put, God's plan in reverse.
Submit yourself daily, to God and His will,
    Receive His instruction, then listen, be still,
Quiet yourself, in His Presence to hear,
    His voice and His will, and His Word to draw near.

Then as you follow, His direction and plan,
    You will walk and live, in His ways, by His hand,
Then when you ascend, in worship to bless,
    You'll receive from His hand, His blessedness.
You'll receive what you need, to do His will,
    You'll decree and declare, His will to fulfill.
You will bring heaven's rule, on earth to dwell,
    To destroy and defeat, all the powers of hell.
For when Jesus Christ, is exalted as Lord,
    And when with His love, you're in one accord,
With all who've received Christ, as Redeemer and King,
    With all who rejoice, in worship and sing.
You'll then have the power, to destroy Satan's plans,
    You'll walk in Christ's Spirit, His will to command,
You'll speak God's will and His Word to redeem,
    You'll give of His Blessing, and His power to esteem,
All others as better, than you, as Christ did,
    For the humble heart, The Saviour will bid!

<u>YOUR HOME</u> - Inspired by Isaiah 48:16.17, & 20.

Your home will be filled, with blessing and peace,
 And those who come in, will find their release,
From all that would trouble, cause fear, and confuse,
 From all of the pain, that the devil would use.
For in the place, that you would call home,
 My Presence will bless, and lead to My Throne.
All who are troubled, confused and alone,
 My Spirit will bless, with joys yet unknown.
There are so many, who know not My Name,
 Who know not the peace, that My Name can proclaim.
They are troubled and tossed, like a ship in a storm,
 They need of My Presence, and My love to form,
Their lives into, My good and My best,
 Their lives to My place, of perfect rest.

You will lead them to Me, in that place you call home,
 You will lead them to Me, they will never more roam;
For in that place, My Presence will dwell,
 To redeem and restore, all those destined for hell.
For you will speak, the words I give you,
 The words that bring life, and speak what is true.
My truth will cut through, every lie like a knife,
 Will expose the deception, that caused all the strife.
Their eyes will be opened, their ears will hear too,
 The plans and the purposes, revealed through you.

You will love with the love, that comes from Me,
 You will show them a life, I have redeemed, set free.
You will show them My heart, and My love for them,
 So they can depart, from their sin and come in.
I will bid them to come, to abide by My side,
 I will hold them real close, as My wife, as My bride.
I'll present them to Father, as the ones I've restored,
 I will call them My blessed, The ones I adore.

MY RULE WILL GO FORTH - Inspired by Zechariah 14:9

My rule will go forth, as you lift up My Name,
    My rule will go forth, as My Name you proclaim,
Lift up My Name, over all mankind,
    For My Name has the power, to heal the blind.
My people have wandered, from the paths I had planned,
    But now I AM calling, drawing by My Hand,
I AM leading to where, the harvest is ripe,
    Where My truth is revealed, in power, not hype.

So preach My Word, and declare My truth,
    With the love and devotion, displayed like Ruth.
She honoured Naomi, in all that she did,
    By her active obedience, she removed the lid,
So the blessings of God, could come down through her,
    Her calling was set, her election made sure.
So obey the ones, I've placed over you,
    Let My love and truth, be displayed through you.
For then I can lead you, to pastures green,
    The place I've prepared, for your spirit to glean.

You have listened and learned, what I've taught you so far,
    But there's much more to learn, before crossing the bar.
As you get your fresh bread, from My Word every day,
    You'll have freshness to give, by My Spirit always.
Therefore taste of My manna, My heavenly food,
    My manna refreshes, and changes your mood.
My manna is the Bread, of Life for your soul,
    My Word, made flesh, by My Spirit, makes whole.
For without Holy Spirit, your life's incomplete,
    But as He dwells in your spirit, you're then made complete.
From this place of completeness, and rest in Him,
    You can lead men to Jesus, who frees from all sin.
There I'll give them joy, like they've never known,
    And the love that comes, from My Father's throne.

HOPE IN THE LIGHT - Inspired by Isaiah 43

Hope in The Light, that shatters the dark,
  Hope in The Light of the world,
For your faith is more, than a walk in the park,
  It's the answer, when life's in a swirl.
The hope that comes, from trusting The Lord,
  Brings faith in The Living Word,
This Word is The Christ, The Son of God,
  By Him, your salvation's assured.
So rest in the promises given to you,
  The words to prosper and bless,
The words He has given, will all come true,
  He'll clothe you with righteousness,
Then clothed in this garment, you will preach of Him,
  You'll preach of His power to save,
You'll preach to the ones, held captive by sin,
  To rescue from hell and the grave.

So fret not, nor fear, what this day will bring,
  But trust in My Word and confess,
That I AM your God, The God who sings,
  Over those who I love to bless.
So listen, My child, and listen real close,
  Listen and don't be afraid,
For I AM The One, who loves you the most,
  The debt of your sin has been paid.
It was paid by the death, of My Son on that cross,
  Paid to redeem evermore,
Paid by His Blood, that redeems all the lost,
  To enjoy, My love more and more.
Now all that receive, the grace that I give,
  The grace that redeems from sin,
Can enter My courts, in heaven above,
  They'll experience My joy, therein!

THIS EARTH - Inspired by Hebrews 13:14

This earth is not your resting place,
   It's only a passing frame,
      Of the picture of life, I have given in space,
        A place to declare My Name.
So when you lift up, My Name in your prayers,
   When you lift up My Name,
      Rest in the knowledge, that your God cares,
        His love over you He'll proclaim.

He'll vindicate you from all that is wrong,
   For you trusted in Jesus to save,
      He'll answer your prayer, He'll make you strong,
        He'll raise you from death and the grave.
For even the faith to believe is His gift,
   His gift of love to you,
      And when you receive His incredible gift,
        His love will bring you through.

So dream with Me, My daughter dream,
   Let me take you to what is unseen,
      Let Me take you into My heavenly place,
        Where you can receive, My esteem..
My grace is sufficient for all of your needs,
   My grace will provide the seed,
      To plant into lives for salvation assured,
        My grace will meet every need.

It will bring forth the life, in ways that ensure,
   A path that is plain and free,
      It will clear all the boulders the devil has placed,
        To hinder men coming to Me!
Keep planting the seed, I've provided for you,
   To bring My harvest in,
   For My will, by My way, will bring men the truth,
      The truth that frees from all sin.

IN YOUR PRESENCE - **Inspired by Psalm 52:8 & 9**

Dear Father in heaven, allow me to hear,
    Allow me to listen, draw near,
Help me to wait for Your presence, Dear Lord,
    For Your voice, is what I want to hear.
Cause us, Your children to worship You Lord,
    In love and in holiness,
For then Your commanded blessing comes forth,
    Your blessing of righteousness.

Our land needs Your healing, Oh Father above,
    Our land needs Your hand to restore,
For death and destruction, pervade our land,
    Prevent men from life evermore.
So help us proclaim, Your holy Word,
    In spirit and in truth to tell,
That sin has a price, and it's wages procure,
    The wages that lead to hell.

You said in Your Word, that all of us sinned,
    But You have prepared a way,
To escape the destruction, the devil has planned,
    You paid with Your life that day.
So cause us to speak, Your Word in love,
    Cause us to tell it all,
To tell of our Saviour, from heaven above
    Who ransomed and saved from the fall.

He came to redeem, from sin and despair,
    From all that would trouble, confuse,
He showed us how we, could believe and be saved
    If we use our free will to choose.
So choose the life He offers, my friend,
    Choose to walk in His light,
You will walk then in faith and light and hope,
    For He has restored your sight

WHEN WE WERE DEAD - Inspired by Ephesians 2

When we were dead, in our trespass and sin,
Lord Jesus came down, our lives for to win.
He showed us how we, could believe and be saved,
He walked with You Father, showed us how to behave.
He taught us how to walk, in love, faith and hope,
To walk in obedience and light, not to grope.

Now until we were brought, into faith By Your Spirit,
Our lives had no meaning, we could not inherit,
The blessings You planned, for us to walk in,
The faith and salvation, that You bring within,
Our hearts and our lives, until Christ Jesus is formed,
In our innermost being, By Your Spirit transformed.

So now by Your Spirit, and His holy power,
Help us to cast off, all the sin that devours.
Help us then to walk, in the light that You've given,
With power to lead, to your courts up in heaven.
These are courts, where those delivered can praise,
Courts of salvation, where we have been raised.

We know, that our works, could never attain,
All what we could do, would be foolish and vain,,
But Your grace and love, You poured out so we,
Could receive Your salvation, Your likeness to see.
Now we are by Your grace, Your handiwork,
Recreated by Christ Jesus, Your body, Your church!

So help us remember, where we have come from,
Remember, give thanks for all You have done.
Remember the love and forgiveness, You've shown,
Remember that we didn't, do this on our own.
Then help us to show, your love and forgiveness,
Till together with all, we sing of Your greatness!

<u>CHOSEN TO ABIDE</u> - Inspired by John 15:16

You didn't choose Me, but I chose you,
    For I have a work for you to do.
To do my work, you must abide in Me,
    For fruit can't be grown, apart from the tree,
I AM The Tree of Life, in you,
    And My Spirit will lead, into what is true.
My truth will cut off, all the lies that blind,
    My truth will illumine, your heart and your mind.
What you have is what, I have given to you,
    Even family and friends, are My gifts to you.

If you live in Me and I live in you,
    You will walk in a way, that declares my truth.
You'll not walk in darkness, or fear or despair,
    For My light and My love, always show you I care.
I care for the hurting, the lost and confused,
    I care for the ones, even those who refused,
My message of love, and My sacrifice given,
    For My love will break down, all of sin's leaven
Leaven puffs up, makes you think something's there,
    But it has no real substance, it's only hot air.
Then when trials come, or troubles persist,
    The leaven dissolves, like a vapour, a mist.

All that is left, is now formless and void,
    The only things left, are the things to avoid.
So let My Word come, and abide deep in you,
    My Spirit will quicken, My Word and it's truth.
This truth will burn, in your heart like a fire,
    Awakening first love, and a holy desire,
To reach for the lost, and show them the way,
    The way to salvation, by what Jesus paid.
He gave of His life to restore and make new,
    He gave so we could receive, what is true!

CHRIST IN YOU - Inspired by John 15:5-8

Do others see Christ, abiding in you?
    Can they tell by your deeds, that He is The Truth?
By your words you give forth, what is deep in your heart,
    But do your deeds back your words, or do they take apart
The faith of the ones, Christ gave His life for,
    The very ones, Christ came to save, as The Door!
He's The Door to salvation, into Father God's heart,
    The Door to real life, with a brand new start.
His love is the way, that must guide your deeds,
    His love, the abundance to meet every need.

So love God in truth, and in spirit to show,
    To all here on earth, that the God who you know,
Is a God who commands us, to love like He does,
    With a love that has substance, and isn't just fuzz!
When you love like that, His abundance you'll see,
    Your life will give fruit, that's refreshing and free!
You will not hoard your money, for you'll know it's not yours,
    You'll give from the substance, of The Lord who outpours.
You will never regret, when you give in this way,
    And The Lord will be pleased, as you serve Him each day.

His abundance provides, to meet every need,
    It flows like a river, to bless every good deed.
What is done in His love, for His Glory will show,
    The way to The Father, to all here below.
For God is The One, who loved us all first,
    Who sent us His Son, to give us new birth.
Christ's Blood was the ransom, to pay for our sin,
    And now He stands ready, to welcome us in,
To the courts of heaven, to live and abide,,
    To the courts of heaven, where we'll never more die,
But live in The Gory, our God has prepared,
    For all those who chose, His great love to share.

OUR DESTINATION - Inspired by John 6:68 & 69

Where could I go, if not to You?
 Where could I go, Dear Lord?
Where could I go, for mercy and truth,
 Who but to You, My Lord!
You are The Author, of all that is good,
 You are The God, who is Love,
You could do more, that I ever could,
 You take me, to heaven above.

You give me the vision, to see what is true,
 What is pure, and holy and kind,
You show me Your mercy, you make me brand new,
 You mold and transform my mind.
You lead me into, Your Word to behold,
 Your love, in it's purest form,
You show me Your Word, my spirit to mold,
 To lift me above, the norm.

You anoint my eyes, with eye salve to see,
 The wonders, You have in store,
You give me a hearing heart, so I'll be,
 Your child forevermore.
Dear Holy Spirit, I ask You now,
 Awaken fresh passion in me,
Awaken my spirit, to seek and to bow,
 In pure adoration to Thee!

You are The One, who brought me to faith,
 In Jesus, as Saviour and Lord,
You quicken God's Word, to cut off like a lathe
 What hinders, from knowing God more!
So teach me and train me, to do as I should,
 So I'll love, my fellowman more,
For You are the source, of all that is good,
 Endow with Your heavenly store!

THE TEACHINGS OF JESUS - Inspired by John 7:16, 28 & 29

Jesus, You taught, what Your Father told You,
    So Your teaching brought life unto me,
What You gave forth, was the Living Truth,
    So all could be brought unto Thee!.
You challenged the ones, who thought they were smart,
    But did not believe what You said,
You healed on The Sabbath, which offended their hearts,
    You even raised the dead!
They looked for the praise, that came from men,
    They wanted to be known as wise,
They talked a big line, to embellish themselves,
    But refused Your Truth that divides.

Your Truth separates, soul and spirit to know,
    The God who calls to abide,
Who says to the ones, who offer their souls,
    I will make you My chosen, My bride.
You will not suffer want, for I will provide,
    What you need to live everyday,
My Spirit will lead you, protect and guide,
    So your feet will not falter or stray.
He will lead you on paths of righteousness,
    Of love and faith and peace,
This life by The Spirit, brings blessedness,
    Salvation and perfect peace..

So listen My child, to My Spirit always,
    Listen and hear and believe,
Listen then speak, what He tells you to say,
    So others can hear and receive.
Then if they will turn, to Christ as their source,
    If they'll leave their sinful lives,
If they'll hear and believe, that Jesus saves,
    They'll receive eternal life

LEAVE BABYLON - Inspired by Isaiah 48:20

Go forth out of Babylon, what it represents,
　　Go forth, for you have been sent,
Sent to proclaim, Christ's coming is near,
　　The veil separating, has been rent.
When Christ cried out, It is Finished, that day,
　　The temple's thick veil, God tore,
From the top to the bottom, He ripped it apart,
　　Christ Jesus, is salvation's door.
No more do we go, through a preacher or priest,
　　To have our sins forgiven,
But now by the Precious Blood of Christ,
　　We've access to God up in heaven.

Christ is coming again, to take to Himself,
　　His Church, His Body, His Bride,
He is coming with power, and glory to rule,
　　And to judge those, who cast Him aside.
So stand dear one, for what's holy and true,
　　Stand for His righteous cause,
Let Your heart seek after, The Lord to pursue,
　　His will with never a pause.
Draw close and listen, to Jesus The Christ,
　　Hear what His Spirit would say,
Reach and receive, what Holy Spirit imparts,
　　For then you'll know how to pray.

Your Saviour, Redeemer is calling your name,
　　Come out, you won't be the same.
Forsake the world, it's charms and allures,
　　Rejoice, for Christ's calling your name.
You'll come out with joy, singing His song,
　　For Your Bridegroom is, Jesus, The Christ,,
He came, He died, to save, to afford,
　　His sacrifice, paid the bride price!

332

<u>YOU - GOD CALLED</u> - Inspired by Isaiah 49

Did you know you were called, before you were born,
    Did you know He is calling, even now to reform?
To change you into, the image of Christ,
    Your Holy Redeemer, who paid your life price!
You thought that your work, was useless at best,
    But you trusted in Christ, and entered His rest.
You brought Him your hopes, and your dreams to His hand,
    You trusted His love, and His power to stand.
He hid you right there, in the shadow of His hand,
    Like an arrow in a quiver, now sharpened to stand,
Along with the others, till He shoots you forth,
    With a message of love, that says: Christ Restores!

He restores the hurting, broken, lost, and forlorn,
    To give them His Word, Come out, be reborn,
The Spirit of God, has sent you to call,
    All that Christ ransomed, to give of their all,
Into the hands, of The One who will bless,
    Will cleanse and make whole, from all their transgress.
The Lord has chosen, and made you His own,
    To stand at attention, before Father's throne.
We're to stand as the ones, He's redeemed and restored,
    Equipped by His Spirit, His Word to give forth.

To decree and declare, to make His Name known,
    To say to the prisoners, come up to God's throne.
Receive the forgiveness, Christ offers to you,
    Receive of the freedom, He purchased for you.
Then enter green pastures, where quiet streams,
    Refresh and restore, all those who esteem
His love and His life, as the greatest gift,
    For then their hearts, and their spirits will lift.
Their eyes will behold then, The Lord that they love,
    They'll be caught up to stand, before God above!

THE LORD - HE IS GOD - Inspired by Psalm 2

Do not fear, the kings of the earth,
 For though they rule and rage,
The Lord is God, over heaven and earth,
 Will rule past the end of the age.
Men make their plans, for glory and fame,
 Thinking that this is the way,
But only what is done, to honour God's Name,
 Will abide forever, will stay.

So what is the will of God for you?
 How can you know what He wills?
Read His Word, He will show you what's true,
 Holy Spirit, will illumine then fill.
He will fill you so full, of God's precious love,
 A love that cannot be compared,
He will give you a faith, that will take you above,
 A faith that can only be shared.

For when God reveals, His plan for you,
 When He opens your eyes to see,
You'll wonder, you'll marvel, at His glorious truth,
 His grace and redemption for thee.
Then your heart will be, so filled with love,
 You will want all others to know,
The grace and the mercy, from God up above,
 Is meant to give out here below!

This hope and faith, in Christ Jesus as Lord,
 As Saviour, Redeemer and Friend,
Will be given to all, then bring to accord,
 The souls of all men to amend!
They will be transformed, into the image of Christ,
 To have the mind of The Lord,
To receive by faith, Christ's sacrifice,
 To be held by Love's strong cord!

OMNIPOTENT GOD - Inspired by Daniel 3 & Zephaniah 3

Oh Holy, Perfect, Omnipotent God,
    You have given us eyes to see,
Then bow and worship, while this earth we trod,
    Your Wonder, Your Majesty!
For there is no other, who can save like you,
    Who delivers from men, and their schemes,
Who gives us the faith, to trust and believe,
    In The Saviour, who ransoms, redeems.

You come like the fourth man into the fire,
    To save and protect, those who fear—
The Lord, our God, to defeat that liar,
    For he only taunts and jeers!
Only You, Lord God, have the power to reign,
    Only You, are The King of kings,
No man and no devil, could ever defame,
    Our Saviour, The God who sings!

You sing over us, with Your song of love,
    You sing to the ransomed, redeemed,
Your song gives us hope, to come up above,
    As Your bride, the one You esteem.
So what can we say, in response to you?
    What can we do to say thanks,
We will give you our lives, in spirit and truth,
    We'll join as Your army in ranks!

We will honour those, You have placed over us,
    To teach and strengthen and guide,
We'll realize that without You, we're lost,
    And then in Your love we'll abide!
So cause us to stand, for Your love always,
    Cause us to always remain,
Your people, Your children, for all of our days,
    To evermore Praise Your Name!

<u>YOUR PROMISES - LORD GOD</u> - Inspired by Psalm 37

Your promises Lord God, are rich and true,
    They teach me what is best,
They give me hope, when all seems lost,
    They lead to Your perfect rest.
They show Your reward, if we treasure the cost,
    The cost that You paid that day,
When Your Son, our Saviour, went to the cross,
    Our sins and our ransom were paid.

I now can enter, For Christ made the way,
    By His Precious Holy Blood,
I receive Your promise, reserved for all,
    Who cry out for Your greater good!
This good is salvation, from sin and loss
    This good You purchased for us,
This good you won, when You died on that cross,
    Delivered from sin and from lust.

You have called us to live godly, in spirit and truth,
    To forsake the sin that defiles,
To receive the blessings You have prepared,
    To live a life that's worthwhile.
So line up our hearts with Yours, Oh Lord,
    Line us up to show the way,
To those whose hearts, need You Oh Lord,
    To know that You hear when we pray!

I commit my ways, unto You Lord God,
    In Your presence, Your peace is found,
All that we need for life and strength,
    You give, by Your grace which abounds.
So I will not fear, when the hard times come,
    For our provision Lord God is in You,
Whether food for the body, or spirit or soul,
    You'll provide for Your promise is true!

HIGHER THAN THE HEAVENS
Inspired by Psalm 97 & Ephesians 1:4

Higher still, Oh Lord, You are, higher than the highest star!
For by Your Word, You made heaven and earth,
You bring us to where You are!
Who are we in Your scheme of things,
Oh Lord, why are we here?
You, who cause all heaven to sing, draw us and bring us near.

You chose us Lord, before all time, to make us wholly Thine,
What awesome love, what rapturous bliss,
For You lift from sin and grime!
Now, those who know Your Love, Your kiss,
Who've received Your love, divine,
Can receive what all, by sin had missed, a life restored, sublime!

You have given us life, like we've never known,
You have washed and made us clean,
And now You bring us before God's throne,
Your child, forever redeemed!
Together with saints and angels we'll raise, our voices in one accord,
To Praise You Lord with all we are, for You are God, The Lord!

We pray Lord God, that You would cause,
Our hearts to now bring forth, Your words that give eternal life
To west, east, south and north.
Cause us to call, to one and all, Come in and taste and see,
The Lord our God is good to all, He came and set us free!

So let's repent, of all our sin, our doubt, our unbelief,
Receive His Holy Spirit now, begin a brand new leaf.
A leaf, that's made alive, brand new, a leaf that's undefiled,
A page, where God can write His truth,
For now we're made worthwhile!

WHO CAN COMPREHEND?
Inspired by Job 37:5 & Matthew 13:23

Who can comprehend Your grace,
Receive Your mercy, see Your face?
Only those who hear Your call, only those who give their all!
For grace like Yours, must be received, so we can enter and believe!

As we go through, each brand new day,
Help us to see by grace, Your way,
Believe Your Word, believe what's true,
Believe that what You say, You'll do!

Help us to see, with sight made new,
Your Word, Your Truth, Your Point of View!
Then we can choose by faith, what's right,
And leave the darkness, for The Light,
Then walk the paths, made plain and pure,
To walk by faith, each step made sure.

You are The substance, of all that is good,
Your life, an example to do as we should,
To walk by faith, and not by sight,
To walk in paths, that You've made right.
For You are The Way, The Truth and The Life,
Only Your salvation, removes the strife!

We know we could never, save ourselves,
No works of ours, could save from hell,
But by Your mercy and Your grace,,
You paid the price, removed each trace,
Of sin and death, of hell and grave,
You gave Your life, to see us saved!

So now equipped to run Your race; the race we're called to win,
Help us to run with strength and grace, for You Lord, conquered sin!

<u>WHY ARE YOU WHERE YOU ARE?</u> - Inspired by Isaiah 55

Why are you there at this House of Prayer,
    If not to minister, to serve and to care?
To lead by example, the life that I want,
    A life that is humble and loving, not gaunt;
But filled with a fullness, from My supply,
    Abounding in grace, for those who will try,
Will try to live, a holy pure life,
    Will cease from all sin, all worry and strife.

I will give you a word, that is faithful and true,
    That shows to all men, I'm The God who makes new,
Who binds up the broken, and comforts the lost,
    Who bears all their burdens, not counting the cost!
For no man can do, what I do for you,
    No man can give you, a life that is true.
No one can redeem, make straight, make pure,
    No one can make, your election sure.

I gave My life, as your Sacrifice,
    My Blood shed for you, will always suffice,
Will purify, purge, and deliver from sin,
    So all who believe, can be cleansed within.
I purify hearts, from all that defiles,
    I cleanse and make new, a life that's worthwhile.
My love and My mercy, will draw you near,
    My Presence will show you, My love pure and clear.
My love will transform, My love will complete,
    All that is lacking, all that depletes.

My love makes whole, what was broken and lost,
    My love made the way, when I took to the cross,
All of the sin and the sorrow and shame,
    All that was used, to destroy and defame.
So rejoice, My child, your life I've made new,
    Rejoice, for My love, has sanctified you!

PRAISE AND THANKS BE UNTO YOU, OH GOD

We praise and thank You, Lord God Almighty!
 Your works and words are strong, not flighty!
You give to all the will to do,
 The plans that make, our lives come true.
No one can add, to what You've done,
 You gave to us, Your Only Son,
To suffer, bleed and die for all,
 So we could answer, heaven's call,
To repent of all, that leads to sin,
 Then enter by, Your grace within!

Oh Heavenly God, You've made us clean,
 By the Blood of Christ, we've been redeemed,
To stand before, Your holy throne,
 To praise and make, Your glories known.

So as we start our tasks, this week,
 Make us Your temple, pure and meek.
Give us a heart and mind, like Christ's,
 To live for You, what 'ere the price.
For then Your joy, will be our strength,
 And love to give, our days the length,
So we can do, what You want done,
 So we can worship, Christ Your Son!
We'll worship with, our heart and hands,
 For Christ fulfilled, the laws demands.

As we've been forgiven, help us to forgive,
 Then help us by, Your precepts live,
In such a way, to honour You,
 For then our lives, will show what's true.
All men will glorify, You Lord,
 When they see our hearts, in one accord,
Reaching out, to save the lost,
 Leading them to Christ, His cross!

LISTEN - Inspired by Luke 8:18

Listen now, all you who hear,
    Draw nigh and hear, The Spirit clear,
For at the cross, God's love is shown,
    His Word made flesh, His grace atones.
He took the wrongs, which we had done,
    Became the sin, we thought was fun.
This so-called fun, brought death and hell,
    Would take us from, God's perfect will.
But God in mercy, had a plan,
    And Christ became, the way for man,
To be forever cleansed, made clean,
    So that by grace, we are redeemed.

Christ takes our broken, misspent lives,
    Creates, makes new, by sacrifice.
Then plants His will, into our hearts,
    To give us all, a brand new start.
His mercies are new, to us each day,
    His Blood alone, has made the way,
The way to come, before our King,
    To worship Him, His praises sing!
So come believe, in Christ who saves,
    You'll have a life, beyond the grave!

Oh don't put off, this saving grace,
    Receive Christ's love, behold His face.
See in His eyes, His look of love,
    For by His grace, He takes above,
To Father God, the ones who choose,
    His life, for then they cannot lose.
Then there with all, who have been redeemed,
    We'll worship Christ, live by His stream.
There we will be, refreshed, made whole,
    By Christ, The Shepherd of our souls.

PRAYER FOR LIFE - Inspired by The Holy Spirit

Holy Spirit, I pray, hover over me,
    Bring forth new life, life pure and free!
Convict me of sin, and righteousness,
    My need to repent, for forgiveness.
Then cause me to hear, Your still small voice,
    Saying come unto Me, make My will your choice.
Come unto Me, with arms open wide,
    Come unto Me, by My side to abide.

Let My word dwell there, richly in you,
    So that your mind, can be changed, renewed,
Renewed to receive, what I have to impart,
    Renewed to receive, from your Father's heart.
A message of love, and the hope that revives,
    A message to share, of a life that's alive;
Alive to behold, what God has for you,
    With eyes that can see, and a word that is true!

From what I impart, you will have to give,
    A message that calls, unto men to live;
Live for The Lord, who paid with His life,
    Live for The Lord, who redeems you from strife.
Live and behold, His unchanging love,
    Live and receive, from your Father above.,
Receive the salvation, prepared for you,
    Receive of His grace, and His mercy too.

Then reach out and give, what He has given to you,
    Reach out in His power, so others can choose,
A life made alive, by Holy Spirit's power,
    A life that can quicken, each day and each hour.
You will see like you have never, seen before,
    The way to real life, for faith is the door.
It's the door to receive, His commission to go,
    To give of His love, to make His grace known!

For the bruised reed, He will not break,
    And the lonely soul, He will not forsake.
He will send you to heal, the broken forlorn,
    To bind up the hearts, that the devil has torn.
He'll use you to be, His arms and His hands,
    For then you will do, what His love demands.
Love The Lord your God, with all of your heart,
    And love your neighbour, with the love God imparts.

Forgive, as He has forgiven you,
    Restore by His grace, and His mercy too.
Don't ask for justice, but let mercy cover,
    All that needs healing, for God to recover,
With His life and His love, to redeem and make whole,
    With His mercy and grace, to quicken men's souls.
Without You, Holy Spirit, we cannot believe,
    But by You, Holy Spirit, we see Christ who redeems.

We see the ones You have chosen, to redeem and restore,
    The ones You want with You, forevermore.
So we will reach out to those, You bring to us now,
    We will reach out in love, and fulfill our vow,
The vow to tell, all men of Your love,
    So they can enter, Your courts up above.
For all need to know, that Christ is The Way,
    They need to receive, of His grace today!

Today is the day, of salvation for all,
    Who hear and repent, and then give their all,
For it is there where they are, You receive right away,
    You take them, and then clean them up to say:
I AM The Lord, who loves and forgives,
    I AM your Saviour, I will cause you to live,
Live in a way, of perfect peace,
    You will live with a joy, that will never cease!

GOD'S CREATIVE POWER - Inspired by Genesis 1,2, & 3

In the beginning, God created heaven and earth,
    With all we'd have need of, for life and new birth,
He made with perfection, according to plan,
    And then in His image, God created man.
God Blessed Adam and Eve, and said multiply,
    Fill the earth and subdue it, for I AM God on high.
I have made you the masters, over all I have given,
    Now live here on earth, as I live there in heaven!
Bring My rule to the earth, so that all living things,
    Will see My power, and the life that it brings.
Only one restriction, God gave unto man,
    One tree was forbidden, to partake of for man;
The tree of the knowledge of evil and good,
    God forbade them to eat, for then they would
Know what would bring them, to death and the curse,
    For then God's commission, for them would reverse!
Instead of dominion over land and sea,
    They would have to labour, to produce what they need.

But they did not know this, when the devil came,
    As a serpent to beguile, to deceive and defame,
He spoke with half-truths, like he always does,
    For he wants to destroy, all the good that God does!
His aim is to sever, all what would bring life,
    He's the author of all, the confusion and strife.
Death and destruction, are what he does best,
    He's a thief of all, that would lead to God's rest!
When he came to Eve, with the forbidden fruit,
    He lied, and his words brought doubt to take root,
He caused her to question, The Word that God said,
    He planted the seed, of doubt in her head.
So when Eve partook of the forbidden fruit,
    She gave to Adam, and he also took.
Their eyes were opened, and then they felt shame,
    They saw they were naked, so hid when God came.

They heard God walking, in the garden that night,
    But they hid, for now they were filled with fright.
No more were they pure, for they had disobeyed,
    The God who had made them, in His image one day!
God wanted for man, to fellowship with Him,
    God wanted communion, with these ones, without sin.
When God called to Adam, and asked where are you?
    He knew they had hid, for He knows what we do.
They came out of hiding, to answer God's call,
    They said we hid, for we were naked and all.
God asked them then, who had told them this news,
    "Have you ate of the tree, which you were to refuse?"
Then Adam blamed Eve, and Eve blamed the snake,
    Who tricked them to eat, what they weren't to partake.
The earth then became, a place of man's toil,
    Now what they needed, had to come from the soil..
Their provision would now come, from struggle and sweat,
    Eve would bring forth children, with pain and yet,
Her desire would be, for her husband to rule,
    He would be her master, and she would be schooled,
To learn submission, to listen, be taught,
    For she was the first one, the devil had caught,

But even then God, our Lord had a plan,
    To redeem His children, by a perfect man.
Holy Spirit hovered over, a virgin one day,
    And a life from God, was created to say,
That God in His love, had sent us His Son,
    To redeem for all man, by the only pure One.
Christ's Blood on the cross, was the pure sacrifice,
    His blood that washed clean, from sin's awful price.
For the soul that sins, it shall die,
    But by faith in Christ Jesus, we'll never die.
All we need to do, is repent and believe,
    Believe in God's Son, and then receive,
The forgiveness, He offers to all humankind,
    And sight to see, where before we'd been blind!

FAITH IS THE EVIDENCE THAT LEADS TO GOD
Inspired by Hebrews 11:1 and Revelation 22

Faith is the evidence of things not seen,
    The substance of things hoped for,
Faith in Christ Jesus, The One who redeems,
    Is the key that opens the door.
This door can't be opened, by what our hands do,
    Our works could not hope to attain,
But by Christ's Blood, The One who is true,
    Our voices can join the refrain,
Of praise and worship, thanksgiving and song,
    We can lift our hearts to God's throne,
Proclaiming The Name of our Saviour, The Strong,
    The God who redeems, who atones.
Then, Oh the joy, of a soul forgiven,
    The wonders of God's awesome grace,
To be made His child, to enter heaven, to there behold His face!
    For when we are privileged to look upon,
    Our Redeemer, The One we adore,
Our minds and our hearts are free, from what bound,
    For Christ Himself is The Door.
He's The Door to real life and joy and peace,
    The door to a brand new heart,
The door that brings to each soul, His release,
    From all that destroys, takes apart.

So Holy Spirit, please lead us on, from faith unto faith until,
    We see The One, who gave us His Son,
    Who chose us and loves us still.
We'll cast our crowns then at His feet, the crowns of righteousness,
    For He is The One, we bow, we greet,
    The One who freed us from death.
We will cast our crowns, at Christ's precious feet,
    We will cast our crowns to say,
That You are The One, who makes us complete,
    The Truth, The Life, The Way.

For no one could come to The Father,
    No one could approach, His Throne,
Until Christ, The Redeemer, our Brother,
    Made the way by His Blood alone!
He alone, could pay the price, He alone could save,
    He alone our sacrifice, redeems from death and grave!

The King of kings, and Lord of lords, will rule forever now
The One we worship and adore, The One to whom we vowed.
To give our lives, what we possessed, without any restriction,
For Jesus Christ, who paid our price, has given us our mission.

So spread this news to all you meet, share His wondrous love,
Give His message, pure and sweet, so more can come above
Above to where The Saviour waits, above at God's right hand,
For there He stands and He awaits, to show His Bride, His land!

This land is heaven, the blessed place, where neither sun nor moon,
Are needed to behold His Face, for Glory lights each room.
No normal day or night are there, for in eternity,
God is The Light, without compare, The Holy Deity!

God's river there is flowing, through the middle of this land,
While trees of life on either side, provide with fruit on hand.
Each month a new variety, fresh fruit and leaves that heal,
What needs to be restored for those, who now have come to kneel.

The Throne of God and of The Lamb, are central to this place,
His servants there will worship Him, receive His warm embrace.
They'll see The One who died for them, then rose on that third day,
The Holy Sinless Son of God, who took their sin away!

So live for Christ, The One who saves, determine now to choose,
The One who ransomed you from death, for then you will not lose.
Oh child of God, please hear me now, confess to God your sins,
Then receive His gift of life for you, He will bid you to come in!

<u>WHY THE BLOOD?</u>-Inspired by Genesis 4, and Revelation 1:5

Blood was shed, in the garden that day,
>   For God to cover, His children to say,
I will cover your shame and your nakedness,
>   I'll protect you from all, that would bring you duress
From then until Christ, sins could not be forgiven
>   Without the shedding of blood,
For the life that is in us, is carried along,
>   In the life stream, in our blood.

Abel knew this, when He brought unto God,
>   A lamb as a sacrifice for sin,
But Cain didn't heed the instruction of God,
>   He wanted his own way to win.
He brought from the fruit of his own toil,
>   From the ground which God had cursed,
Instead of admitting his sin before God,
>   He wanted his way, so perverse.

So let us rely on The Blood of Christ,
>   For only by faith are we saved,
Only by trusting Christ's sacrifice,
>   Are we saved from hell and the grave.
Let us never treat, the grace we've been given,
>   As something to abuse with sin,
For only The Blood of Jesus, The Christ,
>   Paid the way for us to come in.

Holy Spirit, I pray, create in me,
>   A heart that is pure and free,
Free to behold all that God has done,
>   To see with eyes made clean,
Help me never to trust in my own works,
>   For my works could never suffice
To make the way,, to Your heart each day,
>   For Christ's Blood alone, paid my price!,

WHEN YOU SAY OUR FATHER-Inspired by Matthew 6:9-15

Jesus said, When you pray, say Our Father,
    Who is in heaven, Hallowed be Your Name,
For His is The Kingdom and Glory,
    His will we are to ever proclaim.
His kingdom must come on earth as in heaven,
    If ever we are to have peace,
For only His will done His way on earth,
    Will bring us our soul's release.

His will is to have all men believe, believe in Jesus, His Son,
For Christ alone, by the price that He paid, for us salvation has won..
Now we can call God, our Father, by believing in Christ The Lord,
And Christ Jesus becomes our brother, to worship forevermore.

Oh what a brother is Jesus, our Lord, He gave His life for all,
He paid the price to redeem our souls, He saved us from the fall!
Now we are free by His grace, by His mercy and goodness restored,
Free to tell all the others, that for all, Jesus blood was outpoured.

Holy Lord Jesus, You alone are The Christ, The One that we adore,
For You gave Your life as a sacrifice, to become for us The Door.
You left Your home, Your heavenly throne, to save and rescue me,
To be born as a baby, our lives to atone, then die on that cruel tree!

You walked in obedience, in faith and love,
    You did what You saw Father do,
You showed by example, how we are to love,
    To lead men to all of The Truth!
You showed by Your life, what God was like,
    A God full of mercy and truth,
Who longs to show, His goodness to all,
    To redeem what's profane and uncouth!
So help us reach out, as you reached to us, in mercy and in love,
For this is Your call, to one and all, Come up to heaven above,

<u>THE FOURTH MAN</u> - Inspired by Daniel 3 and Isaiah 43

Free with the fourth man, in the fire,
   Free to accomplish, my hearts desire,
To walk unhindered, no longer bound,
   By ropes of sin, for now I've found,
The way that leads, to a life of peace,
   Of love and joy which never cease.

Now I know, who The Fourth Man is,
   I know His love, I know I'm His.
Because I'm His, I no longer fear,
   For He has made, His promise clear.
Now by His Spirit, His Word I believe,
   And now by His Spirit, I can receive,
The faith and trust, that I need in life,
   The faith that removes, all fear and strife.

Christ said, if I will enter into His rest,
   If I'll cease from my labours, then I'll be blest,
For it's only by trusting in Christ, who saves,
   Can I ever be saved from hell and the grave.
No works of mine, could ever produce,
   No works of mine, could ever loose,
The ropes of pride, or fear or sin,
   The ropes that bound me, kept me in.
In this place of faith, I now am free,
   Free to follow, God's destiny.

So whatever furnace is before me now,
   I will not fear, for I trust His vow:
When you walk through the fire, you'll not be burned,
   Or in the deep waters, for I have learned,
That my Lord and Saviour, keeps me close,
   By the will and power, of The Holy Ghost.
The only things, that will be burned off,
   Are the ropes that caused all men to scoff!

For The Lord I trust, is God alone,
    My Saviour, Redeemer, is on The Throne,
From there He issues, His Word of command,
    From there He leads, to His Promised land.
For now promotion, is there if I ask,
    For now provision, is there for the task.
I no longer need walk, in my strength alone,
    I walk in the power, of my Lord who atones.
I'm now one with Christ, by His work on the cross,
    And the only things burned, are the sin and the dross.

The pure gold remains then, the gold that He gives,
    The gold of a life, that's completely His.
He said, Buy from Me gold, that's tried in the fire,
    For only His gold, will fulfill our desires.
Only His gold, is totally pure,
    Only His gold, is the gold that endures.
Earthly riches, will burn on that day,
    But the heavenly ones, can endure come what may.
For God, who makes our election sure,
    Is The God who cleanses, and makes us pure;
Pure by trusting in The Blood of The Lamb,
    Pure by believing, in The Great I AM!

He'll never leave us, or ever forsake,
    The ones He has called, for He will make,
The way for us, who trust in Him,
    The way for us, to abide, come within;
Into the circle, of His loving arms,
    Protected, set free, from all that alarms.
There is no fear, when His arms hold us close,
    There is only His love, by The Holy Ghost.
In this love, we have the peace that we need,
    In His pastures, We will rest and feed,
Feed on what, His hand provides,
    Led by His Spirit, our Holy Guide!

LEAVE YOUR NETS - Inspired by Matthew 4:19-22

Leave you nets, come follow Me,
    Leave your nets, I'll make you free,
Free to follow, the course I've planned,
    Free to travel, throughout the land;
Free to preach, the word I give,
    Free to love, and then forgive,

Forgive, as I have forgiven you,
    Then love, as I have loved you too.
For when you walk, in this My way,
    All then can see, by what you say,
By what you say, and what you do,
    That I AM The Way, The Life, The Truth!

Many streams, are out there now,
    Streams that lead, to disavow,
Streams which lead, to death and grave,
    Streams which say, all ways can save.
But that is not the truth from God,
    For only Christ, is The Way to God!.

So do not dilute, the word you preach,
    Speak My Word, let My Word teach,
Teach The Way, The One Pure Way,
    So men will walk, and never stray,
Walk in truth, and holiness,
    Walk in faith, and righteousness!

Yes I have a job, for you to do,
    Speak and live, each day what's true.
Your life and words, will preach and teach,
    To bring all men, into My reach.
For they must see Me, in what you do,
    Your life a sermon, that speaks the truth!

Let you life be a witness, for all to know,
That The God who loves them, came below!
He left the glories, of heaven to save,
The ones who would hear, and then behave,
Like The Christ, The Anointed, Son of God,
To live by His Spirit, The Spirit of God!

No one can live, like The Christ who atones,
Unless by The Power, of Holy Spirit alone.
Holy Spirit will give, the power to live,
In the steps of Christ Jesus, The One who forgives.

So let the message you preach, be very clear,
Keep it pure and simple, so all can hear,
Hear and believe, that forgiveness is there,
For all who repent, and believe that Christ cares!
He cares enough, to redeem and restore,
He cares to lead, to His side evermore.

So live each day, with your eyes upon Me,
Live in My love, so men can be freed,
Freed from the streams, of deception and lies,
Freed from confusion, and compromise.
Freed to enter, My Life-Giving Stream,
Freed to be cleansed, by My Blood that redeems.

Only My Blood, can cleanse every stain,
Only My Blood, can cause to remain,
What is pure and holy, a spirit made new,
A brand new life, made clean and made true..

So let My Spirit, direct your steps,
Let My will in your hearts, be always kept,
So that ever and always, My Word you will preach
So ever and always, all men can be reached!
Reached with My saving grace, from heaven,
By The love of The Father, in Jesus Christ given!

THE BODY OF CHRIST
Inspired by Philippians 2 & 1st Corinthians 12

We are Christ's body, when He is our head,
    When we walk by His Spirit, and allow to be led,
Into places where we, can be used by Him,
    To tell all men, of God's forgiveness from sin.
We are Christ's body, when we love God first,
    For He sent us His Son, to redeem from the curse,
The curse of sin, and the condemning it brings,
    For Christ ransomed from hell, and the grave with it's sting.
We are Christ's body, when we prefer one another,
    As being better than us, showing love to each other,
And honouring those, Christ has placed over all,
    To teach us His ways, His will and His call.

We are Christ's body, when we reach out to bless,
    Our sisters or brothers, in their need or distress,
Not just with a word, of compassion or hope,
    But with the substance, that helps to live and to cope.
We are Christ's body, when our hearts beat like His,
    When we act with compassion, to those not yet His,
When we show His love, not counting the cost,
    The love that He showed, when He died on the cross.
We are Christ's body, when we ask for eye salve,
    To see what He sees, and then to give what we have,
For nothing we have, is for us alone,
    All that we have, comes from Christ who atones.

We are Christ's body, when our ears hear His voice,
    When we make His will, not ours, our choice,
When we choose to surrender, our lives to His cause,
    For His love is eternal, His grace does not pause.
We are Christ's body, when we join with each other
    To praise and to worship, as sisters and brothers,
To The God Who Alone, is The Ancient of Days,
    The Only Wise God, Who is worthy of praise!

JESUS, WHAT DID YOU MEAN BY THESE WORDS?
Inspired by John 6:48-69

Jesus, what did you mean when You said, Eat My Flesh?
And What did You mean when You said, Drink My Blood?
You said, My Flesh is real food and My Blood is real drink.

Let all of Me, be part of you,
 Be part of My body, where I have placed you.
Do not ever try, to be what you're not,
 For I purchased your life, by My Blood, you were bought!
So when I say to you, eat My flesh,
 I want you to know, that my life is the mesh,
That bonds and binds you to each other,
 As members together, as sister and brother.
And when I say to you, drink My Blood,
 My Life in My Blood, redeems from the flood,
And when you drink of My Blood, you have life,
 The life that I give, that removes every strife.

What you eat and drink, becomes part of you,
That is where I must be, that part of you,
The part that decides, what is best and true,
The part that makes, decisions for you.

Many left My side, when I spoke those words,
 Didn't want to release, their will to serve,
They thought they could live life, without My control,
 But by thinking that way, they brought doom to their souls
For only a life that's presented to me,
 Can live in a freedom, that is pure and redeemed.
Only a life with Me as The Head,
 Can choose what is good, and holy instead.
So eat and drink, from what I give you,
 Eat and partake, so your life can be true,
True to The One, who ransomed your soul,
 True to The One, who alone makes you whole!

THE ROCK - Inspired by Psalm 19

You are The Rock, upon which I stand,
    You hold me up, with Your strong right hand,
When the road seems rough, You clear the way,
    You Word is The Light, that guides each day.
You open the doors, that I'm to walk through,
    You close the doors, that keep me from You,
For You answer my prayers, to keep me close,
    You lead and You guide, by The Holy Ghost.
You speak a word, that leads me to You,
    For there I find, the life that rings true.

Only Your Word, has the power to heal,
    Only Your Word, can cleanse and reveal,
The deepest thoughts, and intents of my heart,
    For it is there by Your Spirit, that You plant and impart,
The Truth that leads to eternal life,
    The Truth that delivers, from heartache and strife.

You are The Powerful, All Knowing God,
    You created the heavens, and the earth we trod.
You spoke, and everything came to be,
    Now everything speaks, of Your Glory, to see,
That You, Lord God, are The Only Wise God,
    You're The Holy God, who is worthy of laud!

We offer to You, glory, worship and praise,
    And we bow and give thanks to you, Ancient of Days!
For You have no beginning, and You have no end,
    Your life is eternal, so on You we depend!
Everything else, is transition at best,
    Only in You, is perfection and rest.
Only in You, is salvation and peace,
    Only in You, do our hearts find release,
For You Lord God, are The lover of souls,
    And in Your great love, we're redeemed and made whole!

LAMB OF GOD WHO WIPES OUR TEARS
Inspired by Revelation 7:17

Lamb of God, You wipe the tears,
    Of all You call, all You draw near,
You wipe the tears, from every eye,
    Of those you've sealed, who never die.
You sent Your angels, to seal Your own,
    All who would worship, You alone.

You know the ones, who have made the choice,
    To hear and live, by Your Spirit's voice
Who answered yes, to Your heavenly call,
    To give their lives, their dreams, their all,
Into Your Holy Hand, Oh Lord,
    There to be kept, by love's strong cord.
Only Your love and grace, make right,
    The souls of men, who will walk in the light.

Oh Light of The World, we come, we bow,
    We worship You, we make our vow,
To love and serve You, all our days,
    To lift our voice to You, with praise.
For no one, can compare with You,
    You are The Way, The Light, The Truth.
Your blood alone, Oh Holy Lamb,
    Can bring me to God, The Great I AM.

Your blood has cleansed and cleans me still,
    It washes fresh, each day to kill,
All wrong desire, so I'll do Your will,
    With joy that brings me strength until,
I reach that golden blessed shore,
    To live with You, forevermore,
Then with the saints, around Your Throne,
    I'll worship You and You alone!

ON TO PERFECTION - Inspired by Hebrews 6:1

On to perfection, The Word of God says,
    On to perfection, to raise the dead,
On to perfection, to decree and declare,
    On to perfection, God's Word to share.
For we have been given, the message that keeps,
    Our hearts and our minds, when the road is steep.
When it seems we cannot, reach the top,
    His Word calls out, come near, don't stop,
So let The Master take your hand,
    He gives the strength, to take the land.

Now when we go, in His strength and power,
    To declare to men, this is the hour,
The hour to receive, Christ's sacrifice,
    As our pure Redeemer, who paid our price,
His Spirit will empower, the word we speak,
    To save the lost, the wounded, the weak!
Our only task, is to preach His Word,
    In the love and the truth, that God assures,
For He puts His Name, above all names,
    So in His Name, all can be saved.

We are not saved, by our pure, holy deeds,
    But by trusting Christ, God's Holy Seed!
Oh let His Spirit, now plant within,
    The life of Christ, that saves from sin.
The Life and Light, that shows The Way,
    The Way to come, to God today.
For today is the day, of salvation for all,
    Who hear His voice, and answer His call,
The call to leave, all sin and vice,
    The call to receive, Christ's sacrifice.
Then forsaking the sin, and the grief it gives,
    You will enter Christ's life, to really live.

GIVING OF THANKS - Inspired by Luke 17:16-19

Like the leper You cleansed, in the gospel of Luke,
    I want to give You, Lord God, my thanks,
For what You have given, and all that you do,
    I thank You, to stand with the ranks,
Of those You've redeemed, the broken and lost
    All those You have healed, and forgiven,
For You have cleansed my soul, from every stain.
    So I could gain entrance to heaven.

Christ's Blood was poured, on The Mercy Seat,
    As an offering, so we could meet,
Our Lord And Saviour, King and God,
    Then bow at His Holy feet!
So give Him glory, all children of men,
    For He has forgiven our sin,
We are washed and made clean, by His Precious Blood,
    We're ransomed, from our failures, within.
No more a sinner, condemned, unclean,
    But now the righteous, redeemed..
For eternal life You have given to me,
    A life in heaven, with Thee.

Oh Precious Redeemer, my Saviour, my Lord,
    You have brought me into Your Place,
No more a sinner or rebel, am I,
    But Your child, beholding Your face!
So I ask You now, Oh Lord, my God,
    Help me to give forth, what You have given,
Your mercy and love, forgiveness too,
    To lead all men, into heaven..
By Your Spirit cause me, to proclaim Your Truth,
    To give forth Your Word, faithfully,
Then with a loving heart and a spirit You've freed.
    All men can be led unto Thee!

<u>A DREAM FROM THE LORD</u> - Inspired by Genesis 37-50

When you get a dream that's too big for you,
    Like Joseph did in The Bible,
Trust in The Lord, to bring it to pass,
    For His Word, is ever reliable
If it seems impossible, look to The Lord,
    For everything is possible in Him,
The One who created, the heavens and earth,
    Will gives you, His Spirit within.

When His Spirit comes in, faith comes too,
    To trust and ever believe,
That what He has planted, will always come true,
    If you will believe, you'll receive.
He speaks in a whisper, to those who will hear
    To those who will listen real close,
He'll awaken your heart, to come and draw near,
    To be led by The Holy Ghost.

He will open the doors, that you're to walk through,
    You won't have to push or shove,
Just stay real close, to your Saviour Dear,
    And always walk in His love.
He will make the dreams, He has given to you,
    Come to pass in His own time,
So don't look at things, that detract from His truth,
    Keep your eyes on your Lord, so sublime!

Holy Spirit, I pray, give me vision to see,
    Your will, Your eternal plan,
So that I will ever believe and keep faith,
    For You, are The Great I AM!
You know the way, that I should go
    You hold me by Your hand,
So let my love for You proclaim,
    Your Word across this land!

<u>WHOM DO YOU TRUST?</u> - Inspired by Proverbs 3:3-10

In whom do you trust, when you face your Red Sea?
　Do you look to The Lord, or do you say, poor me?
In whom do you place, your hope and your trust?
　Don't trust in yourself, for flesh is but dust!
Listen instead, to Holy Spirit within,
　Listen, then flee, from the trap you are in,
Focus on The Lord, who gave you His life,
　He's the Only One, who delivers from strife!

If you will love The Lord God, with all of your heart,
　Then love your neighbour, right from the start,
Love will always conquer, defeat Satan's plan,
　Love will ever deliver, from the fear of man.
Fear has torment, but faith brings peace,
　The faith by His Spirit, in you brings release.
The waters will part, and you will go through,
　For God will make, a plain path for you.

So trust in The Lord, with all of your heart,
　Seek first His Kingdom, and never depart,
For The Word of Life, has been planted in you,
　Trust in His Spirit, He'll bring you through.
The flames will not hurt you, the waters won't drown,
　The hope that's within you, for God has a crown,
A crown of life, if you're faithful to stand,
　A crown that says, Christ has conquered for man.

So listen to what Holy Spirit reveals,
　Listen take heed, do not let Satan steal.
Let your faith grow daily, in God's Holy Word,
　For His Word can be trusted, His Word is sure.
The Word became flesh, and dwelt among men,
　Then died for our lives, to redeem us from sin.
So keep your heart fastened, on The Holy, The True,
　Your Lord, your Redeemer, He lives for you!

REPENTANCE AND REDEMPTION - Inspired by Holy Spirit

What an awesome privilege, to turn from our sin,
    To receive God's salvation, and enter in,
Into His courts, to worship and praise,
    Our Saviour, Christ Jesus, The One Whom God raised!
He was raised from the dead, after paying our price,
    After giving His life, as a pure sacrifice!
No sin was found, in The Son of God,
    No stain or corruption, in The Lamb of God,
But only compassion, and love for the lost,
    So much He became, our sin on that cross!

Our Father in heaven, had to turn from His Son,
    His Only Beloved, His Chosen One,
For sin separates, every man from God's face,
    It destroys and deceives, and produces disgrace.
But The Holy Pure One, Jesus, The Christ,
    Gave freely His Blood, to pay our price.
He ransomed our souls, from death and the grave,
    Took back the keys, so we could be saved;
Saved from the lies, that trapped us in sin,
    Saved us to love, gave a new heart within.

So bow to The One, who paid with His blood,
    Worship Christ Jesus, who saved from sin's flood.
Give Him Your life, give Him Your love,
    Give your all to Christ Jesus, our Lord up above.
Give Him the honour, that is due His Dear Name,
    Give Him Your worship, His praise to proclaim.
For by Holy Spirit, He has called you to come,
    And By Holy Spirit, He calls all, not just some;
Calls to repent and forsake all their sin,
    Then gives of the faith. to believe, enter in;
Into His courts, to worship and praise,
    Our Holy Great God, The Ancient of Days!

THE MORE OF GOD - Inspired by John 14

There is the more for you, My child, more of Me, so come abide,
Abide in the shelter of My arms, abide in peace, free from all harm.
Then wait and watch, My Spirit move,
He will lead the way, He will give you proof,
That what I said, is what I'll do, for Me to be formed into you.

He will lead you to, My pastures green,
    Where you will feed, on what's unseen
You said you want, My more to give,
    So men may see, My more and live,
Live then by what, My Spirit provides,
    Live by the faith, which never dies!
This faith comes not, by word alone,
    But from My Spirit, from My Throne!
He comes by fire, to burn the dross,
    He comes to burn, what causes loss.
He comes to purify, your soul,
    He comes to make, your spirits whole.

He will not trouble, or confuse,
    He'll give you truth, that you can use,
Truth that sifts, and separates,
    Truth that leads men, to My gate.
Then at the gate, they make their choice,
    To come in close, to hear My voice.

If then they make My will their choice,
    I'll enter in and hear their voice,
I'll lead them to, my waters clean,
    For there I'll cleanse, from what's unclean,
I'll purify their hearts, their souls,
    I'll make them pure, I'll make them whole,
Then they will know, for they will see,
    My will, My plan to make them free!

A NEW SONG - Inspired by Psalm 33:3 and Psalm 40:3

I sing to You a love song, a pure song, a holy song,
For You're The One who gives a song, into my heart.
No words of mine could ever sing, what's in my heart today,
So Holy Spirit speak to me, The words that I should say,
Your life of love, inspires me, to give all thanks and praise,
For You have brought me into faith, the faith that's mine today!

A symphony of worship, with blending harmonies,
Is what I want to sing with all, who choose to bow their knees.
Then from that place of highest praise, that shows My love for You,
Help me tuck in, to where You are, to hear Your voice so true.
Bring back the stillness in my life, where I can rest in Thee,
The quiet place, that 's free from strife, Your face alone to see.

Be still my heart and listen now, to hear and make the choice
To let all cares and worries cease, then hear His still small voice,
Now take your rest in confidence, and listen to God's will,
His Word your sure and strong defence, protects and keeps you still.
You'll never faint or fear again, for in His strong embrace,
The things that would confuse, distract, are now removed by grace!

FREE TO EXPERIENCE - Inspired by John 7:38

Free to experience, what I have to give,
    Free to live with a life that gives,
For I did not call you to be a pool,
    But a stream that refreshes, that heals and schools.
A stream that flows, from the river of life,
    That washes away, all sin and all strife.
So come to God's River, for the refreshing you need,
    Then come for His Fire, to cleanse all your deeds.
For you have been called, to walk in The Light,
    The Light that illumines, the darkest night.
Then you can give forth, His Light all around,
    To brighten and lighten, the hearts that are down!

CHRIST'S PRECIOUS BLOOD-Inspired by Colossians 1:14-20

Oh Blood that purifies my soul,
That keeps my mind and body whole,
Oh Blood of Christ, protect me now,
For only blood can seal this vow.
Oh Precious Blood, that never dies,
That purges hearts and sanctifies,
Wash me afresh, this very hour,
So I'll receive, The Spirit's power.

Oh Fire of God, purge now and cleanse
Burn off the ropes, that kept me fenced,
Burn off what troubles, and defiles,
Burn off to make, my life worthwhile.
Then make me salt, that purifies,
Let all my deeds, be sanctified,
So that Christ's Name, is lifted high.
For men to see and live, not die.

Oh, wash us fresh, each day by grace,
So we with all, can see God's face,
And then reflect, the love He gives,
For then we'll really, truly live.
Oh Spirit, give me eyes to see,
The One I love, who set me free,
Then by Your Glory, change my frame,
So I can praise, Your Holy Name.

Oh may my life, lift You up high,
As light to brighten, earth and sky,
With glory rays, that come from You,
To give to all, Your Word of truth.
Your Word will set, all people free,
Your Word proclaims, our destiny,
A destiny of life that gives,
The life of God to all who live!

COME UP HIGHER - Inspired by Revelation 4:1

Come up higher to where I AM,
   Come up behold, The Spotless Lamb,
      The Lamb who takes away your sin,
         Who made The Way, to enter in.
The Lamb of God, became the price,
   The only price, that would suffice,
      To bear the sins, of all mankind,
         To heal the sick, the lame, the blind.

Behold, then kneel here, at His feet,
   For He's The Son of God, the meek,
      The One who left, His glorious throne,
         To ransom men, their sins atone.
For all the good, that we could do,
      Could never cleanse, or make us new,
         Our good at best, were filthy rags,
           No work of ours, could clean the slag!

Therefore, when we were trapped by lies,
   Christ came to save, so we won't die.
      No death you say? but all I see,
         Are death and dying, all round me.
The deaths you see, are but a step,
   To realms of love, where God has kept,
      A place of joy and peace and rest,
         For those who chose, His life as best.

So choose The Lord, as Saviour and then,
   Give Him your life, to cleanse from sin,
      He'll open up, His arms of love,
         And when death comes, you'll go above,
To heaven, to where your Lord awaits,
   To welcome you, at heaven's gates.
      There He'll present you, as His bride,
         As one who in, His love abides!

<u>OUR FATHER'S WILL</u> - Inspired by Philippians 2:13

I come Oh Lord, to Your Holy Throne,
    I come to worship, You alone,
I come to praise, and give You thanks,
    For what You gave, came not from banks!
No cash or gold, could pay the price,
    No wealth of world, could ever suffice,
To ransom me, from death and hell,
    To give me hope, and life as well.

For only You, and what You've done,
    Could buy me back, could bid me come.
Only Your Blood, has paid the price,
    To wash me clean, from sin and vice!
So now I bow, before Your Throne,
    To give You praise, and thanks alone,
For You have made my life, brand new,
    With heart and spirit, and hope renewed.

You've placed a dream, before my eyes,
    A dream that lives, and never dies,
For You make, all Your dreams for me,
    Come true to bring me destiny.
What You have done, and are doing still,
    Is all a part of Father's will,
His will for me, and all who hear,
    His Spirit call to all, Draw near!

Draw near to where, your Saviour stands,
    Draw near, observe, see feet and hands,
The nail prints are, what you will see,
    When Christ became, The price that frees!
His freedom is, for all who choose,
    The way to God, to never lose,
The life He gives, to take us high,
    The life that lives, and never dies!

GOD'S GRACE - Inspired by 2nd Corinthians 12:9

My grace is sufficient for thee,
    The Lord said unto St. Paul,
And if you will let My grace support thee,
    I'll protect and defend, you'll not fall.
For without My grace, My enabling power,
    No man could stand in each hour,
For human strength, is frail at best,
    But by grace, you'll pass every test.

You'll walk in power, like you've never known,
    You'll enter boldly, before My throne.
When you approach each day, what it holds,
    You'll not back down, for My grace upholds!
My grace is the power, that enables you;
    My grace is the equipping, that empowers you.
So do not look, at the size of the task,
    As being too much, for you only must ask,
Ask The Father, in Jesus Name,
    Ask and receive, His grace to sustain.

Grace is God's riches at Christ's expense,
    And if you have grace, you will climb every fence.
No task will seem, too great for you,
    For His grace will equip, and empower you.
So shrink not back, as His vision unfolds,
    But call on The Lord, and His grace to behold,
Your Lord in His glory, at The Father's right hand,
    Your Lord who is with you, and His Spirit that stands.

He stands at the ready, to give you His power,
    With joy as your strength, in every hour!
So trust not in riches, or glory or fame,
    Trust only in Christ, and His grace to proclaim,
That Jesus The Christ, our Redeemer, God's Son,
    Is The One Whom we trust, The Omnipotent One!

BEFORE YOU WERE BORN - Inspired by Psalm 139

What do you have, that I have not given?
    Even your breath, is a gift from heaven!
I saw you before, the worlds were framed,
    I saw you and called you, before you were named.
I formed you and shaped you, in your mother's womb,
    Then brought you forth, and gave you room,
Room to spread, your wings and fly,
    To God who lives, and never dies!

I gave you breath, and the life that sustains,
    The dream I have placed, in your heart to obtain.
I have placed a dream, in each human heart,
    A dream that only, My Spirit imparts.
This dream is so big, only I could conceive,
    Only I could bring forth, to those who believe,
This faith to believe Me, is given to all,
    Then to all who believe, and who answer My call,
I multiply grace and the favour to do,
    The dream I have planted, have planted in you.

So allow me, My child, to bring forth from you,
    The ways and the means, that make dreams come true,
If you'll trust and believe, in My power to do,
    My will and My purpose, will come forth for you.
You'll experience My joy, in it's purest form,
    Then the strength, My joy gives, will renew and transform.
My strength will take you, equip and empower,
    Will give you the faith, to believe Me each hour.

Then in this faith, no path will seem hard,
    Your thanks and your praise, will arise like pure nard.
Your praise and your worship, will give forth the essence,
    That opens the grace, to enter My Presence,
So let praise and thanksgiving, pour forth from you,
    Then I will live in your praises, I'll see you though.

TO LIVE LIKE CHRIST - Inspired by Romans 6

I praise You, my Lord, My God and My Saviour,
    You gave me, Your life, Your grace and Your favour.
You take me and hold me, in Your loving arms,
    You've kept me from sin, from dread and alarm.
So now Precious Jesus, help me live like You,
    Beholding You Father, in all that I do.
Cause me to hear, by Your Spirit, God's voice,
    Then obey what He says, as my primary choice.

Forgive us for thinking, of ourselves first,
    For that leads to selfishness, sin and a curse
Help us instead to give freely to all,
    The love that You give, to stand and not fall.
For only in loving, and extending Your grace,
    Can we ever see clearly, Your Dear Precious face.
Help us treat one another, as we would treat You,
    Remembering Your Spirit, is in us to do,
The will of You Father, in heaven to show,
    Your love and Your grace to all people below!

Let Your love be shown forth, in all that we do,
    Your love and Your mercy, that lead to The Truth.
That You Lord Jesus. are our Saviour and friend,
    That You come to abide, establish, defend,
All those who receive Your forgiveness, Your grace,
    Your mercy, Your love, to redeem from what's base!

Oh help us remember, that without You we're lost,
    Help us remember, and give thanks for Your cross.
Then help us to love, as You first loved us,
    With the love that forgives, all sin and mistrust.
Oh Spirit of God, enable us now,
    With Your grace and Your favour to make this our vow,
To always love others, as You Lord love us.
    With mercy and grace, forgiveness, and trust!

GOD'S UNFAILING LOVE - Inspired by Hebrews 12:1-4

Blessed Redeemer, my Saviour, my Friend,
   Your mercies are new, each day without end.
Who can compare with You, Holy Lord,
   For Your love and Your mercy, and grace outpoured?
In order to save us, You went to the cross,
   Because no one on earth, could redeem what we lost!
Then for the joy, set before You that day,
   You endured the cross, and the tortures to pay,
The price that was needed, to redeem sinful man,
   So we could believe, then enter Your plan.

By Your mercy we do not get, what we deserve,
   And Your grace gives us power, to overcome and endure.
So help us Dear Lord, to look not at what's seen,
   But look to Your cross, where our lives were redeemed.
Then we'll join with all saints, who have gone on before,
   To give worship and praise, for You Lord, we adore.

I know I don't love like You, Blessed Lord,
   For You loved and You gave, Your Blood to be poured,
As the pure sacrifice, that washes us clean,,
   From the sin and the shame, for our lives You've redeemed.
Now all we need do, is come unto You,
   Repent and receive, our forgiveness from You
So Lord, now I come at the start of this day,
   Forgive me for all that I do, think or say,
That is not in keeping, with the love You have shown,
   When You set me apart, called me up to Your throne.

Immerse me in love, the Love that is You,
   Then all of my thoughts, and my words will ring true,
Like a bell with a pure, and a clear ringing sound,
   Calls the faithful to worship, to come and bow down.
When the last trumpet sounds, may I look up and see,
   You, Lord, My Redeemer, The One who saved me!

THE BREATH OF THE SPIRIT - Inspired by Revelation 2:1-7

Holy Spirit, You are hovering over the earth,
  Just like at creation, to bring forth to birth,
To plant Your breath, into the souls of men,
  To give them hope, and faith again.
For we have left our first love, our first love for Thee,
  And entered into striving and trying to please.
Our works and our efforts, although well and good,
  Are not the best You desire, from us who have stood.

We have stood for what's right, and holy and pure,
  Thinking this would make, our election sure,
Like the church in Ephesus, in Revelation, chapter two,
  We've become so busy in serving You,
That the place of intimate communion, we've lost,
  Our first love for You, we have left at the cross.
We are such eager beavers, we want to show all,
  That we stand for You Lord, we answer Your call.

But in grace and in favour and love for mankind,
  You are calling us back, to the place where our minds,
Desire to be transformed, once again,
  To come back to first love, for Our Saviour and then,
Our hearts and our minds and our spirits will say,
  Come Holy Spirit, please change us today.

Oh Lord Jesus Christ, Our Redeemer and Friend,
  You who loved first, who left heaven to end,
The lies and deceptions, and the sins that will kill,
  Call us once again, to return, do your will.
Your will is that first, we receive Your sweet love,
  And then in response, love as we have been loved:
Love You, our Lord God, with all of our hearts,
  Then love one another, with the love you impart!

COME UNTO ME - Inspired by Matthew 11:28-30

Come unto Me, all who long for life's best,
    Your striving will cease, when you enter My rest,
My grace is sufficient, dear child for thee,
    My grace and My mercy, My life is for free.
Grace and mercy are free, when you give Me your lives,
    Free to all who'll believe, in Me and not strive.
For striving is only, done through the flesh,
    And all you achieve, cannot give you My rest.
Only by leaving off sin, and your pride,
    Can you enter My rest, and stand by My side.
So stand by My side, as My bride to say,
    I love You the best, and with my heart, I will stay,
Close by Your side, protected from harm,
    Near to Your heart, enclosed by Your arm,

Then from this position, I will send you forth,
    To east and west, to south and north.
I will give you the love, to preach to the lost,
    I will give you the words, that lead to the cross
The souls who are dying, who don't know My Way,
    Who still are trying, to live life their way.
Your message of love, and The Glory from Me,
    Will bring them to faith, and then they will see!
So come in close, to My heart, My child,
    Let My Spirit, transform, what is wilful and wild,
He will give you the power, and the love that you need,
    To extend My grace and My favour like seed.
Without first love, in your heart for Me,
    You will lack the compassion, to love and to lead.
So come and abide, leave off what divides,
    Your mind and your spirit, your body beside.
Leave off all that causes, to cease from My rest,
    Leave off all that hinders, receive and be blest;
Be blest in the knowing, that I AM in control.
    And I will preserve, spirit, body and soul!

THE TABLE PREPARED - Inspired by Psalm 23:5

Cause me to worship You, Dear Precious Lord,
　　Cause me to bow, at Your feet evermore,
For it is in our praises, that You reside,
　　And it is in our worship, that You abide.
Oh Holy Spirit, come clean me up,
　　So that I can drink, from my Saviour's cup,
Drink and be filled, with the grace that enables,
　　Then eat of The Bread, that He sets on the table.

You prepare a table, in the wilderness,
　　Then You say, come and eat, come and be blessed,
With the righteousness, peace and love that I give,
　　And the life and the love, that you need to forgive.
By Your love and forgiveness, You bid all to come,,
　　To partake of Your goodness, and the life You have won.
Your Blood paid the price, on the cross that day,
　　So we could approach You Lord God, and pray,
Pray to You, Father, In Jesus Christ's Name,
　　Knowing we'll receive, forgiveness from shame.

Christ, You paid the price, for sin, shame and loss,
　　When You went up to Calvary, to die on that cross.
My sins put You there, to pay my life price,
　　To redeem me from all, of rebellion and vice.
But, death could not hold You, for You are The Pure,
　　The Holy Redeemer, and by faith we are cured.
Your blood shed for us, is the cure for our pain,
　　For sickness, disease, and sin with it's shame.

So I bow Precious Lord, I bow and receive,
　　Your grace, Your forgiveness, that meets every need.
Now I am fulfilled, by what You provide,
　　I am cleansed by Your Blood, to stand by Your side;
To stand and then hear, what You have to say,
　　Your words of love, that You speak every day.

PURIFIED GOLD - Inspired by Revelation 3:18

Come buy from Me gold, that's been tried in the fire,
  The fire that purges, all unholy desires.
Let My Spirit burn off, all that distorts the truth,
  So the dreams from My Father, can be seen, pure and true.
Holy Spirit will ignite, bring fresh passion within,
  The passion, the zeal, to be free from all sin.
His fire will burn off, and cleanse what obstructs,
  The way to your holiness, for Him to construct.

I want to live daily, Your pathway to choose
  But my heart and my mind can deceive me, it's true.
So purge me and cleanse me, of what misconstrues,
  So that Your way always, is the way I will choose.
I know Holy Spirit, You don't force or coerce,,
  And Your voice whispers to me, go forward, not reverse.
What is past is past, you cannot change it at all,
  And God's plans for your future, are there in His call.

So live today, in the grace that God gives,
  Live today, to love and forgive.
Then you'll walk unhindered, in a life full and free,
  When you give of yourself, completely to Me.
Your passions and dreams, I will purify,
  And you will see with a sight, that never will die.
You will see with My sight, the ones I've redeemed,
  And you will lead them in love, to My cleansing stream.

So lead by My Spirit, in word and in deed,
  With prayer and with praise, go plant My seed.
My seed that speaks greatness, and hope to each heart,
  That calls them up higher, for what I impart.
I will take all the stony hearts, given to Me,
  And I will give a new heart, that is cleansed and made free.
Free to pursue, with My passion and zeal,
  To reach and transform, to save and to seal!

HOPE IN GOD - Inspired by Psalm 42

Hope not in riches or glory or fame,
> But hope in The Lord, and His powerful Name!
You can hope with assurance, and faith to receive,
> All that God has provided, to meet every need.
He will meet your need, when you walk close to Him,
> He will give you fresh faith, to bring peace within.
This peace and rest, can't be purchased with gold,
> All your striving will make you, prematurely old.

So seek for His kingdom, and all that He gives,
> Seek His will first, so that you can live!
I am living you say, but where is your peace?
> Where is the joy and the love to release?
For as long as you trust, in your strength to achieve,
> You will not have the rest, you so desperately need.
So come all you weary, you broken and sad,
> Come to The One, who will make your heart glad.

God will give you His joy, as your strength that upholds,
> He will give you His love, and the peace that enfolds.
So leave off the fear, that drives you so,
> Trust in The Lord, and His power you'll know.
You will have His provision, that meets every need,
> His plans and desires, for your heart will succeed.
Then you'll have His peace, controlling your heart,
> You will have this assurance, He never departs.

His Spirit will lead you, to what is unseen,
> To pastures to feed in, not fields to be gleaned.
His abundance will be, His provision for you.
> You will have much to give, to bless others too.
Your shoes won't wear out, in the wilderness,
> As you seek out the lost, to save and to bless.
So reach by His Spirit, the ones He has called,
> For He'll save and He'll seal, all those who give all!

THE SOWER - Inspired by Matthew 13:3-23

Purify and cleanse me, Oh Lord, I pray,
    From all that would lead, my heart astray;
Then by Your Spirit, direct me today,
    For You are The Light, The Truth and The Way!
No one can lead, my heart to You God,
    No other but You, Holy Spirit of God.
So cause me to come, to Your river Oh Lord,
    To come and receive, the grace You outpour.

Your grace and Your favour, I need to succeed,
    In all of the paths, where Your Spirit leads.
Your grace is the enablement, that I truly need,
    Your favour brings blessing, to prosper each seed.
So help me plant seeds, in a garden so big,
    That only Your Spirit, gives the power to dig.
Now with proper digging, the soil is prepared,
    For the seed of God's Word, to be planted and shared.

Help me to dig out, the roots and the rocks,
    That would hinder Your seed, that would only be talk!
Help me to prepare, the soil just right,
    By the Power of Your Spirit, and not by my might!
Then water it well, with Your love and Your Word,
    And warm it with grace, by Your Power assured.
Your desire is now, for each seed to grow,
    To produce thirty, sixty, and one hundredfold.

Life can come forth, in the seeds that we plant,
    If we trust in Your Power, never say, I can't.
For we can do all, by Your strength and Your power,
    By Your grace and Your favour, in every hour.
So help me to trust, in Your power to succeed,
    To have in abundance, to meet every need,
Of those You have called me, in grace now to bless,
    With Your love and Your peace, and Your blessedness

COME AND HEAL
Inspired by Isaiah 42 & 2nd Corinthians 3:18

Come Lord Jesus, come and heal,
    And then by Your Spirit, come and seal,
The Words, You have spoken, unto all men,
    The life You have given, to free us from sin.
Inspire me now, Holy Spirit to write,
    The words You want written, to bring to The Light,
All those who read these poems, You gave,
    So hearts can be touched, by Your love and be saved.
Your Word by Your Spirit, gives life unto all,
    Who hearken and hear, His voice when He calls.
He does not yell, or shout in the street,
    But woos us and beckons, with a voice strong and sweet.
For His love and compassion, are His driving force,
    That cause all to hear, and to change their course.

Now, when we were going, our own merry way,
    Our lives had no purpose, and our hearts had strayed,
Away from God's call, and His destiny plans,
    To deliver from sin, and the devil's demands!
But so rich in mercy, and grace are You Lord,
    That You came down from heaven, to see us restored,
To the place in Your kingdom, to live and to dwell,
    To the place where we're free, from the devil's spell.

So we give You our thanks, our worship and praise,
    To You Holy God, for You teach us Your ways.
You, Lord God, have no beginning or end,
    You are The Eternal, The God who defends!
You created us in, Your Image to bless,
    Then to reach out and teach of Your righteousness;
Your righteousness given, by Your gift of grace,
    The grace by faith, to behold Your face.
Your Word says that what we behold, we become,
    So lead us Holy Spirit, to behold God's Son!

CHRIST, THE VINE - Inspired by John 15

Oh Heavenly Vine, whose branches we are,
    Cause us to produce, Your fruit where we are,
For by You and from You, we have this life,
    The life that frees us, from sin and from strife.
The fruit that's produced, can only come,
    By living in You, God's Holy Son.
So cause us to live, so united in You,
    That the fruit that's produced, will refresh and renew.

Oh cause, Holy Spirit, my thoughts to be pure,
    So that by Your life-giving power, I'm sure,
That by abiding in Christ, as my life-giving source,
    My life can be altered, to choose Your new course.
So when the tendrils, of my branch, don't produce,
    I ask You to cut off, what will not give juice.
For only Your pure, and Your life-giving stream,
    Can refresh and renew, restore and redeem.

Only Your life, coming through the branch,
    Can produce the good fruit, by design not by chance.
Oh cause me then, to abide in Your Word,
    For then by grace, through faith I'm assured,
Of life everlasting, that begins when we choose,
    To receive Your salvation, for then we won't lose.

Then when those pick fruit, that's produced from this vine,
    Our hearts will rejoice and give thanks every time.
For the privilege of being, the branch that extends,
    The life and salvation, that redeems and defends,
The ones who partake, of God's mercy and grace,
    The ones who now, can behold Your dear face.
Oh Wonderful, Mighty, Omnipotent God,
    I give You, my praise, my thanks and my laud,
For the awesome privilege, You have given to me,
    To be one of Your branches, on Your Vine, Your Tree!

WHEN GOD BECAME MAN - Inspired by John 1:1-14

Christmas is coming, but do men realize,
    Or have they been blinded, deceived by the lies?
So I ask, dear friend, what does Christmas mean?
    Is it a time to spend and be spent, for what's seen?
Sit back and observe, once again at what's true,
    At what God by Christ Jesus, has done for you.
Reflect on this wonder, that God became man,,
    Christ leaving His Godhood, to be born as a man!
He was called Jesus, God's Only Son,
    And He walked here on earth, as The Holy One.

He sought not for riches, or glory or fame,
    He only did what He did, God's love to proclaim:
That salvation was here, to all who believe,
    Who would answer His call, to hear and receive.
By His coming and walking, as His Father said,
    He gave demonstration, of a life that is led,
By The Spirit of God, in wisdom and truth,
    He showed to all men, what is real, what is true.

He came the first time, as a babe in a manger,
    As helpless, dependent, oh, what could be stranger,
God's Son, our Redeemer, our Saviour from sin,
    Was born as a man, to bring us to Him!
He showed how a man, can walk with his God,
    To show how our lives, could be lived before God!
He only did, what He saw Father do,
    And His life, and His witness, were holy and true.

Then before Christ left earth, in a cloud up to heaven,
    He told His disciples, to wait, to be given,
His Spirit, to give them, the power to tell,
    That by faith in His Name, we're redeemed from hell;
Redeemed and restored, as the children of God,
    To walk in His freedom, while on earth, we trod.

Then to publish His message, to the ends of the earth,
    To lead all mankind, to The Spirit's rebirth.
What is born of the flesh, can never achieve,
    Salvation is only, for those who believe.
Therefore we believe that God in heaven, sent Christ,
    To be our Redeemer, from sin and from vice,
For there is no good work, we could ever do,
    To make our hearts, and our minds brand new.

So let Holy Spirit, birth in you now,
    The faith to believe, in The Christ, who vowed,
To never leave us, or ever forsake,
    The ones who believe, His life to partake.
Now when you partake, of His life, my friend,
    You will enter a life of joy, without end.
His joy will give you His strength, day by day,
    No matter what happens, He will show you the way.
Where He leads, He will feed, where He guides, He provides,
    And all of your dreams, will come true at His side.

As a bridegroom, He takes us, His bride in His arms,
    Our Lord, as our bridegroom, protects us from harm.
Our lives, in this life may perish, it is true,
    But eternal life in heaven, is waiting for you.
All who believe, in Jesus Christ are assured,
    Of a place up in heaven, by God's Holy Word.
Death has no power, for those who believe,
    In The Christ, our Redeemer, for we have received,
The faith by His Spirit, to trust in His grace,
    The faith to receive, His loving embrace.

So as Christmas approaches, and each new day,
    Reach out and receive, His forgiveness and say,
I come to You now, Lord Jesus I come,
    Affirm to me Lord, that I'm Your child, for You've won
My heart, and my life, by Your mercy and grace,
    You're The One that I love, I receive Your embrace!

LIGHTS - Inspired by John 1:1-5

Oh Light of the world, be Thou our light,
    The Light that brightens, the darkest night,
Then make us lights, to shine for you,
    So men will know, and see the truth.
You are The Pure Light, that lights up the world,
    Only You bring clarity, out of the swirl,
Confusion and chaos, the results of sin,
    Muddy the waters, so death can come in.

When the earth was dark, and formless and void,
    Holy Spirit, hovered over it, ready and poised.
Then when God spoke, and said, Let there be light,
    The light appeared, and brought forth sight.
God separated light, from the darkness right then,
    Called the light day, and the darkness night, so men,
Could experience what God, could call, one day,
    To bring order to all, God would make to say,
That He brings order, out of what would confuse,
    If we look for His order, He will bring us to truth!

So Spirit of God, bring order this day,
    Lead us in all, that we do, think or say.
Like an arrow in Your quiver, ready to be used,
    Shoot us forth, to accomplish, by Your Spirit, Your Truth.
Let the words that we speak, bring Your will to be,
    Let the deeds we do, bring honour to Thee,
For we want our lives, to lift up Your Name,
    So men will see You, as God and proclaim,
Your awesome goodness, Your love and Your power,
    Then bend their knees, and worship this hour.

Oh King of all kings, and Lord of all lords,
    Please bring our hearts, into one accord,,
With each of us loving, and preferring each other,
    As father and mother, and sister and brother.

FLAME OF GOD - Inspired by Jeremiah 23:29

Oh flame of God, burn bright and clear,
    Burn off our ropes, and draw us near,
Burn off all sin, that would defile,
    So we can go, the extra mile,
Not with a bitter, vengeful heart,
    But with a joy, right from the start.
May everything, we say and do,
    Be done with love, that comes from You!

Forgive us Lord, wherever we've strayed,
    Away from Your pure, and holy way,
Wherever we have led, away from you,
    All those You love, forgive us too.
Then help us walk, Holy Spirit today,
    Along Your pure, and righteous way,
Dressed in Your robes, of righteousness,
    Dispensing love, and blessedness.

Help us to bless, and never curse,
    The ones You have chosen, to heal and to nurse.
May the love and forgiveness, that You have shown,
    Cause us to lead, everyone to Your Throne;
Then there behold You, Oh Holy God,
    To there embrace, and worship You God!
For who is a God, like unto You,
    Who made this world, and the heavens too!

Your spoken Word, has creative power,
    You give our lives, new life, each hour!
Without You Lord, and Your saving grace,
    We could never behold You, see Your Face.
So I thank You Lord, for extending to me,
    Your grace and forgiveness, that set me free,
Now help me to share, what I have been given,
    So all can see, Your way to heaven.

BY MY SPIRIT - Inspired by Zechariah 4:6

Not by might, nor by power,
 But by Your Spirit, Lord this hour,
For this is the only way to live,
 Your joy, Your strength, and the will to forgive!
Let loving You, be our first desire,
 The love that comes, from Holy fire.
So let Your fire, burn off and cleanse,
 All that would deaden, blur the lenses,
Of what our eyes, were meant to see,
 All that You've done, to set us free.

Then set our feet, on Your brand new way,
 Along Your course, to never stray,
For all Your plans, for us are good,
 So we can stand, like Jesus stood.
He stood for what, was right and true,
 He only did, what He saw You do!
He listened close, to Your every word,
 Then did all what, Your Word procured.

Your Power and love, were His pure clear source,
 And He never sinned, or caused remorse,
But walked in truth, and faith and love,
 His eyes always fixed, on You God above!
His heart was steadfast, to You God alone,
 For He knew what awaited Him, from Your throne!

Now power and might, and dominion are His,
 For He paid the price, to accomplish this.
He gave His pure life, as The Sacrifice,
 His Blood on God's altar, to pay the price,
To redeem us from sin, and death and hell,
 To save us and heal us, and make us well.
Oh, Believe on The Lord Jesus Christ, and be saved,
 Your life will be ransomed, from death and the grave!

GLORY TO GOD - Inspired by Luke 2:9-14

Glory to God, in the Highest heaven,
  Glory to God, for all He has given!
Glory to God, for His love has restored,
  Glory to God, for what He has in store!
Glory to God, for our sins are forgiven,
  Glory to God, for the life He has given!
Glory to God, for heaven awaits,
  Glory to God, He has opened the gates!

Glory to God, for Christ, God's Son,
  Glory to God, The Omnipotent One!
Glory to God, for all He has made,
  Glory to God, for our sins he has paid!
Glory to God, for Christ's blood poured out,
  Glory, to God, He destroyed, Satan's clout!
Glory to God, we are free and redeemed,
  Glory to God,, for our hearts He has cleaned.

Glory to God, for the body of Christ,
  Glory to God, for His pure sacrifice.
Glory to God, for family and friends,
  Glory to God, for He heals and He mends!
Glory to God, for His healing power,
  Glory to God, for our breath this hour!
Glory to God, for the faith to believe,
  Glory to God, for the gifts we receive.

Glory to God, for His mercy each hour,
  Glory to God, for His Spirit and power!
Glory to God, for unmerited grace,
  Glory to God, for the love on His face!
Glory to God, for each new day,
  Glory to God, for the faith to pray!
Glory to God, for His angelic host,
  Glory to God, for He loves us the most!!

HEAR GOD'S WORD AND OBEY - Inspired by 1st Samuel 2

Hear My Word and listen too.
    Then apply My Word, for it is truth!
My Word will be, a strong sharp sword,
    To prune off, all that brings discord.
For what divides and separates,
    Comes from the one, who kills and hates.
But love from God, will break his power,
    Love will conquer, what devours.
Love will heal and make amends,
    Love will triumph, and defend.
Love will give, more than it takes,
    Love redeems, forgives mistakes.
Love will heal, what has been bruised,
    Love will purify, and fuse.
The parts that broke, through hurt and fear,
    Love will brighten, love will cheer.

So when you're tired, and hope seems gone,
    Look to The Lord, to make you strong.
For God is Love, and He will make,
    A way for you, you will not break.
He'll give you faith, to carry on,
    He'll give new faith, new hope, new song.
So let His Spirit, penetrate,
    Remove all pride, all sin, all hate,
For these will give, the devil cause,
    To put your life with God, on pause.
Instead let love and peace, prevail,
    Let Holy Spirit, remove the veil,
To bring your heart, to the place where you,
    Will see what's right, and do what's true!
He will set your life, on a brand new course,
    The place where He, will be your source,
You will live In His Light, no shadow there,
    For He is The Light, that burns the tares!

WHAT GIFT? - Inspired by Psalm 68

What gift can I give You, my Lord and My King,
    What song could I sing, to make rafters ring?
What present would say, how much I love you?
    For all that is good, in my life is from You!
You gave me good parents, who taught me your ways,
    Who took me to church, to worship and praise,
You placed me with family, who love to give,
    Who give from their hearts, so that others can live!

You gave me the pastors, and teachers who showed,
    The way to hear You, and to choose the right road.
You gave of Your Spirit, to teach what is right,
    You gave me Your life, to give me new sight.
You sent us your prophets, to speak hope from Thee,
    To speak life and correction, to set us all free.
You gave us evangelists, as an example of zeal,
    Of passion to preach, Your Word and to heal.

You gave us apostles to teach us to love,
    Like You Father in heaven, our God up above.
You gave missionaries, as examples to be,
    The ones who give, of their lives selflessly;
To preach the gospel, to go and to tell,
    To all everywhere, to save them from hell,

You, showed by example, that when we leave all,
    As You left heaven's portals, to fulfill God's call,
We will really come into, Your plans for us,
    We will realize truly, Your heavenly trust!
This trust is to love, and to serve You Dear Lord,
    And to love one another, with compassion outpoured,
Not seeking our own way, but Your way Oh Lord,
    For then all will come, into Your one accord!
So Lord up in heaven, I give you my life,
    Take me and make me, Your bride and Your wife!

WHAT WILL YOU DO? - Inspired by Matthew 12 & 13

What will you do, with The One called Christ,
    Who redeemed your life, by sacrifice?
Will you bow and worship, before His throne,
    Or will you turn away, go on your own?
The choice to choose, or reject The Christ,
    Is given to all, who will see by His life,
That He alone, is The Saviour from sin,
    It is only by His grace, that we can come within.
Jesus life is a witness, and His Word goes forth,
    To speak to all peoples, change your course,
Choose you this day, whom you will serve,
    Either Christ, or the devil, who will throw you a curve!

The deceiver or Satan, as The Bible calls him,
    Comes with subtle lies, like a wolf in sheepskin,
Like an angel of light, he comes to deceive,
    To steal and to kill, God's Word, God's seed!

If your heart is hard, God's seed can't take root,
    For the devil will steal it, before it's a shoot.
If your heart is a mixture, like gravel and dirt,
    God's seed will die quickly, to your very hurt.
If your heart has weeds, of worry and delusions,
    God's seed will be snuffed, by doubt and confusion.
But if your heart is good ground, prepared to receive,
    The Seed of God's Word, will grow, when conceived.
It will flourish and prosper, and produce much fruit,
    For it's content to be buried, so that life can take root.
Then God in His mercy, will change it to form,
    A brand new creation, away from the norm.

Now what is sown, is a single seed,
    But what it produces, can meet every need.
You can count the seeds quickly, in an apple, it's true,
    But can you count all the seeds, when the tree gives it's fruit?

That's how it is now, with a life that is given,
    To The Lord up above, our God up in heaven.
He will take the life, that's committed to Him,
    He will take it and clean it, from death and from sin.
The He'll change it by Spirit, and Word to receive,
    The faith and the grace, that you need to believe!
If you will trust in The Christ, and His Word that is true,
    The sky then becomes, the limit for you.
He'll reveal to you now, what once was unseen,
    He'll lead and He'll guide you, on the paths that are clean.
He has joys and wonders, for us to behold,
    If we will give Him our lives, to fashion and mold.

So do not delay, in this decision of yours,
    Let your mind and your heart, reach up for God's more.
Come up when He calls, to give you His best,
    Come up. Where He is, to get peace and rest.
In The Lord's presence, is all that you need,
    He will free you from sin, and all of it's greed.
Pride and greed, will destroy your life,
    But love and peace, will release from strife!

Oh come my friend, and receive God's gift,
    Confess your sins, to The One who can lift,
Your life and your heart, from the mire of sin,
    Christ will give you, a new heart within.
This heart, will be pure, and noble and kind,
    A heart that is loving, that changes your mind.

You will love with the love, God has given to you,
    This love will spill over, and bless others too.
For the love God gives, is abundant to bless,
    All those that believe, on His Son and confess,
That Jesus is Lord, and King of all kings,
    Our Saviour, Redeemer, The God who sings.
Let Him sing over you, His song of love,
    Let Him lead you my friend, to His courts above!

HOW DO WE APPROACH GOD?
Inspired by Ephesians 2:1-10 and The Book of Exodus

What would we have, if we didn't have Christ?
    Where would we be, without His sacrifice?
Without Lord Jesus, we'd be dead in our sin,
    Confused and deafened, by the devil's din.
But God, so rich in mercy is He,
    Sent His Son, to die for you and for me.
He could have stayed, in heaven of course,
    But He chose to come, to change our source!
Born in a manger, filled with straw,
    He came to save, all who would call,
Upon His Name, to save and heal,
    To rescue all, who need His seal.
By His Spirit, Christ gives to all men,
    The seal of God's redemption plan.
This seal is given, to all who hear,
    His voice that calls, Come up, Draw near!

Now when Moses came, to the burning bush,
    He came in awe, He did not push.
When God said, Take your sandals off,
    Moses obeyed, he did not scoff!
God spoke to Him, from the bush of fire,
    God gave His call, spoke His desire.
God said He'd heard, His children's cries,
    In Egypt where they slaved and died.
God gave to Moses, what he was to do,
    All that God wanted, to free them too.
God gave His Name, and His Power to perform,
    All what would bring, a bright new morn,
For those held captive, in Egypt's land,
    To bring them out, to His Promised Land.
God rescued His children, from Pharaoh's hand,
    When Moses obeyed, The Lord's command!
He led them to Mt. Sinai, to receive God's law, to hear what's right!

God's law showed them, and us that we,
    Could never by will, be pure and clean.
God used the law, to show our need
    Then sent His Son, as a Holy Seed
Christ was born as a man, to redeem the lost,
    To redeem and restore, Christ paid the cost.
He became our sin, on the cross that day,
    So His Father, had to look away;
Had to forsake, His Beloved Son,
    So that our hearts, could be made one.
By the blood of Christ, now we're redeemed,
    We're cleansed, made whole, our spirit's freed.
No more a captive, by sins curse,
    Our lives are free, our course reversed.
Now heaven awaits, all who receive,
    By faith, God's grace, to now believe,
That Christ, God's Son, The Saviour from sin,
    Has made the way, to enter in!

But this is just, the starting place,
    He calls, come near, behold My face,
Then come, My child, receive My fire,
    For then you'll know, My real desire.
You'll know what I've, prepared for you,
    A life that's real, and pure and true!
The fire I use, will purify,
    Will burn what holds, the ropes that tie
You to the past, the good or bad,
    For what I've prepared, you've never had.
A brand new day, is waiting for you,
    A day when I'll reveal My Truth,
Not just in part, as you have now,
    But in My fullness, that's My vow.
So come buy gold, that's tried in the fire,
    Come and seek, your heart's desire,
If you'll pursue, My righteousness,
    You will walk in faith, and blessedness.

Now a freedom, like you have never known,
    Will bring you close, right to My throne.
My glory rays, will shine on you,
    Will burn off all, that hinders you.
My glory will bring grace, to you,
    To do all I have planned for you.
So come, My child, and do not fear,
    For what I give, gives hope and cheer.
You'll do the greater things, I said,
    To heal the sick and raise the dead.
For men must see, in these last days,
    My power released, so they will pray;
Pray to The Father, in Jesus Name,
    Pray for the freedom, from what defames!
So come, press in, draw close to Me,
    Receive My sight so you can see,
All that God, is waiting to give,
    All He has, so men can live!

WHERE ARE YOU SITTING?
Inspired by Luke 22:53 and Psalm 1

Where are you sitting, when your Lord is reviled?
Be careful, or like Peter, you'll deny, be defiled.
For the devil has asked, to sift you like wheat,
To test your confession, to see if you'll bleat.

Like a sheep that is cornered, by a wolf in the wild,
Be careful your words, will never defile.
For The One who paid, with His body, His life,
Is the One who shed blood, to redeem you from strife.

Call out to Him, in your hour of trial,
For then your life's words, will not be denial;
But you'll stand and you will speak, for The One who saved you,
You will speak out in faith, for what He's given is truth!

WHICH WAY? - Inspired by Proverbs 14:12 and John 14:6

There are some ways, which seem so right,
    But these will not, give light or sight,
Only I, can light The Way, can lead men to, My brand new day!
    So seek My face, My kingdom too, for then I can
Impart to you, the grace you need, My enabling power,
    To do what must, be done this hour.

My voice you'll hear, right in your ear,
    The voice that leads, in paths I've cleared.
For I've removed, the sticks and stones,
    All that would hinder, break your bones.
I strengthen knees, so they can stand,
    For what I want, in this great land.
I purify with holy fire, so men can know, My heart's desire,
    To hold them close, right by My side,
To have My strength, what' ere betides.

So if the path, seems far too steep,
    Just take My hand, for I will keep,
All those who put, their hand in mine,
    I'll take to where, My glory shines.
My presence will, provide and bless,
    Your souls with peace, and righteousness,
For then you will know, even as you are known,
    Your God as Father, on His Throne.

He will hold His sceptre, out to you,
    To show He loves, all those who do
What He has said, what He commands,
    By Spirit's power, to take the land;
To take and cleanse, redeem, restore,
    So men can then, receive God's more.
Christ Jesus is, The More of God,
    So give Him Praise, Rejoice! Applaud!

COME THY KINGDOM - BE DONE THY WILL
Inspired by Matthew 6:10

We pray this prayer, from the depths of our hearts,
We pray this prayer to You,
Oh God of all, as this day starts, may all Your Words, come true!
We bless Your Name, Oh Holy God, for You alone know all,
We bow and worship, give You laud, upon Your Name we call.
You alone, can do all things, Your Word alone has power,
To shape and form the earth to sing, to make the devils cower!

Now when Your Word is proclaimed in Truth,
Your kingdom comes on earth,
You cleanse from all, that's vile, uncouth, reveal to all their worth!
Your revelations make us wise, so we can choose Your ways,
Your light illumines, what's disguised, so we can come away,
Away from every worldly care, away to where You are,
Away to where Your Spirit shares, the love of Who You are!

Your love transforms, makes all brand new,
Your love sets prisoners free,
Your love brings life and light that's true,
Your love has ransomed me.
So Holy Spirit quicken now, Your Word within my life,
Equip me with Your Power, Your Truth,
To speak Your Words of Life!

So hallowed be Your Name Oh Lord, by all in earth and heaven,
Then see Your kingdom come on earth, as it is done in heaven!
Give us this day our daily bread, and the health in which to work,
So that we will not lead astray, but do our work, not shirk.
Help us forgive as You forgive, for then men's hearts are freed,
To hear The Holy Spirit speak, to tend and love and feed.
Now when temptation comes, to test our character,
Help us to stand by Spirit's power, so Your Name won't be slurred!
Deliver us Oh Lord our God, when the tempter comes to steal,
Help us to use Your Word, Lord God, to kill the lies he wields!

TRANSFORMATION - Inspired by Romans 12:1 & 2

Lead and guide Holy Spirit, we pray, Lead and guide our thoughts,
May all we ever do and say, reflect what You have taught.
Transform us then, each day, each hour, transform with Holy Grace,
Transform our minds to never cower, But always seek God's face.
Change us into, what we behold, God's awesome wondrous love,
Help us to do what we are told, to lead, not push or shove.

Let love and grace and mercy lead, the way to reach all men,
To show the way from sin and greed, the way to Christ within.
Holy Spirit, You raised from death, Our Saviour, Christ The Lord,
Now with Your Power, Life, and Breath, make us of one accord,
To all that God in heaven has placed, to all that He desires,
So we may sit or walk or stand, Made pure by Holy fire.

Oh God You're not indifferent, to what we do or say,
You are cleaning lives that are misspent, to watch and seek and pray.
You're burning all that needs to burn, consuming till we're clean,
You call us all, to turn to You, to be what You esteem.
And then You give us brand new minds, transformed to ever see,
Your will, Your plan, to reveal to all, their holy destiny!

Who is a God like You, Oh Lord? A God who is faithful and true?
You alone give the grace that affords, making our lives brand-new!
So purify our hearts we pray, make us wholly Thine.
Keep us close with hearts that stay, abiding in Your vine.
Prune off the branches that grow wild, so good will be produced,
For I would to be your loving child, a branch with fruit profuse.

THERE IS A GOD IN HEAVEN
Inspired by Daniel 2 and Luke 1 & 2

There is a God in heaven who knows, the hearts and minds of men,
And in His love and mercy chose, to save us from all sin.
We had lost the power He gave, by sin, by greed, by pride,
We had lost the will to be saved, to stand right by His side.
Dominion, power and authority, over all the earth and sky,
Was what God planned for all to be, to live and never die.
Now when we were dead in trespass and sin, no eternal life to be,
Our Father God, had a perfect plan, to save and set us free.

Then one day an angel came, to a virgin with God's good news,
That she would be the mother of, Messiah, if she would choose.
How can this be, Mary said to him, for I know not a man?
Then Gabriel spoke and said to her, God has an Awesome Plan!.
He said Holy Spirit would plant God's Seed, by His Holy Power
Into her womb, if she believed, and trusted God this hour.
With God nothing is impossible, His Word shall come to pass
In sweet submission, Mary said, I'll do what God has asked.

Mary went to see Elizabeth, for she was to be mother of,
The one whom God chose to prepare, the way for His Son of love.
As Mary greeted Elizabeth, the child leaped in Elizabeth's womb,
Elizabeth filled with The Spirit, said:
    Blessed is The Fruit of your womb!
And Blessed is she who believed God's Word,
    Who believed what the angel had said,
For Jesus, The Christ, The Messiah of God,
    Would be born as The Saviour of men.
He would do what He saw His Father do, say what His Father said,
He would heal the sick, proclaim God's Word, even raise the dead!

So as this season comes again, to celebrate Christ's birth,
Reflect God's love and grace to men, Receive His life, new birth.
Be born again by The Spirit's power, be born in a brand new way,
Be born to live, each day and hour, in the love Christ gives always!

CALLED GOD'S CHILDREN - Inspired by 1ˢᵗ John 3:1-3

What an awesome privilege, to be called the children of God,
To believe and receive His precious salve, to see The One we love.
No treasure here could ever compare, to this gift that our God gives,
The grace through faith so we can share, the life our Saviour lives.

For though He died on the cross one day, to pay for all our sins,
He rose again, in power to say, I'm alive, I'll come within!
By My Spirit's power, I will live in you, live and never die
I will give you life, that's ever true, to live and never die.

I AM, The Way, The Truth, The Life, by Me if all will come,
I'll save them from all sin and strife, I'll save them everyone!
There is no one, I do not love, no one I would cast aside,
If they will ask, receive My love, I'll keep them by My side.

Look not at what the world provides, look not at what is seen,
But look to Me, I'll truly guide, to pastures lush and green.
The Water of Life I will give to you, My bread you will receive,
If you'll but trust My Word is true, you'll know Whom you believe!

In you God planted His Word as seed, so you can give to all,
A word indeed to set men free, to answer when God calls.
If we would walk in liberty, let Christ bring forth His light,
We would be free from all the lies, that dim and block our sight!

Darkness and sin were put to death, when our Dear Saviour knelt,
And said to God The Father, Your Will not mine be dealt!
Christ's blood not ours has paid the price, to pay for what we lost,
He ransomed us from death and hell, that day upon the cross!

Death is real and hell is too, But Jesus made the way,
To escape the tortures the devil has, if we will seek God's grace.
His grace and mercy, salvation too, are there for our forgiveness,
All we need do, is confess our sin, receive His Blessedness.

READ AND LISTEN - Inspired by 2nd Timothy 2:15 & 16

Where do we go? What should we do?
> How can we hear, Your Word that is true?
Read and listen, come close and pray,
> Then you will be led, by My Spirit each day.
He will tell you what you need to know,
> He will lead and He will guide,
He will give you light along the way,
> When you seek My face, My side.

No path will seem too hard or steep,
> For by My Power and Word, .
You will not falter at the task,
> For I will provide, I'll gird.
A kernel of faith is all you need,
> To move the mountains ahead,
My Word provides, the faith you need,
> To speak to what looks dead!.

Now what you need in the days to come,
> Is the faith to perceive, God's will,
Not by your will or by your hand,
> But by God's Power, be still.
The commanded blessing you will receive,
> When you join with those who believe,
Who believe with all their hearts and minds,
> That by faith in Christ, we're redeemed.

Now by His Blood, we're washed, made clean,
> And by His death, we're saved,
For by His resurrection power,
> We 're raised up from the grave.
Now we can live by grace through faith,
> A life blessed with His substance,
For by His Spirit He gives us life,
> A life with His abundance!

SOUL CLEANSING - Inspired by Psalm 51:6

Holy Spirit we come, with our hearts laid bare,
    We ask You to cleanse us, so that You can share,
Your Word of truth, that will bring to the light,
    The lies and half-truths, that distort our sight.
We ask for Your eye-salve, to heal and restore,
    Your perfect will, so You can give more-
More of Your love and Your will to be done,
    So, Lord Jesus Christ, The Omnipotent One,
Can receive the praise and the honour due Him,
    As our Saviour, Redeemer, and Deliverer from sin!

Forgive us for buying, the lies and half truths,
    For listening to gossip, instead of praying for truth.
Pray through us now, Holy Spirit pray through,
    Your will and purpose, so that we can do,
What You want spoken, decreed and declared,
    What You want prayed, petitioned and shared;
Not out of fear, or anger, or hurt,
    But with mercy and grace, to cover, not shirk,
The responsible task, we have as Your Church,
    To bind up the broken, to heal every hurt.

So wash us afresh, by Your Water and Word,
    Cleanse us, with Your blood, by Your power procured,
All that needs cleansing, in our hearts and our minds,
    So we can be cleansed of all that would blind.
Help us to see, with the sight that You give,
    The way we're to walk, the way we're to live;
In honour preferring one another as better,
    Then we ourselves, to break every fetter!
With love, help us break, plans meant to destroy,
    So every destructive device is made void!
Then restore Holy Spirit, Your destiny plan,
    To walk in love, Your purpose, Your plan!

DAUGHTERS OF JERUSALEM - Inspired by Luke 23:28-31

Daughters of Jerusalem, Daughters of Christ,
    Weep for the sins, that have led to the vice;
Of the sins that have trapped men, body and soul,
    For the sins that captured, divided what was whole!
Weep and mourn, arise from your beds,
    Then by acts of contrition and healing, make dead-
The plans, the devil, has used to destroy.
    By love and forgiveness and mercy, make void,
Every work of the devil, every plan he devised,
    Then come for the cleansing, by The Blood of Christ.

Ask for the love of God to control,
    Your will and desires, the thoughts of your soul,
Then hear what God's, Holy Spirit would say,
    So that you can, intercede when you pray;
Intercede with a heart, that God has made pure,
    Intercede with God's Word, for then He can cure,
All that is sick, and broken and lost,
    All that needs, to be brought to His cross.
Then leave at the cross, what's to be cleansed by His Blood,
    For there God's grace, will lift from the flood.

Holy Spirit will lift then, with grace to behold,
    The mercy by which, God The Father enfolds,
The ones who choose, to leave sin behind,
    And to come to The Christ, to receive His mind!
Oh pray the prayers, that God wants prayed,
    Let your words bring release, to those who're afraid,
Your words can bring, the revelation of love
    The love of The Father, in heaven above.
His love is merciful, gracious and kind,
    His love will reveal, will bring sight to the blind,
Will bring hope and assurance, of sins forgiven,
    Who choose now The Saviour, and what He has given!

REJOICE IN GOD - Inspired by Zephaniah 3:14-20

Oh come let us worship, the King of all kings,
    Let us rejoice, in our Lord God who sings,
Who sings over us, a joyful song,
    Who has come to abide with us, all the day long.
All tears He will wipe, away from our eyes,
    His love and His truth, will destroy Satan's lies.
For when He arrives, in His glory we'll see,
    His wondrous redemption, for you and for me.

Cheer up He says, and don't be afraid,
    Trust in My Power, for you I have saved.
I have saved you from all, of your enemies,
    I have paid the price, to set you free.
No more will you suffer, from fear or disgrace,
    For I will reveal, My mercy and grace.
I'll strengthen you, help you, I'll cause you to stand,
    I'll hold and protect, by My powerful hand.

No one can take you, away from My love,
    For My Spirit has sealed you, for life up above.
No more will doubt, and fears assail,
    For by My power and grace, you will prevail.
You will speak to the mountains, that stand in your way,
    They will not defeat you, or cause you to stray,
For the faith that My Spirit, will impart to you,
    Will give you My power, and the will to be true.

You will help to restore, those wounded and maimed,
    For this is your purpose, the plan I've ordained.
The love and the mercy, I have shown to you,
    Pass on to the ones, that I'll bring unto you.
My truth that I give, by My Spirit will free,
    And the love I impart, will draw them to Me.
There the lost will receive, from My love, My store,
    There they'll receive, My blessing, My more!

THE LIGHT IN YOUR HOME - John 1:4

Mistletoe and holly, and all the trees so bright,
Cannot compare to Holy God, who came one starry night.
He was born so all could see, The Saviour for mankind
He left His throne and power, to heal our hearts and minds.

The angel chorus filled the sky, that dark and holy night,
To tell to lonely shepherds, that The Christ, who is The Light
Was born that night in Bethlehem, to save the world from sin,
Was born to give new life and hope, to those who worship Him.

The Light of the world was born as a man, to restore relationship,
That had been lost, when man had sinned, had made the fatal slip.
But God had created His children to be, His friends forevermore,
So even after man had sinned, God had a plan to restore.

He sent His Son, as The One to redeem, to heal and to forgive,
All who would come, repent of sin, eternal life He'd give!
By grace we're saved and that by faith, if we will trust The Lord,
Salvation and redemption come, to those who seek God's more!

Christ took for us, the punishment, for sin and death and hell,
He took it all, God's spotless Lamb, so we could with God dwell!
The blood He shed that day at the cross, was shed for our salvation,
So we could be saved, everyone, from every tribe and nation!

So as this Christmas comes again, look up to see The Christ,
Who came in grace and love to show, to be our sacrifice!
Draw near and worship Christ, The Lord, listen once again,
To hear the Angel's word proclaim, Peace be to every man!

So if you have no peace within, if your heart is worn and sad,
Come to The Christ, who came for all, He'll make your spirits glad.
If you confess that you have sinned, He'll forgive and He'll restore,
Then peace, like you have never had, Will lead to heaven's door!

DO IN OUR DAY
Inspired by Micah 4:1-7 and Ezekiel 36:26 & 27

Do in our day what before was unseen,
  For it is time for You Lord, to make us all clean.
Take our cracked wineskins, that are dry and hard,
  Transform and restore, so like spikenard,
The praises we offer, will arise to Your throne,
  So glory and honour, will be Yours alone!

Take all of the hardness, out of our hearts,
  Then replace with Your love, that never departs,
Your love will transform, will make our hearts pure,
  For Your love and Your mercy, are the only cure!

We can't in our power, transform our own lives,
  So we ask You Dear Lord, restore and revive,
All that You've planted, in our hearts to grow,
  All You've imparted, so Your grace can bestow-
The faith that we need, to trust and believe,
  The faith that enables, our lives to receive-
The power we need, to live always for You,
  Out of love You impart, for our ways to be true!

Forgive us Dear Lord, for allowing the clutter,
  To hide Your pure love, from our sister or brother.
Help us to always, walk in Your love,
  So all can receive, from You Lord up above,
The mercy and grace, that forgives and restores,
  The faith that enables, and gives evermore.

For You gave us Your Son, as the best gift of all,
  So that our lives, could be saved from the fall.
Oh Father in Heaven, grant us Your pure sight,
  To walk in the faith, that leads to The Light,
The Light of the world, Christ Jesus our Lord,
  The light that will light, our lives evermore!

APPOINTED - Inspired by 1st Thessalonians 5:9

Appoint us Dear Lord to eternal life,
  To cease from confusion and all that is strife,
To receive all that's pure and holy and true,
  All You have planned in Your heart to do.
Make us a light to all those around,
  So that they can hear and receive, Your glad sound,
The sound of Your voice, calling all to draw near,
  For Your message of love is abundant and clear.

The angel announced, Your holy birth,
  The heavenly host sang, Peace on earth,
The peace You give into our hearts,
  Will always abide, will never depart.

The world cannot give, a peace like Yours,
  It always cries out for more and more.
What the world offers never satisfies,
  For all that it offers, eventually dies.
Only In You Lord, are eternal gifts,
  Only what You accomplished, can lift,
Our minds and our hearts to a higher place,
  The place where we can behold Your face!

So come Lord Jesus, establish Your throne,
  Make of our hearts, Your heart alone;
A place where You, can permanently dwell,
  A place from where, our lips can tell,
The greatest news, delivered to all,
  Who hear by grace, Your voice Your call,
Saying, Come unto Me, for eternal life,
  If you are weak or you're weary, cease from all strife,
I will give You My grace, My joy and My love,
  For I have made The Way, to your God up above!

REBUILD THE WALLS - Inspired by Nehemiah 1- 7:3

Rebuild the walls, that have broken down,
    Rebuild and restore, for your city and town,
Rebuild with prayers, and petitions and praise,
    Rebuild for the honour, of The Ancient of Days!
When you see what's destroyed, don't lose heart,
    For God in His power, enables each part,
Of His body to be, fitted in and restored,
    To the place where He, is The Head and The Lord.
He alone makes us holy, He alone has the power,
    To rebuild and restore, to love in each hour.
He has chosen the paths, where we're to walk in,
    To cease from confusion, from pride and from sin.
The paths He has chosen, are love, joy and peace,
    And if we're to rebuild, from our sins we must cease
We must rebuild and restore, with the love God has given,
    Then with love and compassion, lead all to God's heaven.

God has shown to us, what's in need of repair,
    All that is broken, and wounded and bare.
His mercy and love, will cover and cleanse,
    And His grace will enable, our spirits to sense,
His presence surrounding us, drawing us close,
    Then directing our works, by The Holy Ghost!
It is not by our power, that we can rebuild,
    Mere human will and strength, can't fulfill,
The destiny plans, God has to restore,
    The lives that are broken, and searching for more.
Only God, by His grace, and His power can do,
    What will strengthen, redeem, restore and make new.
He will clear all the rubble, and clutter that hinders,
    He will burn with His fire, and turn into cinders,
All that has bound us, to sin and destruction,
    So that in our hearts, He can bring His construction.
What You allow God, to build will endure,
    For His love and His grace, will make your life pure!

<u>PRAYER FOR GOD'S RESCUE</u> - Inspired by Ezekiel 1-13

Rescue Your people, from the grip of sin,
    Rescue from lies, that trap within.
Remove the stoniness, from our hearts,
    Let Your Word, by Your Spirit, purify each part.
Then cut away all, that would defile,
    So we can walk, that extra mile.
We come to You Lord, for the extra oil,
    So our lamps won't go out, as we live and toil,
Help us to occupy, until You come,
    With a heart that is pure, in love with Your Son!

Give us Your grace, Your enabling power,
    To walk in faith boldly, in every hour,
Trusting that You, are directing our way,
    Committing our lives, unto You each day.
Oh, forgive us for blessing, what You would curse,
    For tolerating the sins, that would only reverse,
The plans and precepts, You've ordained for all,
    Who hear Your voice, and obey Your call.

We come to You now, at the start of this day,
    And we ask You to hear, the prayers that we pray.
Cause us to show, with the light You impart,
    So that what's been darkened, will glow in the dark.
Your light will illumine, Your light will bring truth,
    Your light will dispel, will reveal what's uncouth!
Your light like a laser, will cut off the vile,
    Then make us a vessel, that's clean and worthwhile;
A vessel of honour, to carry within,
    The power and glory, that sets free from sin.
For nothing that's vile, will stand in that day,
    When Your glory reveals, Your pure holy way!

PRAYER OF CONSECRATION
Inspired by Psalm 51:10-13 & 2nd Corinthians 4:16-18

Dear Father in Heaven, hold me real close,
    Tuck me in tight, by The Holy Ghost.
Renew my spirit, my body, my soul,
    So I can come in, to Your total control!
I don't want to be, a slave to sin,
    I want Your redemption, to cleanse me within.
Remove from me every, wilful desire,
    Ignite my spirit, with Your Holy Fire!

Consume all that lurks, to destroy peace of mind,
    Then replace with Your power, to love and be kind.
Holy Spirit arrest, and consume every thought,
    Cause my mind to line up, with what Jesus taught.
I need Your miracle, to bring this release,
    I need Your power, to bring this peace.
Your peace passes all, human ways and thoughts,
    For it comes by grace, through faith to be caught;
Caught in a way, that endures to the end,
    With the knowledge that Christ, is Redeemer and Friend!

I thank You for hearing, and answering my prayer,
    I thank You that I,, can bring you my cares.
I thank You for healing, and restoring my soul,
    I thank You for cleansing, and making me whole!
I ask now, Dear Father, in heaven above,
    To remove from my life, all what pushes and shoves,
That pushes and shoves me, away from Your plans,
    That tries to remove, my life from Your Hand!
I come for Your grace, Your enabling power,
    To free me from all, that is morbid and sour,
Make of my body. A temple that's pure,
    A place that is holy, made clean by Your cure!
Baptize me afresh, By Your Spirit's power,
    For I choose to live by faith, in each hour!

PRAYER FOR POWER - Inspired by Hebrews 10:35-39

Holy Father in heaven, I ask for Your power,
 Help me to fast and to pray, to devour,
All that would hinder, Your will to be done,
 All that would take, from what Christ Jesus won!
I surrender my will, and my body to You,
 To cleanse and restore, make everything new.
I put my trust, in Your power Dear Lord,
 To bring my life, into one accord!

Take me up higher to where You are,
 Equip and empower me, to cross the bar,
To enter that place, of perfect rest,
 Content and secured, by Your arms so blest.
Give me Your grace, to endure to the end,
 With the joy and the strength that heals and mends;
All that is broken, and needs repair,
 All that requires, Your miraculous care.

You, are The Miracle Working God,
 All that You do, and are, we applaud!
Nothing and no one, could take Your place,
 Your love and Your mercy, our sin has erased.
Your Blood Precious Lord, redeems and restores,
 Your Blood paid the way, to open the door;
The door to life, and everlasting peace,
 You opened up wide, when You took Satan's keys!

So we come and we thank You, for giving us faith,
 The faith that endures, and that keeps our hearts safe;
Safe in the knowing, our salvation is sure,
 For kept by Your power, our faith will endure.
Our faith will endure, for we know what awaits,
 The ransomed, the faithful, who patiently wait,
For You Lord, our Redeemer, to welcome us home,
 At last with our Father, to never more roam!

PRAYER FOR EQUIPPING - Inspired by Hebrews 11-13

Equip us Dear Lord, with all that we need,
  To do Your will, in spirit and deed.
Remove from our hearts, every wilful thought,
  So that we can live, by what Jesus taught!
Help us to live, by The Spirit's power,
  In the grace through faith, He gives each hour.
Produce in us, what is pleasing to You,
  So our lives can be holy, in all that we do.

Help us give honour, where honour is due,
  With hearts full of mercy, and kindness too;
For You are The Shepherd, of Your sheep,
  You never leave us, or slumber or sleep.
You watch over us, to complete what's begun,
  So we can live faithful, in love with Your Son!
Prepare us each day, with all that we need,
  For Your will to be done, as we sow Your seed.

Cause us to come, before Your Holy Throne,
  With praise and thanksgiving, to You God alone.
For all that we are and have, comes from You,
  Only Christ's Blood, has saved and renewed,
Only His sacrifice, delivers each soul,
  Only His grace, will heal and make whole.
Only His power, enables to stand,
  To stand and proclaim, God's will in our land!

So, teach us to worship, Holy Spirit we pray,
  To worship our Lord, in a pure, holy way;
Not only with outward, signs that men see,
  But from hearts You've made holy, and pure and free.
Remove from our sight and our minds, what would blind,
  Our eyes from the truth, that Christ died for mankind.
Not just for one, or two, or three,
  But for all of Your children, to set us all free.

MY GIFT - Inspired by the Book of Hosea on Christmas Eve

What can I give, as a gift to my King?
   . What song could I offer, what could I bring?
Oh Lord, You're a God who has everything,
   One Word from You, and all heaven sings!
So I give You the life, You have given to me,
   And I ask You Dear Father, for the grace that makes free
From all of the passions, that cause me to stray,
   Away from Your Presence, Your pure, holy way!

Deliver me Lord from sin and disgrace,
   Bring me close to behold, Your beautiful face;
For I would become, a Christ-like one,
   In love with You Father, in love with Your Son!
Forgive me for trusting, in what man can do,
   Instead of trusting, completely in You;
For You alone, are The Giver of Life,
   A life that is free, from hatred and strife!

Help me to love, like You have loved me,
   With a love that is pure, and giving and free;
A love that is willing, to suffer long,
   A love that will heal, the weak and the strong.
For when The Day comes, and we stand before You,
   Only what is accomplished, by Your love will come through.
So help me rebuild, what is broken down,
   To restore, to redeem, to replace every frown.

Let Your love and mercy and grace, rule my thoughts,
   Let kindness and righteousness, release those caught,
Caught up in the sin and the lies Satan weaves,
   To trap and destroy, to kill and deceive.
Oh God, You are love and Your love paid the price,
   To redeem and restore, by Your Blood sacrifice.
So help me to always, reach out in Your Love,
   To all You want brought, to Your courts up above!

THE EXCELLENCE OF GOD'S NAME - Inspired by Psalm 8

Oh Lord, our Lord, how excellent is Your Name,
How excellent is Your Name, in all the earth!
Your glory is greater, much greater by far,
Than all we could see, as we look at the stars!
For with one word, You created all things,
And by Your Word, the heavens all sing;
They sing of Your greatness, Your majestic might,
They reveal to men's hearts, give power and sight.

Your heavens declare, the wonders You make,
When You speak and decree, the universe shakes!
For it is by Your Word, and Your Power, Oh Lord,
That our hearts are laid bare, by Your love, Your sword!
Your Word is a sword, that divides, separates,
That cleanses our hearts, from all that You hate!
Your Word is a lamp, unto my feet,
Your Word is what purifies, and makes sweet.

Your Word removes, the bitter, unclean,
Your Word sanctifies, restores and redeems!
Your Word became flesh, and dwelt among us,
Your Word is The Christ, who went to the cross!
Your Word took the sins, of all of mankind,
Your Word paid our price, gives sight to the blind!
Your Word took the keys, of hell and of death,
Your Word ransomed us, and gave us Your breath!

This breath is Your Spirit, that revives and restores,
The Spirit of God, who gives life evermore.
Holy Spirit of God, revive us again,
Fill us up to flow out, with Your Presence like rain,
For we need Your refreshing, Your awesome power,
So we can sit, walk or stand, by faith in each hour,
Not by the works, which we have done,
But by Your Power, Oh Holy One!

WORDS CAN BE TURNED - **Inspired by the book of Esther**

Words can be turned, when you fast and pray,
    Decrees can be altered, by what you say.
If you do what I tell you, I'll make a way,
    So that you can do, and stand and pray.
When you add fasting, to Your prayers,
    You will see My hand, I will hear and share,
My will for you, as you look to Me,
    For by My Power, I set men free!

So leave off all, the lies and din,
    Leave off what leads, your heart to sin,
Come up to where, I stand and wait,
    Come up, leave off, what causes hate!
Bring unto Me, your fears and cares,
    Your cries and tears, the wounds that tear,
Then trust Me and My power, to heal,
    To save from what, would kill and steal.

I AM, The God, who hears each prayer,
    I AM, The God, who is always there.
I'll save you from, the devil's plans,
    I will make My Church, My One New Man!
When sin contaminates, the whole,
    And clouds the vision, of men's souls,
I will appear, and make things right,
    I will restore, to men their sight!

So come unto Me, and buy My gold,
    The treasure that, will never mold.
Get salve to purify, your sight,
    For then you'll see, when all seems night.
You will see with your spirit, The God who sees you,
    For I have much, for you to do.
You will go and bring, My love to men,
    So they can know, My love for them!

REST - I awoke this morning with this line from a Christmas Carol: "rest beside the weary road and hear the angels sing!"

You cannot fix this present mess,
    So come to Me, I'll give you rest.
The turmoil that would steal and kill,
    I'll quiet by My Word, My Will.
I AM stirring the pot, so the crud will rise,
    I AM skimming off, the devil's lies;
For he was a liar, from the start,
    And he would steal, each human heart.

I have put the heat on, under the pot,
    To reveal what's hidden, to remove the rot!
I will heat till only, the pure remains,
    I AM coming as fire, to remove the stains.
What goes through My fire, without being burned,
    Are the truths I give, The Word you've learned.
My Word will be, a lamp unto you,
    To lead you on, to the path that is true!

So let My Word, dwell in your heart,
    In richness, to renew each part.
Don't look to men, for answers now,
    But look to Me, My Word, My Vow.
What I have said, Is what I'll do,
    To take and make, men's hearts brand new.
My Blood will cleanse, and purify,
    My Blood will heal, each hurt, each cry!

So come to Me, and never doubt,
    Receive by faith, be still, don't shout;
For the bruised reed, I will not break,
    But I will sieve, and I will shake.
Then what 's unshakeable, will remain,
    My Word, My Blood, to cleanse each stain!

THE APPOINTED TIME - Inspired by Galatians 4:4 -7

You weep, you cry, your tears you shed,
　　For me to heal, to raise what's dead,
So watch and see, what I will do,
　　I'll come and save, My Word is true!
When first I came, as a human babe,
　　The world was dark, for sin had made,
The hearts of men, devoid of hope,
　　They lived and breathed, just tried to cope.
But some believed, Messiah would come,
　　To release from sin, and the devil's scum.

So I came at The Father's, appointed time,
　　To remove the sin, the stain, the grime;
To show to all, My Father's love,
　　To heal and save, their hearts with love.
For love alone can heal, restore,
　　Love alone, brings life evermore.
Love destroys lies, by its giving power,
　　Love redeems, by grace each hour.

So forgive, as I have forgiven you,
　　Forgive and restore, the pure and the true.
Extend My love, My mercy and grace,
　　So all can behold, My Love, My Face!
What you behold, you will become,
　　So behold My Word, read all, not some.
I will lead you then, on paths made sure,
　　My grace will give, the faith that cures;
That heals and gives, new hope to all,
　　Who hear My voice, My Spirit's call.

I will take the hurt, and pain away,
　　I will give the strength, to watch and pray.
So watch and see, what I will do,
　　To make My Bride, My Church, brand new!

RIP UP AND TEAR OUT - Inspired by Jeremiah 45:4 & 5

Rip up and tear out, what we've built by ourselves,
  Rip up and tear out, what the world calls wealth,
Then place a new heart, in us we pray,
  A heart that is willing, to love and obey.
Give us ears to hear, what Holy Spirit says,
  Then a heart to obey, and to enter God's rest;
For in Your rest, comes the power to choose,
  A life that is pure, a life that can't lose.

You, Oh Lord, are our source of real life,
  A life that's eternal, a life freed from strife.
The life You give, gives power to all,
  Who forsake their sin, to answer Your call.
You call us to leave, the world and its sin,
  You call us to give us, new life within.
You call us to be born, of the spirit, not flesh,
  You call us to say, let your hearts be enmeshed,
With Your heart Oh God, to experience Your grace,
  The grace that enables, to behold Your Face!

Then change us by what, our spirit's behold,
  To hear and obey, what Your Word unfolds.
Holy Spirit we ask, for revelation to know,
  The ways we're to walk in, Your grace to show-
The love of God, by Christ Jesus revealed,
  The love and mercy, by which we are sealed;
For we are sealed for redemption, by Christ's Holy Blood,
  Saved and delivered, from sins awful flood.!

So at this new year, we humbly pray,
  Oh Lord make us pure, and spotless each day.
Put to death all, what would defile our minds,
  By the Power of Your Spirit, revive and refine,
The Words You have planted, in our hearts to know,
  Your will, Holy Father, Your love to bestow!

THE END OF THE AGE - Inspired by; Matthew 13

The end of the age, will soon be here,
    When Christ with His angels, will soon appear.
The thorns that grew, with the wheat will then,
    Be plucked out and gathered for the burning bin!
Then at the same time, the ripe holy lives,
    Those matured to adorn, their Father beside,
Will be gathered to come, before His throne,
    To worship, adore, their God alone!

Thorns are sown, by the enemies lies,
    Thorns that try, to quench God's life,
But the life of God, that is sown in our hearts,
    Has power to quench, all the devil's darts.
The life of God, is in His Word,
    By which our salvation, is assured.
Salvation is not by works, we've done,
    But only by grace, through faith in God's Son.,
And when we turn, to Christ in faith,
    No thorn of hell, can quench the grace,
That God extends, to those who call,
    Upon His Son, to conquer all.

So when the thorns of doubt assail,
    To try and steal your faith - prevail!
Prevail by faith, in grace to know,
    God's power is there, by love bestowed.
God's love will conquer, cleanse and heal,
    If we call out, for Holy Spirit's seal.
He watches those, who call out to Him,
    And He will come, to live in them!
That is where, God's power is seen,
    To stand and grow, as His redeemed!

WHAT CAN WE TAKE? - Inspired by 1st John 4

What can we take, to Your courts above,
    What can we bring to You, God of love?
For all that we are, and we have is from You,
    Your grace, gives faith, to bring us through!
So let my life, and my words proclaim,
    The honour and the glory, that is due Your Name!
Your Name Lord Jesus, is above every name,
    You came and You gave us, freedom to gain,
A life that's redeemed, and forgiven to live,
    In love with You Jesus, and ready to give.

You, Lord Jesus, showed The Father's love,
    When you left heaven's glory, and courts above,
You came out of love, to redeem our souls,
    You gave Your life, for our lives to be whole.
So we bow and we worship, on bended knee,
    We give You our lives, for You set us free.
Now we're free to love, and live and forgive,
    All those You have chosen, among us to live!
Now unless we love those, that we can see,
    How can we say Lord, that we truly love Thee?

Loving You Lord, means loving like You,
    You loved us first, gave us power to choose,
The way to heaven, and all God bestows,
    Then show forth Your love, to all here below.
You gave us Your life, to redeem us from sin,
    Even when we were sinners, did not welcome You in
You loved us first, though dead in our sins,
    And Your love conquered all, to bring us within-
The place of safety, where sins are forgiven,
    The place of grace, for those who choose heaven.
So cause us all, to love one another,
    As You have loved us, as our Father, our Brother!

GOD'S THRONE - Inspired by Hebrews 12:22-29

Dear Lord, I come, to Your throne of grace,,
    I come to behold, Your beautiful face.
I come to receive, the grace that I need,
    I come to love You, in truth and in deed.
So give me Your strength, to walk day by day,
    Equipped by Your Spirit, to watch and to pray;
Watch what you are doing, and give You praise,
    Then pray for Your Spirit, to empower each day.

It is not by my might, or my power I live,
    It is by Your Spirit, I can give and forgive.
Give to all men, the love You gave me,
    When You came and You died, on that awful tree!
When I think of all, of the love You have shown,
    How could I say, that my life is my own?
For I was condemned, to death and to hell,
    I could not by my works, or my deeds be made well!

But You, Lord Jesus, reached out in Your love,
    You picked me up, for Your courts above,
Your Blood cleansed the grime, that defiled my soul,
    Your Spirit brought faith, and the grace to make whole.
Now I can walk, in Your light every day,
    Knowing You as The Truth, The Light and The Way!
Knowing I am loved, I can now extend love,
    To all You are calling, to come up above!

Now I can rise like an eagle, to soar with Your Wind,
    I can see and believe, in The God who rescinds,
Who rescinds and redeems, by love and grace given,
    All those who repent, to be cleansed of sin's leaven.
Pride is the leaven, that puffs up our self,
    But a humble heart, can receive God's wealth.
Now this is the wealth, God gives in His Son,
    The faith to believe Christ, for the battle is won!

RETURN - Inspired by Jeremiah 15:19-21

Return to the place, where I first met you,
    Where I baptized you, in Spirit and Truth,
Where I touched your life, with My power divine,
    Where I placed My seal, to make you Mine!
Think, My child, what happened there,
    When you sought for Me, with heartfelt prayer?
You wanted from Me, what alone I can give,
    You wanted My life, so that you could live!
You were hungry then, for My Spirit's touch,
    For you knew your life, didn't amount to much.
I placed that hunger, within you My child,
    The hunger to know Me, as The Pure Undefiled!
You needed to know, The Father's love,
    A love that transcends, then takes above,
All that would trouble, confuse and defile,
    So that your life, could be made worthwhile.

I came that day, when you sought My face,
    I came and touched, with My power, My grace.
My warmth suffused you, body and soul,
    It quickened your spirit, to envelope, make whole.
The touch you received, was My love, My child,
    That touch turned your life, from what would defile.
No more would anything less, satisfy,
    For what you received, ever lives, never dies!
Now you are seeking, My face once again,
    For My touch to re-fire your faith, so that men,
Will hunger to know Me, in spirit and truth,
    Then lay at my feet, in submission like Ruth;
Who came for the covering, of a cloak to protect,
    For she knew what she needed, to save and perfect.
The plan You had placed, in her heart to believe,
    To be part of God's family, to know and receive
The Robe of Your Righteousness, is the cloak that we need
    For it covers, and cleanses, nurtures and feeds!

THE ROCK - Inspired by 1st Corinthians 10:4 & 1st Peter 1:7

Fear not the fire of God, My child,
    My fire will only burn off what defiles,
It will purify, the intents of your heart,
    It will deaden the things, that tear you apart.
You will have a pure, and holy soul,
    When My fire consumes, to make you whole;
Whole and holy, set apart for Me,
    For the plans I have planned, for destiny.

My plan is perfect, My plan is true,
    My plan will bring you, to a place that is new;
A place you have never been before,
    To the place I've prepared, a brand new door.
I will open the door, just ask and knock,
    Just seek My will, for I AM The Rock;
The Rock of salvation, for all who will call,
    The Rock upon which, you can build, not fall.

No more will you stumble, or walk aimlessly,
    For My hand is guiding, to a place that is free,
A place I've prepared, where you can drink up,
    And then pour out, from My loving cup,
The blessings, the words, the touch that men need,
    To release them from all, of their sin and their greed;
The place where My arms, are opened up wide,
    To receive and to welcome, to draw by My side.
There they'll experience, the love that I give,
    There they'll receive, a real life to live.

Therefore, follow My leading, and don't deviate,
    I'll lead you and guide you, I'll open the gate.
You will enter and dwell, in My garden of love,
    And there I'll prepare you, for heaven above.
Worry and fear, have no entrance there,
    For there in My presence, I take every care!

BEHOLD THE LORD - Inspired by 2nd Corinthians 3:18

I love You, my Lord, and I ask for Your grace,
    The grace that illumines, that reveals Your face.
Your Word has declared, that we shall become,
    What we behold, when we gaze at Your Son!
So Lord God Almighty, give me eyes that can see,
    My Saviour, Redeemer, to purify me.
Make me like gold, that's tried in the fire,
    Purge me and cleanse me, so I can desire,
All that is of You, and for Your Great Name,
    All that would give You, the love we proclaim.

All that is good, in our lives comes from You,
    Only Your life, in us brings us truth.
Your Truth penetrates, like a two-edged sword,
    It cuts off what defiles, so Your Blood that You poured,
Can cleanse and make new, every inward part,
    To give us a pure and a holy heart.
So I ask, Holy Spirit, let Your sword penetrate,
    To reveal and cut off, what delineates,
All what would cause me, a double mind,
    Then see with Your sight, to lead the blind,
To the place where they, can receive Your love,
    The love that redeems, for Your courts above.

I know I can't do this, on my own,
    I need the power, from Your Holy Throne.
So I come to You Lord, on bended knee,
    Reach out with Your sceptre, to empower me,
With Your Spirit's anointing help me speak and do,
    All You have planned, for a life that is new.
I place myself now, before Your Throne,
    To live for You Lord and You alone.
Lead me, Oh Lord, by Your righteousness,
    Lead by Your Spirit, to blessedness.

COME TO MY SIDE - Inspired by John 15

What, Oh Lord, would You have me to know,
How should I give, Your grace to show?
How can Your love, best be portrayed,
So that Your glory, will never fade?

Come unto Me, sit by My side, come unto Me and there abide,
Sit real still and listen close, for the still small voice of Holy Ghost
Pray in the spirit and don't let up, until I fill your loving cup.
I will refresh, I will make whole, and I will heal your troubled soul.

As you pour out Your heart to Me, I will redeem, I'll set you free.
So cast your cares upon Me now, I paid the price, I'll show you how,
To walk by grace in faith to see, My will, My hand, enabling thee.

You cannot walk this path alone,
For you would stumble o'er the stones.
So let Me take your hand in Mine,
To lead you in the path divine.

The path I have prepared for you,
Is the path to lead men to My Truth
My truth will set each captive free,
To see My love, My destiny.

Oh come before My face each day,
So I can lead your thoughts to pray.
Then as you pray, My will on earth,
As is in heaven, life comes to birth.

This life comes not by man's desire,
But comes by Holy Spirit's fire,
It comes with anointing and power to bless,
It comes to bless with righteousness!

THE VISION - Inspired by Habakkuk 2:1 - 4

Print the vision, make it plain,
   So My will may be proclaimed.
      What I've given you are to share,
         So all can see I hear, I care.

I love, I care, for every soul,
   I died and rose, to make men whole.
      Sin had fractured, My perfect man,
         But by My Blood, new life began.

This life doesn't come, by man's will to be,
   For by My Spirit, life comes to thee,
      As a life of love, which has no end,
         A life of peace, and joy which sends,

A message clear, to every soul,
   God's love is here, to make all whole.
      So tarry not, do not delay,
         Print out the words, that I will say.

Write the vision, and make it plain,
   So man from sin, can now abstain,
      From all that would, destroy and kill,
         So they can know, and do My will.

My will for man, is eternal life,
   A life of joy, without the strife.
      A life of peace, a life of grace,
         A life of love, which sees My face.

For when men see, My love for them,
   They'll come to know, My love again.
      For I have planted, in each heart,
         A place to know, what I impart
A faith to live as those atoned, redeemed to stand before My Throne!

INASMUCH - Inspired by Matthew 25:31-40

In the night, I had a dream, about a little boy,
Who came to sit beside me, he was not shy or coy,
As he sat there, I saw his feet, he had no socks on them,
His toes stuck out the front of shoes, the leather was so thin.
His smile lit up his little face, his eyes looked right at mine,
And then He opened up and spoke, of what he'd seen one time.
He saw a pair of shoes one day, and Oh they were so fine,
Five fifty was the cost of them, but he didn't have a dime.

He said the children laughed at him, and at his shoes and clothes,
I knew exactly how he felt, I felt his pain and woes.
Then in my heart, I heard God speak, what will you do for him?
For He had shown me of this need, this little lamb so thin!
I knew then, I must always be, ready to give and share,
Of all the blessings I'd received, to show God's love and care.
Then in my heart, I asked The Lord, how can I meet the need?
Of all the ones who lack the means, to clothe and care and feed?

I knew I could not care for all, the ones He dearly loves,
But I should do what I could do, for then I'd come above;
To heaven to where My Saviour stands, to give what I must give,
For He'll provide, what must be given, so that His children live.
I knew I had to tell you friend, about this dream I had,
To tell you, do what you can do, you'll make The Father glad!
For if we'll give what we can give, from all He's given to us,
If we will give, to show God lives, our treasures will not rust!

Now what we give to show God's love,. to all the least of these,
Will add up to the blessings that, we get as we believe.
So open up your heart my friend, and open up your hand,
For as You give, God gives to you, His blessings from His hand..
The more you give, you will receive, for God's a giving God,
And He would have us give like Him, while on this earth we trod,
So when you see a need my friend, ask God how you can give,
He'll speak into your heart the way, to show His love that lives!

GOD'S PLACE - Inspired by John 14:1-3

There is a place I have for you,
   A place where you will stand,.
A place where you can speak the truth,
   Where you can show My hand.

There will be room to come away,
   Alone to seek My face.
I have prepared a room for you,
   A quiet secret place.

But until then, be still My child,
   Be still, wait patiently,
For what I have prepared will come,
   For those who wait on Me.

This world is just a resting place,
   Until you come on home,
To where I have prepared a place,
   A place like none you've known.

So take what I have given you,
   Give freely, what I've given
For then you will have treasure there,
   When you arrive in heaven!

THANKS BE TO GOD! - Inspired by 1st Corinthians 15:57

Thank You Lord for what You do,
   To set my mind at ease,
Thank You Holy Spirit too,
   For giving perfect peace.
Your Words inspires my heart to hear,
   They cause my eyes to see,
The things You want to make real clear,
   For then I can be free!

THE WORDS OF THE SPIRIT - Inspired by Revelation 2 & 3.

Listen to The Wind Words, as My Spirit calls,
   Listen to The Wind Words, calling one and all.

Listen to The Wind Words, blowing through The Church,
   Listen to The Wind Words, let My Spirit search.

He is calling to enlighten, to gather to Himself,
   The souls of all, who heed His call,
      The abundance of His wealth.

The wealth He gives will never rust, corrupt or bruise or kill
   For what He gives enlightens, and equips to do God's will.

And when we heed The Spirit's call, to listen and obey,
   We'll hear God's voice to enter in, God's pure and holy way

We will not stumble when we walk, the path He has prepared,
   For then we'll see His blessings, the blessings to be shared!

The gifts God gives will always be, much more than we could hold
   These gifts will bless with peace and rest,
      Give warmth instead of cold.

The Lord comes as we enter in, to God's extended arms,
   There to receive the love He gives,
      His protection from all harm.

Healing grace God there bestows, and faith to trust in Him,
   Forgiveness we'll receive as well,
      When we confess we've sinned.

So listen to The Wind Words, His Spirit speaks today,
   Listen to His Spirit, and heed what He would say.

ASCEND AND ENTER - Inspired by Revelation 4

Ascend and enter God's Spirit calls,
    Ascend and enter today.
Come up to God's own banquet hall,
    Come up, do not delay.
He has a feast prepared for you,
    A feast with bread and wine.
A feast of all that's pure and true,
    So enter, come and dine.

What do you need My bride My child,
    What do you need today?
I'll give you food that is worthwhile,
    As you come up and pray.
When you come up and see what all,
    The Father has prepared,
You'll want to give your heart your all,
    Your worship, praise and prayer

You'll see the beasts and elders,
    And worship round God's throne,
You'll see your Lord in glory stand,
    For God is God alone.
You'll worship then for you will see,
    Your God upon His throne.
You'll worship then on bended knees
    For Christ, your sins atoned.

He is the Lord The Worthy One,
    Who gave His Life, His Blood,
For when our hearts were hard as stone,
    He rescued from sin's flood
He took out all our story hearts,
    When we confessed our sin,
And then a new heart did impart,
    So we could live with Him.

IT IS FINISHED. - Inspired by John 19:30

It Is Finished, our Lord cried out, as He gave up His life,
He gave a shout and with that shout, removed all sin and strife
His shout penetrated the regions of hell, He opened the gates for us,
Salvation was made, our sins were paid, our Lord had died for us!
The temple curtain was torn in two, an earthquake shook the land,
Many believers dead in their tombs, came out to walk the land.

After Jesus arose upon the third day, those resurrected would say,
What happened to them, when the debt was paid,
By Christ on the cross that day.
His provision procured, our salvation and grace,
Redemption to see His face.
Oh, behold with me the Lamb of God, behold the King, give praise!

For He alone has redeemed our souls, His blood alone has cleansed,.
For you or I could not begin, to redeem our souls from sin.
Only the Christ, The Perfect One, could set us free from sin,
God's Holy Son. became a man, so we could enter in.
Then He gave back, what man had lacked, a life set free, God's plan
To live a life, a perfect life, a life set free, to stand!

So ponder now on Christ's sacrifice, what Jesus did for you,
Commit your life to The Lord Jesus Christ, He paid the price for you.
Confess you've sinned, that you've missed the mark,
Confess and then believe,
That what He said, is what he'll do, If we will but receive.
The grace He give is not a license, to continue in our sin,
For Christ The Lord redeemed our lives, so we could enter in!

This life we have, right here on earth, can be renewed right now,
Our eyes can see, His plans for us, as we believe, then bow,
Before The Lord, our King and God, before His majesty,
To there proclaim, for all to hear, our love, our fealty;
Towards The One, who gave His life, to save and set us free
Towards Our Precious Jesus Christ, His friend forever be!

DON'T BORROW - Inspired by Matthew 6:19-34

Don't borrow from tomorrow, what belongs to today,
    Just listen and learn, and watch and pray.
Listen to what, My Spirit will say,
    Learn from My Word, how to watch and pray.
Your needs I will meet, when you sit at My feet,
    Your needs I will meet, each day.
As you cast every care on Me, I will keep,
    Your heart and your life, on My way.

So leave off the past, with its worries and tears,
    Look, it's a brand-new day.
It's a day where My mercies, are new to share
    With all you will meet, on the way.
My faithfulness and My righteousness,
    Are yours to strengthen and keep,
My comfort, peace and blessedness,
    Will be there to comfort, the weak.

So come at the start, of each new day,
    Sit quietly at My feet,
Be careful to hear, every word I say
    For My words have the strength to keep.
My words will keep your heart and mind,
    Will purify, your walk
Go forward then, I'll protect your back,
    Your walk, will match your talk.

You will not suffer want or lack, in the place I have prepared,,
I will give from My abundance, so you can always share.
So open up your home to those, the ones I bring to you,
Then give of what I've given to you, My Word, My Love, My truth!
My truth will set each captive free, from all that would control,
My truth will bring, My mercy near, to heal and save each soul!

GOD'S SECRET PLACE - Inspired by Psalm 27.

Hide me in your secret place,
    Where the world can't find me.
Hide me as I seek Your Face, away from all until I see:
    Your wondrous beauty, matchless grace,
        Your awesome place above the base.

Forgive me for neglecting You,
    For in this place, I find what's true.
One touch from You is all I need,
    One word from You will always feed.

So touch me once again I pray,
    For by Your side I long to stay;
Protected by Your loving arms,
    Away from all that steals and harms

Take me away from the world's noise,
    Into Your place of peace and poise,
For there my soul is truly blessed,
    With peace and joy and perfect rest!

Lord you have heard my heart, my prayer,
    Now I will sit in silence where
Your still small voice can speak to me,
    Where I can hear what sets me free.

You are hearing and you always will,
    When you come near, to sit, be still.
My love for you will never fail,
    New strength I'll give, you will prevail.

You'll stand when all are falling down,
    You'll stand and then receive My crown.
This crown of life, I've saved for you,
    The crown I have prepared for you.

I know that you delight in Me,
    So I will set your spirit free.
I'll take you up to where I am,
    To there behold, My Son, The Lamb.

My Son, The Lamb takes away all sin,
    For all who choose to enter in.
You'll stand then with the ones redeemed,
    You will stand and praise for you've been cleaned.

The precious blood has cleansed your soul,
    The Lamb of God has made you whole.
So look not at what now is seen,
    But look to what's above, unseen.

With eyes of faith look up above,
    Look to your Lord your God above.
Then when His revelation comes,
    When you behold the Christ, God's Son,
You'll know as fact that you are loved,
    My grace through faith took you above.

SPEAK WHAT GOD WANTS - Inspired by Proverbs 18:21

Speak what I want spoken, speak the Word of Truth,
Heal what has been broken, then pledge like faithful Ruth.
In living or in dying, to trust and to obey,
For then your words will build a bridge, that will not rot or sway.
Hold fast, stand firm, whatever the cost, for that is how you'll win,
The victory over what was lost, a life set free from sin.
Sin is not entertainment, it only destroys and kills,
So stay away from defilement, and all it's deadly ills.
Present yourself to The Lord, at the start of each new day,
Then you'll be freed from each device, that leads your heart astray.
Then what you bring as an offering, I'll purge with holy fire,
I'll burn off all the sin that clings, till I'm your one desire.

<u>WAKE UP AND PRAY</u> - Inspired by Holy Spirit, after the murder of a mother of five children.

Wake up church, it's time to choose,
    For if we snooze, then we will lose!
It's time to get, the extra oil,
    To ask our Lord, to cleanse the soil.
For death has raised, its ugly head,
    And taken one of ours, instead.
It's time to cover, each other in prayer,
    It's time to seek, the Lord who cares.
Death and hell, must be destroyed,
    The church must rise, and then employ,
The weapons, God has given her,
    To save the lost, the sick to cure.

Oh Church lets rise, in righteousness,
    And in God's power, reach out to bless:
With goodness, love, and mercy too,
    So men can see, our God anew.
The world must see, God's love in us,,
    Or all they will do, is spout and cuss.
Let's pray: God cleanse our hearts, and then,
    Let's ask to cleanse, our cities again.
Let's make a stand, for what is right,
    Let's take His light, into the night.
Let's rise above, to where He stands,
    To receive fresh fire, to cleanse the land

Send the fire, Oh God, of Your holiness,
    To purge this land, of lawlessness.
We pray for those, in charge to rule,
    With wisdom from, Your holy school.
We pray for judges, in our land,
    Who'll make the choice, to take a stand.
A stand against, all lawlessness,
    A stand for God's, own righteousness!

432

REND THE HEAVENS - Inspired by Isaiah 64

Rend the heavens, and come down Lord,
 It's time to swing, the sickle, the sword.
It's time to cleanse, from godlessness,
 It's time for peace, and righteousness.
Anoint Your Church, with fire anew
 So we can rise, to all that's true.
Help us strip off, what holds us down,
 For then we can run, to receive the crown.
Let's run with purpose, run with a plan,
 Run with Your Word, Oh God to man.

So anoint us Lord, with your love to speak,
 The words You give, to equip the weak,
To strengthen the hands, that have fallen down,
 To strengthen the knees, to erase the frown!
Your joy is the strength, that equips and keeps,
 Our soul in the peace, and the faith it needs.
Your joy comes afresh, as we bow our knees,
 To repent and confess, our sins, our deeds.
For all that is done, without Your will,
 Can lead us to, the pride that kills.

Forgive us Lord, when we've acted in pride,
 When we've sought for men's praise, and didn't abide,
In The Vine where Your life, could refresh and renew,
 In The Vine where Your blessing, produces what's true.
Bring us back to The Blood of the Lamb, to be cleaned,
 Help us die to what all, of the world esteems.
Immerse us afresh, with Your pure sweet love,
 Then by Your great glory, to lead up above,
To Your Throne Holy Father, those who receive Your grace,
 Your mercy, salvation, Your holy embrace.

THE LORD'S LAMP - Inspired by Psalm 119:105 & 130.

Your Word Oh Lord, is a lamp to me, The Light to lighten my path,
So use Your Word to set me free, from all of Satan's wrath.

Let every word You give bring life, and hope into my soul,
Strip off what causes fear and strife, renew and make me whole.

Holy God to You I come, wash off the grime, wash off the scum,
Anoint my eyes so I can see, the truths you give to set me free.

Reveal your will Oh God I pray, write it upon my heart of clay
Then with Your Holy Fire burn, till all that's left is Your Pure Word.

A vessel of honour, make of me, so I can give Your Word that frees,
Give it pure and lovingly, give with grace, and mercy like Thee!

Oh Holy Spirit come now with fire, so that Your Will be my desire;
The Will of God that shows to man, the path of light away from sin.

Your path Oh Lord, leads us to life,
    In your path, love conquers strife.
        Your love forgives, shows mercy too,
            Your love reveals, the lies of fools.
Your love enables, Your Word to heal,
    The wounds and scars, so men can feel:
        Your loving arms, Your warm embrace,
            Your peace, as they behold Your face.
For there is no, condemning there,
    When humble hearts, release their cares.
        When they confess their sins, their need,
            You save Oh Lord, You gently lead.
To where our souls, are satisfied,
    To where we live, and never die!

DAY BY DAY - Inspired by Philippians 1:6

Day by day and moment by moment,
    My Spirit is working in you
Day by day and moment by moment,
    Inspiring and speaking to you.
Oh listen my child to His still small voice,
    Listen and be not afraid,
For The Words that He speaks, will bring life to you,
    The foundation where faith is made

Conformed to the image of Christ you will be,
    When His Spirit completes His work,
If you will allow Him, the freedom to mold,
    He will give you a faith that won't shirk!
A destiny God has planned for each child
    Each child of His own to perform,
His dreams and His plans will take you above
    All that is mundane and norm.

When God first revealed His love to you,
    And saved you from Satan's plan,
Your heart and your mind, were made fresh and new
    With a peace not given by man.
Oh this wondrous peace, and the joy God gives,
    When His grace by faith we receive,
How precious in Christ is this gift of life,
    When we know His love and believe.

So leave for a moment your thoughts and your plans,
    Come focus your heart now on Him,
Draw near and behold your Saviour, The Christ,
    The One who ransomed from sin.
Behold His face and the love that is there,
    Come near and abide with Him.
He'll tenderly wrap, His arms around you,
    He'll give you His peace within.

JERUSALEM - Inspired by Zechariah 8:20 -14:21

Jerusalem, Jerusalem, the city where tribes go up,
Jerusalem, Jerusalem, they come to fill their cup.
Jerusalem, Jerusalem, the Lord cried out one day,
For He had come to save all men, from sins they could not pay.

He walked your streets Jerusalem, He taught God's Word to you,
God signs and wonders followed Him, for all His words were true.
He preached to scribes and Pharisees, the teachers of God's law,
He came to show He was God's Way, God's Son, without one flaw.

He preached to all The Way to God, was not in what men do,
But by the heart receive God's grace, and faith that He'll make new.
Jesus wept over you that day, He wept for He saw your end,
For you would not believe He was, The Messiah, God had sent.

Your pride in what you did put scales, before your very eyes,
You trusted in Your words and works, you bought the devil's lies.
You tried the very Son of God, then crucified Him too,
Outside your city walls He died, to pay the price for you.

Soon He'll return to earth again, return to claim His bride.
He will gather to His heavenly home, all those who hear His cry:
Come unto Me you weary and sad, come unto Me and live,
Come unto Me I'll wash you clean, your sins I will forgive.

The tribes still come to Jerusalem, they know it is special there;
For this is where Messiah will come, He'll come to answer prayer.
All tribes call this their holy place, Jerusalem The Fair,
The Christian, Jew & Muslim claim, that God will meet them there!

Jerusalem, Jerusalem, call out to the Lord with your vow.
Jerusalem, Jerusalem, Christ Jesus will save You now.
He'll save you from the terrors without, and all the terrors within,
He'll come again as Messiah and Lord, if you confess you've sinned.

Jerusalem, Jerusalem, Your Father is waiting to hear
To hear you call The Lord, His Son, to enter and draw near.
Jesus, The Christ, The Anointed One, is waiting for your call
He is waiting with your Father God, for you to give Him all.

So call to Him, Jerusalem, call out to Jesus Christ,
Call out in faith believing, for He is The Sacrifice,
The Pure and Holy Son of God, who paid the price for sin,
Who is standing, waiting and loving you, for you to say, come in.

He'll come and be Your Lord and Christ, He'll save and rescue you,
From all the sin that kept you bound, He'll give you life that's true.
No more a wanderer, lost, forlorn, but now His child redeemed,
For by His blood, you're ransomed now, from all that is unclean.

Together now with angels, and all those Christ redeemed,
You'll have the harps of God in hand, beside the glassy sea.
You'll sing the song of Moses, and the song of The Holy Lamb,
To worship God Almighty, The Lord, The Great, I AM!

At this the tent of testimony, in heaven is opened wide,
And seven mighty angels, go forth, to turn the tide.
No more will those who are unclean, who rebelled against The Lord,
Be left unpunished for their sin, for now God's wrath is poured.

Oh read The Revelation, of Jesus Christ The Lord,
For this was given to the Apostle John, so we could be restored.
Hell and condemnation, were not prepared for men,
But were prepared for Lucifer and all who left with him.

So pray for the peace of Jerusalem, this city where tribes still come,
Pray they will look to the Christ of God, for He is The Saving One!
Pray that men's hearts will turn again, to Jesus the Saviour of all,
Who came and became God's sacrifice, to redeem all from the fall.

THE KINGDOM OF GOD - Inspired by Matthew 24:14

You eat The Bread, you drink The Cup,
    But do you know, the time is up?
The time has come, for My Kingdom to come,
    The time when men, will worship The Son!
But for My Glory to be revealed,
    My church must open, what has been sealed;
Must open by My Spirit's Power,
    To bring The Light of God this hour!

So pray now church, for revelation,
    Pray in every place, and nation,
Pray for Holy Spirit to come,
    To cause to worship, Christ, God's Son!
Many now say, that they know Me,
    But they refuse, to bend their knees,
They want My Kingdom, on their terms,
    They fail to see, My love they've spurned.

They want to fit Me, in their box,
    But I have come, to break the locks,
Of sins that bound, in chains for death,
    The ones who need, My Spirit's breath!
So seek My will and not your own,
    For then you will, prepare a throne,
Within your heart, where I may dwell,
    For I have saved, from death and hell.

Christ is Lord, and reigns on high,
    So men can live, and never die;
But rise to where all heaven waits,
    To see God's saints come through the gates
Then take the hand, of The One who gave,,
    His life as ransom, from the grave.
For you're The Bride, His blood paid for,
    His life He gave, He is The Door!!

BEHOLD YOUR GOD
Inspired by Isaiah 25:1-9 and Matthew 25:1-13

Men and women, boys and girls,
    Hear The Word of The Lord,
He is coming in power, coming in glory,
    Coming His Church to restore!

The saints through the ages, have longed for this day,
    Longed for His Kingdom to come,
And now He is coming with angels to claim,
    All those who look to The Son!

So raise a glad cry, to your God on high,
    Praise His Name evermore,
For The King is coming, to claim His Bride,
    To reveal what He has in store.

Christ's Thousand Year Reign, will seem but a day,
    For those who love God alone,
They will see The Lord, in His Glory arrayed,
    Ruling from God's Holy Throne!

So prepare your hearts, and your minds my friends,
    Prepare for your coming King,
He will set in place, restore, make amends,
    So His Bride, can rejoice and sing!

There are no words, that can express from my heart,
    The longing for that blessed day,
When my Saviour, my King, my Wonderful Lord,
    Will appear in His glorious array!

Therefore children, prepare your hearts and your minds,
    Put off all that hinders and spoils,
Get your wicks and your lamps ready to find,
    The source for His fresh new oil!!

THE GIFT OF GOD'S LIFE
Inspired by Matthew 1, Luke 2 and John 1

Let my prayer reach to heaven, and my praises arise,
To You Lord God Almighty, Omnipotent, All Wise!
For by The Word of Your Power, we all live and breathe,
By Your mercy and goodness, our lives were conceived.
For when we were but, a seed in the womb,
You created a life, that would say, give me room.
This life was a child, a child destined to grow,
To be formed in Your likeness, to be born and to know,
That You, Lord God, are Creator of all,
The God whose Word, redeemed from the fall.

Now The Word became flesh, and was born as a man,
To fulfill God's will and His destiny plan!
Now God who created, all life from the start,
Hovered over a virgin, to plant, to impart,
His Seed in her womb, to bring forth The Messiah,
The Lord Jesus Christ, who'd defeat the old liar!
When Joseph, the bridegroom of Mary found out,
That she was now pregnant, he had many doubts.
According to the law, he could have her stoned,
This one who'd give birth, to The Lord who atones!

But instead he decided, to divorce her quietly,
For He was just and upright, a man of God was he.
But as he was thinking this over, one night,
An angel appeared, in a dream for insight.
The angel said to Joseph, Don't be afraid,
To take Mary as your wife, she's God's honourable maid.
What is conceived in her, is by The Holy Spirit,
She will bear a Son, by Whom, all will inherit,
Everlasting life if they have faith in Him,
For He is to be The Messiah, The Saviour from sin!

You're to call His Name Jesus, which means Saviour,
For He will save His people, from their sinful behaviour.
This all took place, to fulfill the prophecy,
That the prophet Isaiah, said was to be.
He said a virgin would conceive, and give birth to a Son,
He'd be called Emmanuel, God with us each one.
After Joseph aroused from his sleep, he obeyed,
What the angel had said, and married Mary, God's maid.
But he had no sexual relations with her,
Until after The Lord Jesus, was born to ensure,
That Jesus, The Christ, The Pure Holy Child,
Would be born of a woman, God's Seed Undefiled!

Now Joseph and Mary lived in Galilee,
But in order to fulfill, Micah's prophecy,
Which said that Messiah, would be born in Bethlehem,
God caused the Romans, to call a census right then.
Each one must return, to their ancestral home,
So they headed for Bethlehem, where David had grown.
In the land of Judea, our Messiah was born,
Our Lord Jesus Christ, was Mary's Firstborn.
Jesus, The Holy, Sinless Son of God,
Was born to be Saviour, for the children of God!

The first to be told of God's Awesome Gift,
Were shepherds watching sheep, so that wolves wouldn't lift,
The ones who needed the shepherds' good care,
The ones who were grazing on the hills around there.
An Angel of The Lord, came and stood by them,
Said Don't be afraid, I have news for you men;
This day in David's city, a Saviour is born,
God's Son, The Messiah, as Christ, The Lord!
The Angel told them, how to recognize Him,
This Child, sent from heaven, to take away sin;
You will find The Baby, wrapped in swaddling clothes,
Lying in a manger, in the place that God chose!

Then suddenly with the Angel, there appeared a great throng,
Of God's Holy Army, filling the skies with their song.
Glory to God in The Highest Heavens, they sang,
And Peace to all men, was the message that rang,
Into the hearts and the minds of those men,
For God's promise in Eden, had now come to them!
God's Son was not born, in a castle so fine,
But in a small stable, This Child, The Divine!
He came to lift up, what had been torn down,
He came to give life and salvation's crown,
To those who would believe, and forsake their sin,
Who would give Him their lives, ask Him to come in.

So as you celebrate Christ's Birth this year,
Take time to be quiet and pray,
Give thanks unto God in heaven, for sending His Son that day!
The first day He came, only a few people knew,
That Messiah had come, to make new,.
But the next time He comes, every eye will see Him
For salvation or judgement for sin.
He is coming in glory, with His angels to claim,
His Bride, His Redeemed, for they acclaimed,
Christ as Saviour and Lord, Messiah and King,
The One who makes heaven sing!

If you haven't asked Jesus, to be Lord of your life,
If you're still caught in sin, and in strife,
Confess that you've sinned, then believe in Him,
He will hear and forgive, every sin.
Then He will give you, a brand new life,
A life of God's vision for you.
Then God's peace which passes, all understanding,
Will guard and keep you in truth.
The trials and tests now, won't take you off course,
For you are a child of The King,
And when He arrives, with the hosts of heaven,
You'll rejoice with the angels who sing!

Printed in the United States
144446LV00002B/1/P